Healthy Heart Cookbook

Healthy Heart Cookbook

By the Editors of Sunset Books

Sunset Books • Menlo Park, CA 94025

SUNSET BOOKS

Vice President Sales: Richard A. Smeby
Editorial Director: Bob Doyle
Production Director: Lory Day
Art Director: Vasken Guiragossian

STAFF FOR THIS BOOK

Developmental Editor: Linda J. Selden
Recipe Development and Text: Karyn I.
  Lipman and Cynthia Scheer
Copy Editor: Rebecca LaBrum
Design: Robin Weiss
Dietary Consultant: Patricia Kearney,
  R.D., Stanford Health Services
Principal Photographer: Chris Shorten
Principal Food Stylist: Susan Massey
Assistant Food Stylists: Gabrielle Massey
  and Victoria Roberts Russell
Production Coordinator: Patricia S.
  Williams

For additional copies of *Healthy Heart
Cookbook* or any other Sunset book, call
1-800-526-5111.

Front Cover: Jeweled Chicken (page 71)
Frontispiece: Sourdough Chili Chicken
Salad (page 77)
Photos by Chris Shorten.

A WORD ABOUT THIS BOOK

Our recipes conform to the American
Heart Association's recommendations for
fat intake; in each, fat provides no more
than 30 percent of the total calories. Every
recipe is accompanied by a nutritional
analysis prepared by Hill Nutrition Asso-
ciates, Inc., of Florida. We are grateful to
Lynne Hill, R.D., for her advice and
expertise.

Our nutritional analysis states calorie
count; percentage of calories from fat;
grams of total fat and saturated fat; milligrams of cholesterol and sodium; grams
of carbohydrates, fiber, and protein; and
milligrams of calcium and iron. Generally, the analysis applies to a single
serving, based on the number of servings
given for each recipe and the amount of
each ingredient. If a range is given for the
number of servings and/or the amount of
an ingredient, the analysis is based on the
average of the figures given.

The nutritional analysis does not
include optional ingredients or those for
which no specific amount is stated. If an
ingredient is listed with a substitution,
the information was calculated using the
first choice.

For each recipe, we provide preparation and cooking times. Keep in mind
that these times are approximate and will
vary depending on your expertise in the
kitchen and on the cooking equipment
you use.

We extend our sincere thanks to Sur
la Table of San Francisco for their generous loan of props used in our photographs.

Contents

Living a Healthy

Lifestyle

Design for Heart-healthy Living

You can resolve to learn and strengthen healthful habits for living, starting at any age. It takes commitment to put aside harmful routines and take up more beneficial ones. But if you approach the changes one by one, gradually building on each success, it won't take long to form good habits that can influence the health of your heart in very positive ways.

THE FIRST STEP

Reading the information in *The Healthy Heart Cookbook*—and then acting on it— can be the first step toward more healthful living. Have a look at our strategies for reducing the risk of heart disease and stroke. Take note of our techniques for heart-healthy cooking. Leaf through the recipes and see how delicious and satisfying nutritious eating can be. Foods low in fat and cholesterol can most certainly be enjoyed by everyone.

Of course, not even the most healthful diet can change certain risk factors: age, sex, and heredity. Nonetheless, making healthful choices in every aspect of your life can help you beat the odds of developing heart disease—and increase your chances of living longer.

WHAT IS CORONARY HEART DISEASE?

The underlying cause of coronary heart disease is **atherosclerosis**, or hardening of the arteries. In this process, cholesterol, fat, and scar tissue are deposited in the walls of arteries. Often referred to as **plaque,** this buildup narrows the vessel, decreasing the amount of blood that can reach organs or muscles normally supplied by that vessel.

If a **coronary artery** (one of the arteries supplying the heart with oxygen and nutrients) is sufficiently narrowed, the heart does not receive enough blood. This causes **angina,** or chest pain, which usually occurs during exertion, when the heart must pump harder than usual. If an artery is completely blocked—usually by a blood clot forming in a vessel narrowed by plaque buildup—blood and oxygen will be prevented from reaching a portion of the heart. The result is a **heart attack.**

If sufficient narrowing occurs in one of the arteries in the neck that supply blood to part of the brain, a **stroke** can result. Depending on the location of the blockage and the part of the body controlled by the affected portion of the brain, stroke symptoms can range from brief confusion to paralysis of one side of the body to loss of functions such as speech and swallowing.

Though the actual causes of atherosclerosis are not fully known, scientists do know that it is a slowly progressive disease. Plaque buildup begins in childhood, particularly in countries such as ours where diets are typically high in saturated fat and cholesterol.

RISK FACTORS FOR CORONARY HEART DISEASE

Some risk factors associated with coronary heart disease are uncontrollable. Men are more likely than women to develop heart disease—until women reach menopause, at which time a woman's risk of heart disease begins to increase dramatically. If you have a family history of heart disease before the age of 55, your risk for a heart attack is also increased. And the risk of heart disease definitely increases with age.

You do, however, have some control over several other primary and secondary risk factors, whether through diet, exercise, style of living, or medication.

PRIMARY RISK FACTORS

Circumstances having a direct adverse effect on heart health include high blood cholesterol level, high blood pressure, smoking, and physical inactivity.

Cholesterol is necessary to the body (see page 13), but excess cholesterol is also a major component of plaque. **High blood cholesterol levels** can indicate a high risk of heart disease.

Some cholesterol, enough for the body's needs, is manufactured in the liver. Your blood cholesterol level also depends to a certain extent on the amount of cholesterol in your diet. A more important dietary factor, however, is the quantity of **saturated fat** you consume. Excess saturated fat consumption is thought to be responsible for excess cholesterol production by the liver; that excess cholesterol, in turn, produces plaque.

Cholesterol cannot move through the bloodstream on its own; it must be carried by substances called **lipoproteins.** Among these, **low-density lipoproteins (LDL)** are the "bad guys" in the cholesterol-coronary heart disease story. They are the most abundant lipoproteins, carrying 65 percent of the cholesterol circulating in the blood. LDL carries cholesterol to cells and deposits excess cholesterol in arterial walls. Thus, high levels of LDL-cholesterol increase the buildup of plaque, elevating the risk of heart disease.

In contrast to LDL, **high-density lipoproteins (HDL)** carry only small amounts of cholesterol, but their role is a vital one: they transport cholesterol *away* from arterial walls, decreasing the risk of coronary heart disease. You can increase your HDL-cholesterol level by exercising consistently, losing weight, and not smoking. Diet, however, is not thought to affect HDL-cholesterol.

When your blood cholesterol is tested, request measurements of HDL- and LDL-cholesterol in addition to total cholesterol. Also ask that your **triglyceride** level be checked. Triglycerides are fats that circulate in the blood and are thought to contribute to atherosclerosis. A

LOWERING BLOOD CHOLESTEROL

Some experts consider blood cholesterol level the single most important correctable risk factor in the development of heart disease. Here are a few steps you can take to lower your blood cholesterol.

- Eat fewer high-fat foods, especially those high in saturated fats.

- Replace part of the saturated fats in your diet with unsaturated fats (see page 12).

- Eat fewer high-cholesterol foods.

- Choose foods high in complex carbohydrates (see page 14).

- Reduce your weight if you are overweight.

BLOOD PRESSURE FACTS

Blood pressure tends to increase with age; a young person with normal blood pressure may develop high blood pressure later in life. Up to about age 50, men are more likely to have high blood pressure than women; after that, high blood pressure is more common in women. In many cases, however, the cause of high blood pressure is not known. But experts do agree that blood pressure can be lowered by exercising regularly, losing extra pounds, reducing alcohol intake, and not smoking. Limiting sodium intake is effective for some people. If these measures aren't sufficient, medications can be used to reduce blood pressure to the normal range.

high triglyceride level usually corresponds to the high LDL-cholesterol levels and low HDL-cholesterol levels that increase the risk of heart disease. When you receive the test results, consult your doctor for an explanation. (You'll also find information on desirable cholesterol levels on page 14.)

High blood pressure is another serious risk factor. Blood pressure is the measure of the force of blood against arterial walls. It is reported in millimeters (mm) of mercury (Hg)—that is, in units reflecting how many millimeters the pressure can raise a column of mercury.

Each time the heart beats, blood is pumped out, creating a surge called the **systolic pressure**—the top number in a blood pressure reading. The pressure in the arteries between heartbeats is the **diastolic pressure,** the bottom number.

People with high blood pressure or **hypertension** also have narrowed, or tightened, vessels, so their hearts must work harder to pump blood throughout the body. This strains the heart and, over time, causes it to enlarge and weaken. High blood pressure can also damage arterial walls, increasing the chances of developing atherosclerosis.

It's best to keep blood pressure around 120/80 (or even 120/70) mm Hg; a reading greater than 140 mm Hg systolic or 90 mm Hg diastolic needs treatment. Lowering blood pressure lowers the risk of heart disease and stroke.

Cigarette smoking has been clearly documented as injurious to your health. It contributes to atherosclerosis by damaging arteries (including those that supply blood to the heart) and enabling plaque to build up. It can raise total blood cholesterol, lower protective HDL-cholesterol, and increase the stickiness of blood platelets, making blood clots more likely to form. What's more, the carbon monoxide in smoke reduces the amount of oxygen the blood can carry, while nicotine causes the heart to beat faster and use more oxygen. Smoking may also constrict coronary arteries, interfering with the supply of oxygen to the heart during physical exertion. And smoking can increase blood pressure. All of these effects create conditions for a heart attack.

Physical inactivity has a significant relationship to coronary heart disease. Those who exercise regularly have fewer fatal heart attacks than those who are sedentary, and they stand a better chance of surviving a heart attack should one occur.

Regular physical activity is one of the few things known to raise levels of protective HDL-cholesterol. At the same time, it lowers levels of potentially harmful LDL-cholesterol and triglycerides.

Exercise strengthens the heart and improves its overall fitness. A strong heart doesn't have to work as hard to circulate blood, since it can pump more efficiently with each beat. Exercise also improves the ability of other muscles to use the blood and oxygen they receive.

The American Heart Association recommends 30 to 60 minutes of **aerobic activity**—the kind that makes the heart beat faster—three to four times a week. Aerobic activities include running, swimming, cycling, hiking, climbing stairs, jumping rope, cross-country skiing, brisk walking, raking leaves, and mowing lawns.

If you're over 40 or have any risk factors for heart disease, check with your doctor before you begin an exercise program.

SECONDARY RISK FACTORS

Factors that affect heart health indirectly are known as secondary risk factors. They include diabetes mellitus, obesity, and stress.

Diabetes mellitus is a condition in which the body is unable to metabolize glucose properly. It occurs as Type I (insulin-dependent), which usually begins in childhood, or Type II (non–insulin-dependent), previously called adult-onset diabetes. Type II accounts for at least 90 percent of cases; it is usually associated with obesity, and losing excess weight is the chief treatment.

Diabetes of either type raises levels of abnormal blood fats and cholesterol and causes increased damage to artery walls, accelerating the development of atherosclerosis and heart disease.

Obesity strains the heart, increasing the risk of high blood pressure, diabetes, and high blood cholesterol. People who exceed their ideal body weight by 30 percent or more are more likely to develop heart disease and suffer strokes, even if they have no other risk factors.

You can lose excess pounds by eating fewer calories and increasing regular physical activity. Doctors and nutritionists recommend a nutritious, varied low-fat diet of foods such as whole grains; lean meats, poultry, and fish; fruits and vegetables; and low-fat or nonfat dairy products. Watching portion size is another important factor in weight control.

Stress may also be involved in coronary heart disease. Those under a good deal of stress may simply find it too difficult and time consuming to adopt heart-healthy habits such as eating right, exercising regularly, and refraining from smoking.

NUTRITION & A HEALTHY HEART

The dietary guidelines listed on page 12 form the basis of the American Heart Association (AHA) eating plan for healthy American adults. You'll find more detailed information on each of these points in the following pages. In considering points 1 through 4, keep in mind that the total amount of all fats consumed each day should add up to no more than 30 percent. That is, if you consume the maximum recommended levels of saturated and monounsaturated fats (10 percent and 15 percent, respectively), you'll need to limit your polyunsaturated fat consumption to just 5 percent of total calories.

Pasta, Pears & Gorgonzola (page 173)

FAT INTAKE

Most Americans consume at least 10 percent more fat than they should each day. Trimming your intake from 40 percent down to 30 percent of calories from fat is a significant reduction.

To start with, of course, you'll need to know just how much fat adds up to 30 percent of calories. If you eat a total of 1,800 calories a day, then 30 percent of your total is 540 calories (1,800 x .30). Because most product labels (see the example on page 16) show amounts of fat in grams, however, you'll probably find it more useful to know your daily limit in grams of fat rather than in calories. To calculate fat grams, simply divide fat calories by 9 (there are 9 calories in a gram of fat); thus, 540 calories equals about 60 grams of fat. The chart below shows fat limits in calories and grams for a variety of daily calorie totals.

WHAT'S YOUR FAT LIMIT?

CALORIES PER DAY	30% OF CALORIES	TOTAL FAT (g)	SATURATED FAT (g)
1,200	360	40 or less	11 to 13
1,500	450	50 or less	13 to 17
1,800	540	60 or less	16 to 20
2,000	600	67 or less	18 to 22
2,200	660	73 or less	20 to 24
2,500	750	83 or less	22 to 28
3,000	900	100 or less	27 to 33

There are two major types of fat—**saturated** and **unsaturated. Saturated fats,** found in animal products and a few vegetable products, are usually solid at room temperature. Animal foods such as high-fat meats, lard, poultry skin, and whole-milk dairy products contain large amounts of saturated fat. The so-called tropical oils are saturated fats that come from plants; they include coconut, palm, and palm kernel oils and cocoa butter. They are used in many prepared snack items, such as crackers, cookies, and candy.

Saturated fats have a greater effect on raising blood cholesterol than anything else in your diet and should be limited to no more than 8 to 10 percent of total calories. Even if you eat almost no cholesterol, your blood cholesterol level may remain high if you don't restrict saturated fats.

Unsaturated fats, usually liquid at room temperature, are classified as either **monounsaturated** or **polyunsaturated.**

Polyunsaturated fats, found mainly in vegetable oils such as safflower, sunflower, corn, soybean, sesame, and cottonseed, help lower blood cholesterol. They should account for up to 10 percent of total calories. **Monounsaturated fats** may be even more effective than polyunsaturated fats in reducing blood cholesterol. These fats include canola, olive, avocado, and peanut oils; most nut oils and most of the fats found in nuts are also monounsaturated. These fats should provide no more than 15 percent of total calories.

COMPARISON OF FATS

Legend:
- Saturated Fatty Acids
- Monounsaturated Fatty Acids
- Polyunsaturated Fatty Acids

	Saturated Fatty Acids	Monounsaturated Fatty Acids	Polyunsaturated Fatty Acids
Canola oil	7%	58%	35%
Safflower oil	10%	13%	77%
Sunflower oil	11%	20%	69%
Corn oil	13%	25%	62%
Olive oil	14%	77%	9%
Soybean oil	15%	24%	61%
Peanut oil	18%	49%	33%
Margarine	19%	49%	32%
Vegetable shortening	28%	44%	28%
Lard	41%	47%	12%
Beef fat	52%	44%	4%
Butter	66%	30%	4%

Source: Composition of Foods, Agriculture Handbook No. 8-4. Washington, D.C.: USDA, 1990.

RESTRICTING FAT IN CHILDREN'S DIETS

For children under 2 years of age, the "30 percent or less calories from fat" guideline does not apply. Children this young should not be subject to any type of fat restriction; fat is needed during the formative years to ensure proper development of the brain, bones, and muscles. Heart disease does begin early in life, however—so once children are older than two, they (like their parents) should consume no more than 30 percent of calories as fat, with no more than 8 to 10 percent coming from saturated fat. Likewise, children over 2 years old should consume no more than 300 milligrams of cholesterol per day.

You'll also see fats described as **hydrogenated.** Hydrogenation is a process that changes vegetable oils from their natural liquid state to a more solid form. During hydrogenation, air is rapidly incorporated into the oil, filling all the empty spaces in the molecules with hydrogen and forming trans fatty acids. As the oil becomes more solid, it also becomes more saturated, with a correspondingly greater potential for raising blood cholesterol. Completely hydrogenated oils, such as vegetable shortening, resemble saturated fats in their cholesterol-raising ability. Partially hydrogenated oils, such as margarine, are acceptable if they contain twice as much polyunsaturated or monounsaturated as saturated fat; look for the breakdown on the label.

CHOLESTEROL INTAKE

Cholesterol is a soft, waxy, fatlike substance. It helps waterproof the skin and slow down evaporation of water from the body; it is also involved in the formation of nerve sheaths and cell membranes and in the synthesis of certain hormones and vitamins.

The liver manufactures enough cholesterol to satisfy the body's requirements; **dietary cholesterol** comes from the foods we eat. Both types affect the amount of cholesterol circulating in the blood. As noted on page 9, excess blood cholesterol can lead to the formation of plaque on artery walls, narrowing or blocking the vessels and leading to coronary heart disease.

For a healthy heart, dietary cholesterol intake should not exceed 300 milligrams per day; limiting saturated fat is crucial as well.

The National Cholesterol Education Program states that people should aim for total cholesterol levels of 200 milligrams per deciliter (mg/dl) or less. At this level, the risk of heart disease is relatively low, though not necessarily nonexistent: be aware that a low HDL-cholesterol level can increase the risk of heart disease even when total cholesterol is in the desirable range.

A blood cholesterol level of 200 to 239 mg/dl is considered borderline high; people in this category have twice the risk of heart disease as those with levels below 200. Levels of 240 mg/dl or greater are considered high and carry over twice the risk of heart disease as levels of 200 mg/dl or less.

BLOOD CHOLESTEROL LEVELS

	TOTAL CHOLESTEROL	LDL LEVEL	HDL LEVEL
Desirable	Less than 200 mg/dl	130 mg/dl	More than 45 mg/dl
Borderline High	200–239 mg/dl	130–159 mg/dl	
High	240 mg/dl	160 mg/dl	Less than 35 mg/dl

SODIUM INTAKE

It's hard to believe, but the human body requires only 250 milligrams (about ⅛ teaspoon) of sodium each day. Yet present consumption in the United States has been estimated at 4,000 to 6,000 milligrams (4 to 6 grams or 2 to 3 teaspoons) per day.

The American Heart Association recommends decreasing sodium intake to 2,400 milligrams per day, the amount in only about 1¼ teaspoons of salt. For some people, cutting back on sodium may help lower blood pressure.

CARBOHYDRATE INTAKE

Carbohydrates are classed as **simple** (sugars) and **complex** (starch and fiber). Both types are found naturally in foods such as fruits, vegetables, whole grains, and milk. Carbohydrates contain just 4 calories per gram—under half the amount provided by fat, which weighs in at 9 calories per gram.

Simple carbohydrates may be either fruit sugars or concentrated sugars such as the familiar granulated sugar, corn syrup, and honey.

Complex carbohydrates are found in whole-grain breads and cereals, pastas, legumes, vegetables, and fruits; they're an excellent substitute for foods high in saturated fat and cholesterol. Besides being lower in calories than fats, they supply a variety of vitamins and minerals. They're also the main sources of **dietary fiber,** an important part of a healthful diet.

ADDITIONAL NUTRITION GUIDELINES

• **Proteins** consist of amino acids linked together. The body manufactures some amino acids, called *nonessential* amino acids; dietary protein provides the *essential* amino acids that the body cannot make on its own.

Protein contains 4 calories per gram. It is necessary for building and repairing tissue and manufacturing enzymes, but you need surprisingly little protein to meet these needs—just 10 to 15 percent of each day's total calories. The average American diet contains more than enough protein. Even vegetarians can easily meet their protein needs by choosing good sources of vegetable protein such as tofu, peas, and beans.

• **Alcoholic beverages** need not be completely excluded from a healthful diet. However, the USDA's *Dietary Guidelines for Americans* do advise that if you drink alcoholic beverages, you should do so in moderation: no more than one drink a day for women, no more than two drinks a day for men. (One drink counts as 12 ounces of regular beer, 5 ounces of wine, or 1½ ounces of 80-proof distilled spirits.) Those who drink alcohol should also aim to do so with meals and when consumption does not put themselves or others at risk.

• **Variety in the diet** is the best way to get all the many nutrients you need for good health. In fact, a varied and wholesome diet usually provides sufficient vitamins and minerals to make supplements unnecessary.

Fennel with Mushrooms & Prosciutto (page 207)

Dietary fiber can help lower blood cholesterol and may reduce the risk of colon cancer. It falls into two groups: **water insoluble** and **water soluble.** Foods typically contain a mixture of both types, but they often provide more of one kind than the other. **Soluble fiber**—gums and pectin—helps reduce blood cholesterol and has been shown to stabilize blood sugar levels (an important benefit for people with diabetes). It's found in fruits, vegetables, legumes, oats, oat bran, barley, brown rice, and seeds. **Insoluble fiber** is less important in fighting heart disease than the soluble type, but it too is necessary for overall health. It occurs mainly in whole grains, fruits, and vegetables. Aim to eat a total of 20 to 35 grams of fiber each day, with about a third of that coming from soluble fiber.

Americans today get an estimated 47 percent of their calories from carbohydrates—less than the 55 to 60 percent recommended in the AHA guidelines. To boost your consumption of carbohydrates, you should eat at least six servings of breads, grains, and cereals and at least five servings of fruits and vegetables each day.

TOTAL CALORIES

When you consume a greater total number of calories than your body needs to function, you put on weight. Studies have shown that even a gain of just 10 percent over ideal weight increases the risk for heart disease. Excess body weight is also linked to high blood pressure and diabetes.

Eating Right for a Healthy Heart

Eating right is easier than it seems. In the following pages, we'll spell out the best ways to shop for healthful, low-fat foods and share our secrets for cooking with a light touch.

FOLLOWING THE GUIDELINES

When you plan your meals, let the goals of the AHA guide you. Over half the calories in every meal should come from carbohydrates, 10 to 15 percent from protein, and no more than 30 percent from fat.

To sort out these numbers, check the nutritional data that follows every recipe in this book. Another, more general way to accomplish the same job is to remember these three easy rules:

- Emphasize complex carbohydrates.
- Eat no more than 6 ounces of lean meat, fish, or poultry each day.
- Avoid added fat and high-fat food.

Use this cookbook as a guide when you experiment with low-fat cooking techniques and modify your family's favorite recipes to make them leaner and more healthful. Once you've familiarized yourself with the basics of heart-healthy dishes and how they're prepared, you'll also gain a better sense of which foods you can enjoy without guilt when you eat away from home.

IDENTIFYING HEART-HEALTHY FOODS

If you learn how to read food labels, you'll be able to make the most healthful choices at the grocery store. These labels consist of two parts: the nutrition label and the ingredient label.

NUTRITION LABELS

Headed "nutrition facts," a nutrition label must be provided for any food product for which nutrition claims are made, as well as for foods that are enriched or fortified. A sample label is shown at left.

Serving size is listed first on these labels, followed by the number of servings per package. *Calorie count* comes next, letting you determine how a serving of the food adds to your daily total. *Calories from fat* and *total fat* also appear prominently.

Saturated fat is noted as well. Though part of the total fat in food, it's listed separately due to the key role it plays in raising blood cholesterol and increasing the risk of heart disease.

Cholesterol and *sodium* are listed next. Following these, you'll find the amount of *carbohydrates* a serving of the food provides. In your meals, go easy on choices such as soft drinks and candy (these are high in *sugars,* one form of carbohydrate). Instead, emphasize nutritious high-carbohydrate foods such as breads, fruits, and vegetables. These same foods are likely to provide *dietary fiber.*

Protein is important for good health. Opt for small servings of lean meats, fish, and poultry; low-fat or nonfat dairy products; and veg-

Nutrition Facts

Serving Size 1 cup (228g)
Servings Per Container 2

Amount Per Serving

Calories 260 Calories from Fat 120

	% Daily Value*
Total Fat 13g	**20**%
Saturated Fat 5g	**25**%
Cholesterol 30mg	**10**%
Sodium 660mg	**28**%
Total Carbohydrate 31g	**10**%
Dietary Fiber 0g	**0**%
Sugars 5g	
Protein 5g	

Vitamin A 4%	•	Vitamin C 2%	
Calcium 15%	•	Iron 4%	

* Percent Daily Values are based on a 2,000 calorie diet. Your daily values may be higher or lower depending on your calorie needs:

	Calories:	2,000	2,500
Total Fat	Less than	65g	80g
Sat Fat	Less than	20g	25g
Cholesterol	Less than	300mg	300mg
Sodium	Less than	2,400mg	2,400mg
Total Carbohydrate		300g	375g
Dietary Fiber		25g	30g

Calories per gram:
Fat 9 • Carbohydrate 4 • Protein 4

CHECKING INGREDIENT LABELS FOR FAT, SUGAR & SODIUM

Fat. Check labels to see how many different fats and fat-containing ingredients a food has and where each falls in the listing. If any kind of fat is one of the first ingredients, you'll know that the food is high in total fat. But beware of less obvious sources of fat, as well—nuts, cream cheese, whole milk, cheese, and poultry skin, for example. These too add to the fat total.

If the following appear toward the beginning of an ingredient list, the product is high in saturated fat—the kind that raises blood cholesterol levels:

beef tallow	palm oil
butter	partially hydro-
cocoa butter	genated vegetable
coconut oil	oil
cream	poultry fat
lard	shortening
meat fat	suet
palm kernel oil	

Sugar. Even if the word "sugar" isn't listed first, sugar may still be the principal ingredient in many prepared foods. Check the list for corn syrup, fructose, honey, molasses, sorbitol, and so on—all are types of sugar.

Some products, especially cereals, provide extra information about carbohydrate content. Most food manufacturers break down this information into starch and related carbohydrates; sucrose and other sugars; and dietary fiber. Use such information to compare cereals, particularly where sugar and fiber are concerned.

Sodium. You can also judge a food's sodium content by reading the ingredient list. The following all contain significant amounts of sodium:

baking powder	salt
baking soda	seasoned salt
bouillon	sodium caseinate
brine	sodium citrate
disodium inosinate	sodium nitrate
meat tenderizer	sodium phosphate
monosodium glutamate	sodium saccharin

etable foods such as beans and grains. *Vitamins and minerals* are listed as well. Don't count on any one food to provide all the vitamins and minerals you need; combine foods to reach the total.

Percent of daily value (listed to the right of total fat, sodium, and so on) has been calculated for a diet of 2,000 to 2,500 calories per day. If your daily calorie count differs, percentages will vary accordingly.

INGREDIENT LABELS

Always read a food's list of ingredients carefully; when you're choosing among similar products of different brands, comparing ingredient lists can help you make the most healthful selection.

Ingredients must be listed in descending order by weight—that is, from the ingredient present in largest quantity down to the one used in smallest quantity. If no ingredients from animal sources are listed, the food will be naturally cholesterol free. It may still be high in saturated fat, though, so be sure to note the types of fats used.

For help in evaluating ingredient labels for fat, sugar, and sodium, see the box at left.

HEALTH CLAIMS

You'll often find various health claims made on food packages. What does it mean when the label on a favorite food boasts that it's "light" (or "lite")? How does "lean" differ from "low fat"? For an explanation of a number of these claims, review the box on page 18. As you'll see, similar foods bearing one or the other of these designations can differ substantially in grams of fat per serving.

TAKE YOUR HEART-HEALTHY KNOW-HOW TO THE SUPERMARKET

You'll find a mind-boggling number of foods on display in today's supermarkets. The shopper of only a generation ago would be astonished at many of today's products—and new items seem to appear every week! That's why reading nutrition and ingredient labels wisely is so important.

Scanning every label will take extra time, especially in the beginning. But once you've narrowed down your selection of pantry staples and frequently purchased items, the task becomes easier. You'll soon be wheeling your cart right past the high-fat sectors, stopping almost automatically in front of the more healthful alternatives.

The information in the next ten pages will guide you up and down the supermarket aisles and around the perimeter. Use these tips to make the most nutritious selections from among the many possibilities.

FRESH PRODUCE

With few exceptions, fresh fruits and vegetables are naturally low in fat, calories, and sodium; as a class, they're also high in fiber, nutrients, and flavor. What's more, fresh produce almost always gives you the most nutrition for your money.

When used on labels, the following words and phrases must now meet specific government criteria.

Fat free Less than 0.5 g fat per serving

Low fat 3 g fat or less per serving

Reduced fat (less fat) At least 25 percent less fat per serving than a higher-fat version

Lean Less than 10 g fat, 4 g saturated fat, and 95 mg cholesterol per serving

Extra lean Less than 5 g fat, 2 g saturated fat, and 95 mg cholesterol per serving

Light (lite) One-third fewer calories or no more than half the fat of the higher-fat, higher-calorie version; or no more than half the sodium of the higher-sodium version

Low in saturated fat 1 g saturated fat or less per serving and not more than 15 percent of calories from saturated fat

Low sodium 140 mg sodium or less per serving

Reduced sodium (less sodium) At least 25 percent less sodium per serving than a higher-sodium version

Cholesterol free Less than 2 mg cholesterol and no more than 2 g saturated fat per serving

Ideally, produce should be harvested and eaten the very same day. You may be able to accomplish this goal if you shop almost daily at a farmers market for locally grown vegetables and fruits—but most of us save time by making a single trip to a supermarket for the major part of the week's food needs. The produce there may have been shipped in from a considerable distance away, and some fragile nutrients will inevitably have been lost during transport and storage. To make the most of the abundant vitamins and minerals these fruits and vegetables still provide, serve them while they're as fresh as possible.

MILK & OTHER DAIRY PRODUCTS

What was once called "skim milk" is now usually labeled "fat-free milk"—and it's much tastier than the bluish, watery product some may remember from the past. You'll find various lower-fat milks available, as well.

These are the terms currently in use on milk cartons in the dairy case:

- Fat-free milk (also called skim or nonfat milk): 0.5 gram fat or less per cup
- Low-fat milk (also called light or 1 percent milk): 2.6 grams fat per cup
- Reduced-fat milk (also called 2 percent milk): 4.7 grams fat per cup

Note that lower-fat milks are described by the amount of fat they contain by weight. So reduced-fat milk, though it contains only 2 percent fat by weight, actually derives 35 percent of its calories from fat—and at 5 grams of fat per 1-cup serving, it's too high in fat to be considered a low-fat food. However, you may find it a useful ingredient in baked products and sauces when a lower-fat milk would compromise the quality of the recipe. Low-fat or fat-free milk is the best choice for an everyday beverage.

Chocolate milk, a favorite of children, is generally made from whole milk. But it's sometimes available in a low-fat version—a good choice for youngsters over 2 years of age, as well as for adults with a taste for chocolate.

Also look for buttermilk in lower-fat forms. Different dairies offer a range of lowered-fat options. Fat-free buttermilk is occasionally available, too.

Cheese can contain as much as 70 percent of calories from fat, a fact that's prompted many fat-conscious shoppers to strike it from the grocery list completely. But times are changing, and numerous reduced-fat cheeses have been created in response to consumer demand. These products are still relatively high in fat (be sure to read the labels), but if used in moderation they offer a fine way to add interest and flavor to many recipes. You'll also find entirely fat-free cream cheese, cottage cheese, and pasteurized process cheese slices; try them to see which ones suit your taste and cooking style.

COMPARING MILK & MILK PRODUCTS

MILK OR MILK PRODUCT (1 CUP)	CALORIES (g)	FAT (g)	SATURATED FAT (g)	CHOLESTEROL (mg)
Reduced-fat (2%) milk	122	4.7	2.9	19.5
Low-fat (1%) milk	102	2.6	1.6	9.8
Fat-free milk	86	0.4	0.3	4.9
Evaporated milk	338	19.0	11.6	73.0
Evaporated fat-free milk	199	0.5	0.3	10.2
Reduced-fat (1½%) buttermilk	120	4.0	2.5	15.0
Low-fat buttermilk	98	2.2	1.3	9.8
Chocolate milk (whole)	208	8.5	5.3	30.0
Low-fat (1%) chocolate milk	158	2.5	1.6	7.3

Among regular cheeses, soft dessert cheeses such as Brie are very high in fat, as are firm cheeses such as Cheddar, Swiss, and jack. Part-skim types such as mozzarella and ricotta contain less fat than their whole-milk counterparts, but should be used sparingly even so.

Yogurt is simply milk that has been fermented and coagulated by adding beneficial bacteria. The amount of fat in yogurt depends on the milk it's made from. Some yogurts are made from whole milk, but the more healthful ones start with low-fat or nonfat milk.

EGGS & EGG SUBSTITUTES

To help keep down cholesterol intake, the AHA recommends limiting eggs to three or four per week. All of an egg's cholesterol is found in the yolk; the yolk of a large egg contains about 213 milligrams of cholesterol, more than two-thirds the recommended amount for one day.

You may want to try the cholesterol-free egg substitutes sold in the freezer or dairy case. Egg whites are the main ingredient in these products; additions such as oil, sodium, and coloring help simulate the appearance and flavor of whole eggs. The package labels offer suggestions for using the substitute in egg dishes and in baking.

When you cook and bake, you can use egg whites in place of some or all of the whole eggs, as we do in many recipes throughout this book. You'll find more information about making this substitution on page 32.

CANNED & PACKAGED FOODS

Until frozen foods appeared on the supermarket scene, canned and packaged foods were widely used for their convenience. Even now they're useful pantry-shelf commodities. When you buy them, follow these guidelines:

- Watch for phrases such as "in its own juice" and "no sugar added" on the labels of canned fruits; "water-packed" on canned fish and shellfish; and "no salt added" and "reduced-sodium" on canned tomato products, canned beans and other vegetables, and canned broth.

BUYING EGGS & EGG SUBSTITUTES

- When you buy eggs for their whites, select large eggs. Two large whole eggs yield about ¼ cup egg whites (the equivalent of one whole egg).

- Check eggs carefully before you buy them to be sure they're clean and free of cracks that can admit harmful bacteria.

- Buy eggs only from a refrigerated case, and refrigerate them as soon as possible after purchase.

- Always check the expiration date stamped on the carton before you buy.

- Select canned soups or dry soup mixes containing 5 grams of fat or less per serving, preferably with a low level of sodium. Look for the new "healthier" canned soups that are lower in fat and sodium than the "regular" products.
- Pasta sauces should contain less than 6 grams of fat per ½-cup serving; they should contain no added salt or less than 500 milligrams of sodium per ½-cup serving.
- Choose canned fruit juices without added sugar or corn syrup.
- Instead of hydrogenated peanut butter, buy the kind with the oil on top (it may be labeled "natural" peanut butter). Some brands of this sort of peanut butter are now available in reduced-fat versions. You can also find unsalted peanut butter.

PASTA, GRAINS & LEGUMES

Include plenty of pasta, grains, and legumes in your meals. They provide an abundance of complex carbohydrates, protein, fiber, vitamins, and minerals—and better still, they're naturally low in fat, calories, and sodium. Just be sure the sauces and seasonings you use with them are also low in fat and sodium.

Pasta has become one of the stars of heart-healthy meals. It's conveniently quick to cook, and the seemingly endless array of shapes, sizes, and colors brings welcome diversity to the dinner plate. When possible, select whole-grain pastas for their fiber and flavor. And when you spoon on a sauce, choose one that's almost as lean as the pasta underneath. You'll find many fat-saving pasta dishes in the pages ahead.

Grains are among the oldest cultivated dietary plants. Thanks to worldwide interest, it's now possible to find previously obscure grains on your supermarket shelves. Look for amaranth, barley, bulgur (cracked wheat), hominy, grits, millet, oats, polenta, quinoa, triticale, and wheat berries. All can bring new flavor and texture to familiar soups, salads, stews, and saucy dishes.

Rice, the principal food for more than half the world's population, contains only a trace of fat and no cholesterol. Brown rice provides more fiber than white rice, and the bran it contains has been shown to have some effect in lowering cholesterol. Other rices to explore for their subtle differences in texture and flavor include arborio or pearl, basmati, texmati, wehani, and wild rice. (Purists will note that wild rice is actually a marsh grass, not a rice, but it's usually served the way rice is.)

Seasoned mixes for rice and other grain products are increasingly popular because they're such time-savers. When you select these, be sure they aren't overly high in sodium. And when you prepare them, try using less fat than the directions specify.

Legumes are plants that produce pods with edible seeds. Think of familiar types such as kidney beans, pinto beans, garbanzo beans, lentils, and peas (split and whole, green and yellow). Newcomers to specialty markets include multihued and variegated dried heirloom beans. Some of these are so colorful they evoke thoughts of Jack and his fairy-tale beanstalk.

All legumes are a good source of soluble fiber (the kind that lowers blood cholesterol levels), complex carbohydrates, protein, vitamins, and minerals. Serve them often as a substitute for higher-fat meats and poultry.

When you buy legumes in canned form, look for no-salt-added versions. If these aren't available, be sure to rinse and drain the beans thoroughly before using them.

BREADS & CEREALS

Most breads and cereals are low in fat and a good source of complex carbohydrates. Those made from the least refined grains are the most nutritious, since they contain more fiber, vitamins, and minerals.

Breads made without shortening and entirely or in part from whole-grain flour are the best choices for heart health. But identifying truly whole-grain breads can be tricky; looks alone aren't enough, since loaves that are dark colored or brown aren't necessarily whole grain. To be sure you're getting what you want, check for one of the following listed first on the ingredient label:

- 100 percent whole wheat flour
- Stone-ground whole wheat flour
- Whole-grain flour
- Rye flour
- Multigrain flour
- Cracked wheat flour

French, Italian, and sourdough breads and rolls are usually made without fat and often come in whole-grain varieties. Other nutritious choices include bagels, pita rounds, breadsticks, English muffins, corn tortillas, and low-fat or fat-free flour tortillas.

It's especially important to read labels when you buy commercially baked quick breads such as biscuits, scones, cornbread, and muffins. They tend to be higher in fat, particularly saturated fat, than plain yeast breads. When time permits, bake your own; the chapter beginning on page 208 offers some delicious possibilities.

Cereals can be a truly healthful part of your diet. The key to making good choices is understanding the information on the nutrition label—ignore it and you may inadvertently select a cereal that's as sugary as candy or as salty as potato chips! Check the box at left for pointers on cereal shopping.

CHOOSING HEALTHFUL CEREALS

Here's a handy checklist for cereal shopping.

- Read the ingredient list; the first item should be a grain. The shorter the list, the less refined (and more nutritious) the cereal.

- Look for whole-grain cereals. The word "whole" must appear unless it is an oat-based cereal; on these, the words "rolled oats" or "whole oat flour," not simply "oat flour," will appear.

- Choose a cereal with at least 2 grams of dietary fiber per serving.

- Check the nutrition label for grams of fat; select cereals with no more than 1 to 2 grams per serving. Also scan the list for the kind of fat contained in the cereal. Avoid products made with coconut, palm, or palm kernel oils; these are all saturated fats. If you buy granola, choose a reduced-fat kind (or try our Gingersnap Granola, page 41).

- Remember that most ready-to-eat cereals have 200 to 300 milligrams of sodium per serving. If you're cutting back on sodium, choose shredded wheat, puffed rice, or puffed wheat; these generally have little or no added sodium.

- Hot cereals are often a good choice for heart-healthy nutrition, especially the regular and quick-cooking types. The instant kind may have more salt and sugar; check nutrition labels carefully.

VEGETABLE OILS & MARGARINES

All vegetable oils and margarines are a combination of polyunsaturated, monounsaturated, and saturated fats. Monounsaturated and polyunsaturated fats help lower blood cholesterol levels, reducing the risk of heart disease. Saturated fats, on the other hand, can cause blood cholesterol levels to rise.

Vegetable oils, used sparingly, are an important part of a heart-healthy cooking and eating plan. Choosing an oil that's totally free of saturated fat is impossible, since all oils contain at least some; but some oils have less saturated fat than others. Look for one with a higher percentage of monounsaturated and polyunsaturated fats than saturated fats.

Because monounsaturated fats can lower artery-clogging LDL-cholesterol, oils high in these fats should be your first choice. Canola, olive, and peanut oil are the three oils highest in monounsaturated fats.

The best choices for oils high in polyunsaturated fats are safflower, sunflower, corn, and soybean oils.

To compare the amounts of polyunsaturated, monounsaturated, and saturated fats in various oils, look at the chart on page 13. And do remember that no matter what oil you choose, its makeup is 100 percent fat—each tablespoon provides about 120 calories and 14 grams of fat. Use it with discretion.

Asparagus with Rosemary & Prosciutto (page 194)

Margarines have undergone changes in recent years to make them more heart friendly. Take a look at the ingredient list; if water or an acceptable liquid vegetable oil (canola, safflower, sunflower, corn, or soybean) is the first entry, the product is probably a heart-healthy spread. Also make sure that the product provides no more than 2 grams saturated fat per 1-tablespoon serving.

The first ingredient in reduced-calorie and diet margarines is water. When water is whipped into margarine, volume is increased without adding calories. Soft margarines in squeeze bottles and tubs are less saturated than stick margarines.

You can also create your own spread by blending ½ cup (one stick) of butter (at room temperature) with ½ cup of canola oil. This spread is lower in saturated fat than butter, and it's free of the trans fatty acids found in hydrogenated margarine. Once you've prepared the spread, store it in the refrigerator.

WHERE THE LEAN MEAT IS

LEAN BEEF CUTS

Tenderloin: This long, tapering muscle extends the full length of the loin. It's costly but very tender. As long as outside fat is conscientiously trimmed, it can be included in a low-fat diet.

Top loin: Top loin steak is the larger portion of a sirloin or porterhouse, separated from the tenderloin by a center bone. This cut is sometimes labeled New York, Delmonico, club, or strip steak.

Sirloin: The largest of the loin steaks, sirloin comprises several tender, juicy, and flavorful muscles, which are usually sold separately as top sirloin, fillet, and culotte steak.

Flank steak: Robustly flavored flank steak comes from the area below the loin. It has a coarser, more fibrous texture than the loin and is less tender.

Round tip: The round is lean and mild in flavor. The entire round can be seen clearly in cross section, muscle by muscle, in a full-cut round steak; it consists of round tip (often sold as sirloin tip), top round, eye of round, and bottom round. Round tip is the most tender of the four.

Top round: This second-tenderest portion of the round is often served as "London broil," sliced thinly across the grain at a slant (it is often labeled as such, as well).

Eye of round: This very lean, compact, fine-grained portion of the round needs help—in the form of pounding and/or moist-heat cooking—to be fork-tender.

Bottom round: Though similar to eye of round in tenderness, bottom round is more flavorful and has a coarser grain.

Lean ground beef: To be sure ground beef is truly lean (no more than 17 percent fat), insist on well-trimmed meat from the round.

MEATS

Health-conscious cooks may wonder if meat has a place in a heart-healthy eating scheme. The answer is yes! Today's meat animals are all bred to be leaner than in the past, and you may have noticed that the fat on the meat you buy has been trimmed more closely than it once was. Still, it's important to buy the leanest cuts available, then trim away as much of the remaining fat as you can at home. Watch portions, too: the recommended serving size is 3 ounces of cooked meat (about 4 ounces uncooked).

Beef contains saturated fat and cholesterol, but it fits smoothly into a heart-healthy eating plan when you pay attention to the grade and cut. The U.S. Department of Agriculture (USDA) divides beef into three grades: prime, choice, and select.

- Prime beef contains the most fat, accounting for its tender, juicy appeal. Unfortunately, it is also high in saturated fat.
- Choice beef is the grade most often found in the supermarket. Marbling, the tiny streaks of fat that interlace the muscle, is evident in naturally fatty cuts of choice beef. But naturally lean choice cuts can be low in fat; see the list at left.
- Select beef is the leanest. It contains approximately 20 percent less fat than choice beef and nearly 40 percent less than prime beef. Because select cuts are low in fat, they tend to be less tender. Hints for cooking them successfully can be found on page 33.

Veal is the meat of 1- to 4-month-old calves. It's higher in cholesterol than other lean cuts of meat but lower in saturated fat, so you can include lean cuts in your heart-healthy menus.

Lamb also comes from young animals. Several lean, distinctively flavored cuts fit nicely into fat-conscious menus; they're listed on page 24. Be sure to trim away any surface fat before cooking.

Pork is leaner than in the past; in fact, lean pork can contain less saturated fat per serving than a comparable cut of beef. The best cuts for heart-healthy cooking are listed on page 24.

Unlike fresh pork, processed pork products are rarely appropriate for healthy eating: regular bacon, sausage, cold cuts, and hot dogs simply contain too much saturated fat and cholesterol. As leaner versions of these processed meats become available, check the labels to verify the nutritional advantages claimed for them. Be sure the percentage of calories from fat per serving is low enough to make the product truly acceptable.

If sodium is a concern for you, avoid all cured and processed pork products.

LEAN VEAL CUTS

Veal is typically regarded as all lean meat. It's not always cut the same as beef, though veal cuts generally do correspond to beef cuts. Some veal cuts may require moist-heat cooking to become tender and flavorful.

LEAN LAMB CUTS

Leg: Meat from a leg of lamb is juicy, full flavored, and tender. It may be sold in slices or smaller sections, which are handy for stir-fries and small-scale stews.

Loin: Tender, juicy lamb loin adjoins the leg; sirloin steaks can be cut from this large end of the leg. The loin is usually divided into chops, but may occasionally be available in a boneless form similar to pork tenderloin.

Rib: Cuts from the rib lie next to the loin, toward the front of the lamb. Trim away surface fat thoroughly before cooking.

Shoulder: Lamb shoulder comprises several small muscles separated by layers of fat and connective tissue. Trimming all the fat can be a considerable job, and the meat is usually cooked using moist heat.

Lean ground lamb: To make sure ground lamb is truly lean, it's best to buy well-trimmed leg or shoulder, then grind it at home or have it ground for you at the meat market.

LEAN PORK CUTS

Leg: Most pork legs are cured and sold as ham, but more fresh boneless legs are being offered today than in the past, either whole or cut and packaged as boneless slices or cubes. The meat is moist and quite tender.

Tenderloin: Pork tenderloin is a boneless strip of meat that lies inside the rib cage along the back. As the name suggests, it's exceedingly tender.

Loin: All the meat from the loin section is tender and relatively lean when scrupulously trimmed of surface fat.

BUYING MEAT

Adopted by most retail food stores nationwide, the uniform labels on packaged meats can help shoppers make good choices.

The label identifies the meat, states the part of the animal from which it was taken, and gives the standard retail name for the cut. A retailer may also show (either on the label or with a separate sticker) some other name for the cut—"London broil" for top round, for example. Another sticker may suggest good ways to cook a less familiar cut.

The date stamped on the label tells when the meat was packaged or the last date it should be sold. Ask the meatman for help if you aren't sure what the date signifies.

How much meat should you buy to yield that model 3-ounce serving of cooked meat? It depends on the nature of the cut. Lean, boneless meat with little or no fat, such as ground meat, fillets, or boned, rolled roasts, will yield four such servings per pound. For meat with a medium amount of bone and some fat at the edges—loin and rib roasts, steaks, and chops—estimate 6 to 8 ounces raw weight to yield 3 ounces cooked meat. With very bony cuts, such as veal or lamb shanks or breast, you'll need to buy 12 to 16 ounces for each 3-ounce serving of cooked meat.

POULTRY

Versatile chicken and turkey are naturally lean, almost made to order for heart-healthy cooking. A 3-ounce serving of boneless, skinless cooked chicken breast has about a third fewer grams of fat than the same amount of lean beef, and turkey breast is even leaner.

The virtues of lean poultry, however, can be undermined by a misguided cooking method. A broiled or poached 3-ounce serving of skinless chicken breast has 140 calories and 3 grams of fat; if that same portion is coated with batter and fried with the skin intact, the calories soar to 221 and the fat to 11 grams! Be sure to read the cooking tips on page 33; then browse through the recipes beginning on page 140.

Chicken. Frying and broiling chickens are leaner than roasting birds, which, in turn, are leaner than capons. Breast meat is leaner than that of the leg and thigh—a point to keep in mind if you buy chicken in parts.

Turkey breast is one of the leanest meats you can find. If you buy a whole turkey, look for a natural-style bird rather than one with a fat-laden basting solution.

Ground turkey and chicken are now widely available. The leanest form is 100 percent breast meat, with no added skin or fat.

Rock Cornish game hens aren't as lean as standard chickens. If you cook them as a rare treat, split each hen to make two servings. Be sure to discard all the fat from the cooking juices, and don't eat the skin.

Duck contains more fat than any other kind of poultry, so it's best to limit it to very special occasions.

COMPARING NUTRITIONAL CONTENT OF MEATS AND POULTRY

3 OUNCES COOKED	CALORIES	FAT (g)	SATURATED FAT (g)	CHOLESTEROL (mg)
BEEF				
Tenderloin	179	8.5	3.2	71.4
Top loin	176	8.0	3.0	64.6
Sirloin	166	6.1	2.4	75.7
Flank steak	176	8.6	3.7	57.0
Round tip	157	5.9	2.0	68.9
Top round	153	4.2	1.4	71.4
Eye of round	143	4.2	1.5	58.7
Bottom round	161	6.3	2.1	66.3
Ground beef (17% fat)	218	13.9	5.5	71.4
VEAL				
Shoulder	169	5.2	1.4	110.6
Leg (cutlets)	128	2.9	1.0	87.6
Loin	149	5.9	2.2	90.2
LAMB				
Leg	162	6.6	2.3	75.7
Loin	172	8.3	3.2	74.0
Rib	200	11.0	4.0	97.4
Shoulder	174	9.2	3.5	74.0
Ground lamb	174	9.2	3.5	74.0
PORK				
Leg (fresh ham)	187	9.4	3.2	80.0
Tenderloin	139	4.0	1.4	76.2
Center loin	169	7.7	2.8	67.2
CHICKEN				
Breast (skinless)	140	3.0	0.9	72.3
Leg (skinless)	162	7.2	1.9	79.9
Thigh (skinless)	178	9.3	2.6	80.8
TURKEY				
Breast (skinless)	115	0.6	0.2	70.6
Dark meat (skinless)	157	5.9	2.0	74.8
Ground (dark and light meat)	195	11.7	3.2	58.7
Ground (breast only)	115	0.6	0.2	70.6

FISH & SHELLFISH

Fresh, frozen, and canned fish and shellfish from around the world are as close as your neighborhood supermarket. They offer a multitude of choices for low-fat cooking.

Fish served as an entrée two or more times a week will introduce a healthful element into your diet: omega-3 fatty acids, which protect against heart disease (see the box at left). By replacing meat or poultry with fish, you can decrease the levels of saturated fat and cholesterol in your diet.

Of course, much depends on how you cook the fish. Review the cooking techniques described on pages 28–29 and see which apply to fish. For more ideas, take a look at the recipes beginning on page 156.

At the market, look for firm, moist fresh fish; it should smell clean, not fishy. Any skin should be shiny; edges of whole or cut fish should be moist, not dry. When you buy packaged fish, avoid packages that are strong smelling and those in which liquid has collected. If you're purchasing frozen fish, check carefully for signs of mishandling: discoloration, buildup of ice crystals, or drying (especially around the edges).

Canned fish such as salmon, tuna, and sardines are useful to keep on hand in the pantry; buy the water-packed kind.

Shellfish, including mollusks (oysters, scallops, mussels, and clams) and crustaceans (shrimp, crab, crayfish, and lobster), were thought in the past to be a significant source of cholesterol. In fact, however, most shellfish are actually low in cholesterol. The exceptions are shrimp and crayfish: the AHA has recently concluded that they are higher in cholesterol than most fish and shellfish. Even so, they're lower in cholesterol than most meats and poultry—and *all* shellfish are naturally very low in saturated fat. To preserve that lean character, be sure to prepare shellfish without extra fat.

Fresh shrimp and scallops should look firm and have a mild, slightly sweet aroma. Live oysters, clams, and mussels should have tightly closed shells. If the shells are not closed, they should close when tapped; if they remain open, discard them.

If you buy shellfish frozen, be sure it's frozen solid and free of odor; reject any packages with accumulated liquid.

Snacks are the downfall of many a well-intentioned heart-healthy regime. It's difficult to do without something salty, crunchy, or sweet at odd times of day, and sorting out the healthful choices from the jumble of possibilities can be discouraging. How can one dodge fat, saturated fat, cholesterol, calories, sugar, and salt and still enjoy a satisfying munch? In fact, the task isn't that tough. Beyond such clearly wholesome selections as baby-cut carrots, cherry tomatoes, seedless grapes, and long-stemmed strawberries, you'll find quite a few packaged snacks that meet your criteria.

Cookies, in general, get 40 to 60 percent of their calories from fat. A more healthful cookie has less fat than average (preferably 30 percent or less calories from fat) and is made with an acceptable fat, not coconut oil, palm oil, or animal fat. Satisfying choices include vanilla wafers, gingersnaps, animal crackers, graham crackers, and fig and other fruit-filled bars.

Pretzels, if unsalted or lightly salted, are a great heart-healthy snack. Mostly flour and water, they're baked, not fried. Most kinds contain 20 percent or less calories from fat, but check the label to be sure.

Popcorn can be made at home in a hot-air popper or microwave popper with little or no oil, keeping the fat well below 30 percent. If you buy microwave popcorn, try to find a low-fat version; some kinds are high in fat (and salt).

Specialty chips made from bagels or pita bread can be a healthful snack if they're baked and contain a minimum of fat.

FROZEN FOODS

By now, frozen foods are an acknowledged part of most American diets. Main dishes, accompaniments, sauces, desserts, and complete dinners abound. Some prepared frozen foods are high in fat and sodium, so be sure to read the labels before you buy.

Frozen dinners and entrées are hard to beat when time is short. Choose them carefully, looking for those with no more than 30 percent of calories from fat (10 grams fat or less per 300-calorie serving). Many products labeled "light" or "healthy" meet this goal, but don't assume that every item of a particular brand will meet your specifications simply because one product in the line does.

Beware of high sodium levels. For a frozen dinner, sodium content should be less than 850 milligrams—about a third of the recommended daily allowance for most people. Also be sure the cholesterol content doesn't exceed your limit for a meal.

For a complete meal, complement a frozen dinner with fat-free milk, a slice of whole-grain bread, extra vegetables or a salad with fat-free dressing, and fruit for dessert. That way you'll be sure to get the fiber, vitamin A, and vitamin C a nutritious meal should include.

Frozen vegetables are a great time saver when you need to prepare a meal in a hurry. A wide variety is available year-round, and the nutritional content can be as good as or better than that of fresh produce. When you buy bagged frozen vegetables, be sure they're loose in the package; this lets you know they haven't been thawed, then refrozen.

Frozen desserts such as nonfat and low-fat yogurt, sherbet, sorbet, and ices are sensible alternatives to ice cream. Fruit frozen without sugar is also a good starting point for a dessert sauce.

CONDIMENTS

Like other prepared foods, condiments are often high in sodium and fat, so read labels closely.

When you buy soy sauce, catsup, salsa, mustard, Worcestershire sauce, and teriyaki sauce, look for low-sodium or reduced-sodium versions.

Standard preparations of mayonnaise and salad dressings are high in fat, cholesterol, and sodium. It's best to buy a fat-free mayonnaise; the next best choice is a reduced-fat product with only half to two-thirds the calories of regular mayonnaise and less than half the fat.

Select bottled salad dressings with monounsaturated or polyunsaturated oils listed on the ingredient label. Steer clear of those made with cheese, egg yolks, and cream. You'll find a wide variety of commercial low-fat and nonfat dressings, and the salad recipes beginning on page 94 include some tempting dressings you can make at home.

EQUIPPING YOUR KITCHEN FOR HEART-HEALTHY COOKING

To make heart-healthy cooking easier, you may want to invest in the utensils and small appliances described below.

A **food processor** and/or **blender** makes quick work of chopping, slicing, mincing, shredding, and puréeing. A blender or small food processor is ideal for making fresh fruit beverages such as smoothies (pages 232–233) and puréeing vegetables for wholesome soups.

A **broiler pan** is standard equipment with most new ranges; if you don't have one, it's well worth the investment. The pan's rack lifts the food above any fat that drips from it. For easy cleaning, coat the inside of the pan with vegetable oil cooking spray before you use it.

A **gravy skimmer** or **fat-separating cup** lets you pour skimmed cooking liquid from the cup's bottom; fat rises to the top and can easily be discarded. A **fat-off ladle** works on the same principle and is useful for smaller amounts of liquid.

A **perforated loaf pan** makes it easier for meat loaf lovers to have a favorite food in low-fat form. The pan liner has holes that let fat drain into the outer pan, away from the meat.

Nonstick baking pans and **muffin pans** need no greasing or oiling in order to turn out low-fat baked treats. **Paper pan liners** and **baking cups** achieve the same results, as does **baking parchment.**

Nonstick frying pans can be found in a wide range of sizes and shapes. They're a good investment, allowing you to cook with a minimum of fat.

A **steamer** can be as simple as a collapsible metal basket that fits into a variety of ordinary pans. For more ambitious jobs, look for a covered two-piece steamer consisting of a perforated container that fits into a deep pan.

COOKING SMART FOR A HEALTHY HEART

You've made wise choices at the supermarket. The next step is to cook those healthful foods wisely, using low-fat cooking techniques and utensils that facilitate heart-healthy cooking.

COOKING TECHNIQUES

Some methods are better than others for cutting fat, cholesterol, and calories while bringing out flavor and preserving nutritional value. As you prepare the recipes in this book, you'll learn the advantages of each of these techniques.

Baking is cooking food in an oven with dry heat. The technique is essentially the same as roasting (see page 29), but the term "baking" is most often used in reference to cooking fish, soufflés, casseroles, breads, and desserts such as cakes, pies, and cookies.

Oven-frying is a low-fat baking technique in which food is arranged on a rack or in a shallow pan (exposing all sides to the heat) to produce a crisp coating suggestive of deep-fat frying. Oven-frying is ideal for lean pork chops, chicken (see Chicken Fingers, page 92), and fish (see Cornmeal-crusted Fish, page 57).

Braising, also called stewing or simmering, is particularly good for developing tenderness in lean cuts of meat that benefit from long, slow cooking. You can use this technique for range-top or oven cooking. Braised foods such as large cuts or substantial cubes of meat are usually browned first, then covered and cooked in liquid at low heat for an hour or more. This gentle process relaxes fibrous meats until they're fork tender. You'll find some tempting variations on this method in such recipes as Beef Stew with Almonds & Olives (page 67) and Green Chile Stew (page 138), cooked with a technique we call "sweating."

Broiling, like baking, is a dry-heat cooking method. Food is placed directly under the heat source, usually in the oven. To raise or lower the cooking temperature, you move the food closer to or farther away from the heat source.

Grilling is similar to broiling, but the heat source is below rather than above the food. You place the food on a grill above hot charcoal or a gas flame; any fat in the food drips down onto the heat source, creating a flavorful, aromatic smoke.

Poaching keeps food moist and tender without added fat. You cook the food in simmering water, broth, or other liquid; the cooking liquid absorbs flavor and can later be used to make a sauce. Jeweled Chicken (page 71) and Poached Seafood with Potatoes & Fennel (page 161) are two elegant examples of this technique.

Roasting refers to baking at a constant moderate temperature (usually around 325°) to produce a well-browned surface and moist interior. (Roasting meat along with vegetables at a higher temperature can also be successful; see Roast Beef with Fennel, page 125, for example.) Most poultry and reasonably tender cuts of meat can be roasted with good results; use a rack that elevates the food above its drippings and enables heat to penetrate evenly.

Sautéing is defined as cooking food quickly in a small amount of fat in a frying pan over direct heat. Using a nonstick frying pan or sauté pan (deeper than a frying pan) helps limit the amount of fat needed. You can also coat the pan with vegetable oil cooking spray, or—for even leaner results—brown the food in a small amount of broth, wine, or water.

Steaming is a nutritious cooking method; because foods are cooked over, not in, boiling water, water-soluble vitamins and minerals are preserved. You need not add fat when you steam foods. To increase flavor, add herbs or spices to the water.

Stir-frying is associated with Asian dishes, but the technique works just as well for other cuisines. It involves cooking small pieces of food over high or medium-high heat, all the while keeping the food moving so it doesn't stick. You can accomplish it with little or no fat (see Stir-fried Pork & Asparagus, page 134), and a wide, heavy frying pan is nearly as effective as the traditional wok.

MODIFYING RECIPES WHILE KEEPING THE GOOD TASTE

We hope that many of the recipes in this book will become regulars in your menu plans. But what of your longtime favorites? Don't think you must abandon them all; you can still prepare many of them—in healthier guise—by following the fat-lowering techniques in our recipes. As a start, use these guidelines.

One way to modify a recipe is to change the cooking method. For example, instead of pan-frying chicken chunks for an appetizer, you can oven-fry them (see Chicken Fingers, page 92).

You can also slim down a recipe by changing one or more ingredients. This can be a bit more complicated than changing the technique. Begin by identifying the sources of fat in a recipe; then take steps to alter those ingredients so the dish will be lighter and more nutritious. Keep in mind that there are three basic ways to modify a high-fat ingredient: reduce the amount of the ingredient, omit it entirely, or use something that's lower in fat. In the oven-fried chicken above, for instance, you can simply substitute lean skinless chicken breasts for higher-fat chicken pieces with skin. For other recipes, though, you must determine if an ingredient trade-off can be made without damaging the finished dish.

As you plan your make-overs, ask these questions:

- Will the recipe work if high-fat ingredients are reduced?
- Are all the ingredients—particularly those that are high in fat—essential?
- If there is a high-fat topping, can it be omitted? If not, can the topping be made with lower-fat ingredients?
- Do any of the ingredients exist in a nonfat, reduced-fat, lower-calorie, or lower-sodium version?
- Do any of the proposed ingredient modifications require a change in technique to make them practical?

Heart-Healthy Macaroni & Cheese

HEALTHY HEART RECIPE MAKE-OVER

With a few judicious ingredient substitutions, you can make your family's favorite recipes more healthful. Have a look at these before-and-after versions of a basic macaroni and cheese recipe. The old-fashioned goodness remains unchanged—but some simple substitutions for the high-fat ingredients have significantly reduced the calories, fat, saturated fat, and cholesterol.

TRADITIONAL MACARONI & CHEESE

PREPARATION TIME: *About 20 minutes*
COOKING TIME: *20 to 30 minutes*

   12 ounces dried elbow macaroni
    5 tablespoons butter or margarine
    1 cup soft bread crumbs
    1 tablespoon grated Parmesan cheese
    1 cup chopped onion
   ¼ cup all-purpose flour
   ½ teaspoon paprika
   ⅛ teaspoon ground nutmeg
    3 cups milk
    3 cups (about 12 oz.) shredded sharp Cheddar cheese
       Salt and pepper

1. In a 5- to 6-quart pan, bring about 3 quarts water to a boil over high heat; stir in pasta and cook, uncovered, until just tender to bite (6 to 8 minutes). Or cook pasta according to package directions. Drain well.

2. While pasta is cooking, melt 1 tablespoon of the butter in a small frying pan over medium heat. Mix in bread crumbs and Parmesan cheese; set aside.

3. In a 3- to 4-quart pan, melt remaining 4 tablespoons butter over medium-high heat. Add onion and cook, stirring often, until soft but not brown (3 to 4 minutes). Blend in flour and cook, stirring constantly, until bubbly. Then mix in paprika and nutmeg. Remove pan from heat and gradually stir in milk; return to heat and continue to cook, stirring, until sauce boils and thickens (5 to 7 minutes). Add Cheddar cheese and stir until melted. Remove pan from heat. Season sauce to taste with salt and pepper.

4. Add pasta to cheese sauce and mix lightly. Pour into a shallow 2½- to 3-quart casserole; sprinkle with crumb mixture. Bake in a 450° oven until crumbs are browned (5 to 8 minutes).

MAKES 6 TO 8 SERVINGS

Per serving: 559 calories (47% calories from fat), 29 g total fat, 18 g saturated fat, 89 mg cholesterol, 486 mg sodium, 51 g carbohydrates, 2 g fiber, 23 g protein, 508 mg calcium, 3 mg iron

HEART-HEALTHY MACARONI & CHEESE

PREPARATION TIME: *About 20 minutes*
COOKING TIME: *About 20 minutes*

   12 ounces dried elbow macaroni
    2 slices whole wheat bread (about 2 oz. *total*)
    1 tablespoon grated Parmesan cheese
   ¾ teaspoon paprika
    1 cup chopped onion
   ¼ cup all-purpose flour
    2 cans (about 12 oz. *each*) evaporated fat-free milk
    1 cup vegetable or fat-free reduced-sodium chicken broth
    3 cups (about 12 oz.) shredded reduced-fat sharp Cheddar cheese
   ⅛ teaspoon ground nutmeg
       Salt and pepper

1. Cook pasta as directed at left for Traditional Macaroni & Cheese. Drain well.

2. While pasta is cooking, tear bread into ½-inch chunks. In a food processor or blender, combine bread, Parmesan cheese, and ¼ teaspoon of the paprika; whirl until mixture forms coarse crumbs. Set aside.

3. In a 3- to 4-quart pan, combine onion and 2 tablespoons water. Cook over high heat, stirring often, until onion is soft (about 4 minutes). Stir in flour and remaining ½ teaspoon paprika. Remove from heat.

4. Blend milk and broth into onion mixture, stirring until smooth. Return to medium-high heat and cook, stirring, until sauce boils all over (about 5 minutes). Remove from heat, add Cheddar cheese, and stir until melted. Add nutmeg; season to taste with salt and pepper.

5. Add pasta to cheese sauce and mix lightly. Pour into a shallow 2½- to 3-quart casserole; sprinkle with crumb mixture. Bake in a 450° oven until crumbs are browned (3 to 4 minutes).

MAKES 6 TO 8 SERVINGS

Per serving: 455 calories (20% calories from fat), 10 g total fat, 6 g saturated fat, 39 mg cholesterol, 599 mg sodium, 58 g carbohydrates, 2 g fiber, 32 g protein, 776 mg calcium, 3 mg iron

DAIRY PRODUCTS

It's important to keep dairy products in your meal planning; they're excellent sources of the calcium your body needs. Low-fat and fat-free versions of milk and other dairy items can be used in many recipes.

Milk, half-and-half, or cream in many recipes can be replaced by reduced-fat, low-fat, or fat-free milk. If the result doesn't seem creamy enough, try mixing in a tablespoon or more of instant nonfat dry milk. You'll see that we call for evaporated fat-free milk in the sauce for the Heart-healthy Macaroni & Cheese on the previous page; it's a product that often can be substituted for whole milk or half-and-half for added body and creaminess.

Cheese with reduced fat is now found in increasing variety, but because many such cheeses still contain over 50 percent calories from fat, you should use them discreetly. See the box at left for a few pointers on cooking with cheese.

Sour cream and yogurt are often dolloped over soups and desserts. Fat-free and reduced-fat versions make fine replacements. When you cook with these lean products, however, you should be aware that, because they lack fat, they react differently to heat.

- When you add fat-free sour cream or yogurt to other ingredients, fold it in to prevent thinning.
- Bring fat-free sour cream or yogurt to room temperature before adding it to hot food; blend in a little of the hot food first to prevent separation.
- When finishing a sauce with yogurt, keep temperature low and heating time short to preserve a smooth texture.

EGGS

Eggs account for more than a third of the cholesterol in American diets. But because all the egg's cholesterol is in the yolk, you can use egg whites freely. In cooked dishes like scrambled eggs and omelets, and in baked goods such as cookies, pancakes, muffins, and other quick breads, you can use two egg whites in place of each whole egg. In a recipe that makes more than one serving, you can retain one or more whole eggs for color and flavor. As examples, see Chocolate-Orange Cheesecake (page 226) and the scrambled eggs that fill Breakfast Pocket Sandwiches (page 45).

When you substitute egg whites for whole eggs in scrambled eggs, frittatas, and the like, cook them slowly over low heat; because they're so much lower in fat, they can be toughened by high heat.

MEATS, POULTRY & FISH

If you choose lean cuts and cook them appropriately, you can still include red meats in your heart-healthy regime. To control fat intake, however, it makes sense to eat poultry, seafood, pasta, grains, and legumes more frequently than meat.

COOKING WITH CHEESE

When you cook with cheese, heed the following tips.

- Shred or grate cheese to extend it.

- Decrease the amount of cheese called for in a recipe by a third to a half. Using a more robust-tasting cheese—Romano rather than Parmesan, for example—will give you more total flavor.

- Substitute reduced-fat Cheddar, jack, jarlsberg, and Swiss cheeses for their higher-fat counterparts.

- Choose low-fat or nonfat cottage cheese and part-skim ricotta cheese. Lower-fat cottage cheese can often replace ricotta.

- Light cream cheeses such as Neufchâtel can be used in many recipes, as can the fat-free version.

TIPS FOR COOKING LEAN MEAT

- Use a meat thermometer. An instant-read thermometer will enable you to check the internal temperature of even a thin piece of meat so that it cooks just to the rare to medium stage.

- Marinate lean meats in an acid-based marinade. There's some question about whether a marinade can actually tenderize meat, but it will certainly add moistness and flavor.

- Braise large cuts of lean meats in gently simmering liquid until they are tender and juicy.

Meat contributes fat, saturated fat, and cholesterol to the diet. To minimize these, select the leanest cuts (see pages 23–24) and trim away all visible fat. If you're unaccustomed to cooking such lean fare, it may seem dry to you, since there's less fat to keep it juicy. To keep lean meats as moist as possible, it's important to avoid overcooking (which will indeed make the meat dry). For advice on cooking lean meats, see the box at left.

Poultry will contain only half as much fat if you skin it before cooking. Keep it moist by using a lower cooking temperature and checking it often near the end of cooking time to avoid overcooking. As is true for meat, a thermometer can help you determine doneness.

Remember that the white meat of chicken or turkey is lower in fat than the dark meat.

Try substituting poultry for red meat in some of your favorite recipes to decrease saturated fat and cholesterol.

Fish and shellfish should be enjoyed at least two or three times a week to meet heart-healthy dietary goals. With the exception of types high in beneficial omega-3 fatty acids (see page 26), fish is naturally low in fat. What makes all the difference is the preparation method. Learn to select varieties of fish that take well to the low-fat cooking methods described on pages 28–29.

Go easy on higher-cholesterol shellfish such as shrimp and crayfish; other shellfish can be eaten as often as desired. You might wish to substitute scallops for half the shrimp in recipes in which shrimp is the main ingredient.

GRAINS, FRUITS & VEGETABLES

Prepared simply or eaten in their natural state, fruits, vegetables, and grains (including whole-grain products such as breads and pastas) are some of the most healthful foods you can eat. But the way you prepare and serve them can make a big difference in their nutritional value. It's best to cook pasta, rice, grains, and vegetables with little or no added fat; for vegetables, focus on steaming, sautéing, and stir-frying.

When you buy bakery breads, look for those made with no added fat or with monounsaturated oils or margarines.

SUGARS & FATS

Sugars and fats are needed in many recipes, especially those for baked goods. Granulated, brown, and powdered sugars as well as butter, margarine, and vegetable oils act as tenderizers and also help provide the crisp, brown crust characteristic of many breads and desserts. Still, you should try to use sugars and fats sparingly when you bake.

Sugars are not known to play a direct role in the development of heart disease, but they may contribute to obesity, a secondary risk factor (see page 11). And if your triglycerides (see page 9) are elevated, your doctor may advise you to cut down on the sugar in your diet.

LIVING A HEALTHY LIFESTYLE　　**33**

When preparing recipes that contain sugar, try cutting the quantity by a third to a half. Brown sugar and honey taste sweeter than granulated sugar, so you may be able to substitute one of them—and use less in so doing.

Accent flavor in desserts by slightly increasing the amounts of spices such as cinnamon, nutmeg, or cloves; or use a bit more vanilla or other flavoring. You can also add natural sweetness in the form of dried fruits such as raisins, cranberries, apricots, or dates, or with a dollop of applesauce or mashed banana.

Fats behave differently in cooking and baking for many reasons, starting with their sources and structures. Some come from animals, some from plants; some are natural, some manufactured. Fats are solid at room temperature, while oils are liquid.

In cooking, you can switch from butter to margarine or vegetable oil to cut cholesterol and saturated fat. But that change doesn't cut calories: butter, margarine, and oil all have 100 to 120 calories per tablespoon.

Decreasing cooking fat can be as simple as omitting added fat, reducing the amount of fat called for, or sautéing in a nonstick frying pan with a spritz of vegetable oil cooking spray.

Cutting or substituting fats in baking presents certain problems, because fats aren't always interchangeable. However, you can usually reduce fat in recipes for quick breads and baked desserts by a fourth to a third. But should you substitute a light margarine for butter—in cookies, for example—the results may not please you. That's because light versions of butter and margarine contain more water and less fat, by volume, than regular butter and margarine. That changes the proportions of ingredients in a recipe just as if you'd not only added less fat, but also increased the amount of liquid.

Mayonnaise is an emulsion of oil and eggs, so it is very high in fat. In salads and dressings, you can use fat-free, reduced-calorie, or cholesterol-free mayonnaise in place of the higher-fat version.

WHEN THE HEALTHY HEART DINES OUT

You shouldn't assume that only the food you prepare and eat at home "counts" as part of a heart-healthy diet. It's also important to know how to make healthful choices from restaurant menus, whether you dine in the restaurant or purchase the food to enjoy at home or on a picnic. You'll find a number of pointers in the box on page 35.

EATING IN SPECIALTY RESTAURANTS

Successful restaurateurs know it's smart today to offer heart-healthy choices. Because the traditional foods of many cuisines are inherently healthful, you'll be able to make wise selections from their menus if you know what to look for.

Chinese menus include many steamed and stir-fried chicken and seafood dishes abundant in vegetables. Choose steamed rice over fried

FATS USED IN COOKING

- **Butter** is a natural fat containing about 20 percent water. The water is emulsified, or suspended throughout the butter.

- **Margarine** consists of hydrogenated vegetable oils processed to resemble butter through the addition of color, flavor, and moisture. The conversion of oil to solid fat produces the controversial trans fatty acids, which are thought to play a role in raising cholesterol levels.

- **Light butter and margarine** contain added water (or other nonfat ingredients), which gives them more volume. Thus, measure for measure, you get less fat.

- **Vegetable shortening,** like margarine, is made from hydrogenated vegetable oils. But as the fat cools and firms, air is incorporated rapidly to make it soft and malleable.

- **Vegetable oils** are, in general, made from seeds, grains, beans, nuts, or fruits. For the most part (olive oil is an exception), they're refined until clear in color and neutral in flavor.

TIPS FOR EATING OUT

Fortunately, many restaurants now use a special menu symbol to indicate dishes made with a minimum of fat. Even if you're looking at an unannotated menu, however, you can let the following suggestions guide you.

• Order entrées and appetizers that are broiled, grilled, steamed, roasted, poached, or stir-fried.

• When possible, select entrées such as pilafs, stir-fries, or curries made with vegetables and grains.

• Watch portion sizes. If you get more than you should eat, ask for a container so you can take the rest home for another meal.

• To keep portion size manageable, try ordering a healthful appetizer in place of an entrée.

• Order a low-fat appetizer. It will take the edge off your appetite, so you'll be satisfied with a light main dish.

• Choose vegetable, bean, or tomato-based soups over creamed soups.

• Ask for low-fat or reduced-calorie salad dressing, and request that it be served on the side.

• Choose whole-grain breads and rolls; avoid croissants and other butter-rich breads.

• Order a turkey or chicken breast sandwich, and hold the mayonnaise and cheese. Avoid sandwiches made with such high-fat meats as corned beef, bologna, meatballs, pastrami, sausage, luncheon meats, and meat loaf.

• For dessert, choose fresh fruit, fruit ice or sorbet, low-fat frozen yogurt, or angel food cake. A fruit sauce rather than whipped cream, custard sauce, or chocolate sauce will complement your dessert without adding fat.

rice, and make the rice a substantial part of your meal. If sodium is a concern, be sure the food is prepared without monosodium glutamate; use soy sauce sparingly.

French restaurants might seem hazardous to the health-minded. But remember *nouvelle cuisine!* Though its heyday is over, this one-time trend resulted in big changes in the way French food is prepared today. Sauces rich in butter, cream, and egg yolks are no longer *de rigueur.* Now you can usually find fish and shellfish, chicken, and lean meats that have been poached, broiled, or grilled, then seasoned with fresh herbs and wine-based sauces. And French bread is as lean as it is crusty and delicious.

Italian food includes plenty of healthful choices. Start with minestrone or another broth-based vegetable soup. Top your pasta with seafood such as clams or mussels or a tomato or vegetable sauce. Good main-dish options include shrimp, chicken, rabbit, or veal, lightly sautéed or in a tomato or mushroom sauce. Italian ice is a virtually fat-free dessert.

Japanese food is for the most part so lean that you can enjoy it often. Start with a delicate broth-based *miso* soup or one that's hearty with noodles. Then savor broiled teriyaki-seasoned fish or chicken—or the same foods quickly seared with vegetables on a grill at your table or counter. Enjoy the rice and fish combinations of the sushi bar. Just stay away from battered and fried *tempura*.

Mexican and other Latin-American and Caribbean cuisines are based on beans, rice, and corn. As long as they are prepared with a minimum of fat, these foods can be ordered without qualms. For a starter, savor gazpacho, black bean soup, or a spicy seafood broth. Fajitas made with grilled chicken or fish are fine, as are soft tacos and burritos filled with chicken, seafood, or vegetables. Stay away from over-generous cheese and sour cream toppings; often you can ask that these be omitted. Fresh fruit such as melon, banana, or pineapple is a refreshing dessert choice.

TIPS FOR EATING ON THE ROAD

Traveling presents a serious challenge to the healthy heart. Low-fat choices are limited at the most accessible fast-food establishments, and they may grow monotonous on a lengthy trip.

To make sure you get enough fiber and other vital nutrients, consider taking along a cooler and a few basic implements so you can have a picnic of fresh fruit, peanut butter on whole-grain bread, and fat-free milk en route. Carry along a basket of heart-smart snacks such as fruit, baby-cut carrots, part-skim string cheese, and pretzels.

When you go into a roadside restaurant, order the lowest-fat poultry, fish, or lean meat offered. And keep your trips to the salad bar nutritious by going heavy on lettuce and vegetables and limiting fatty embellishments.

When you're pressed for time and the dinner hour looms, can you cook up something light and fresh in a twinkling? If it's a chilly afternoon and you yearn for an old-fashioned, stick-to-the-ribs supper, can the menu be nutritious as well? You've invited friends for a get-together, and you'd like to offer fare that's both healthful and hospitable. Is there an entrée to fill the bill?

The answer to all these questions is a resounding yes. On these two pages, you'll find plenty of ideas for nutritious, quick-cooking dinners, comforting suppers, and menus for entertaining. All feature recipes from this book, rounded out with everyday foods requiring little or no preparation. (For still more suggestions, see pages 40–81.)

SUMMER SALAD LUNCH

Feature fresh summer fruits in this refreshing menu for four. For dessert, heap strawberries or cherries in your prettiest bowl. With a ¹/₂-cup serving of strawberries, the calorie total per serving is 415; with cherries, 441 (grams of total fat: 6 to 7).

Fruit Salad with Lemon–Poppy Seed Dressing (page 98)

Lemon-Date Tea Bread (page 217)

Strawberries or Sweet Cherries

Iced Tea

EASY BUT EXOTIC

The sophisticated flavors that enliven this Mexican-style chicken dinner for four are surprisingly quick and easy to produce. Complement the main dish with a dessert of sliced papayas drizzled with fresh lime juice. The calorie total per serving, including two tortillas and a half papaya, is 661 (grams of total fat: 9).

Quick Chicken Mole (page 142)

Steamed Rice

Warm Corn Tortillas

Sliced Papayas with Lime

WINTRY WEEKEND SUPPER

To warm up a cold evening, serve big bowls of colorful, vegetable-rich lentil soup and wedges of home-baked soda bread. The soup serves eight, so you can invite the gang in after an afternoon hike or bicycle ride. With a ¹/₂-cup serving of carrots, a banana, and 1 cup of milk, calories per serving total 596 (grams of total fat: 9).

Lentil & Kale Soup (page 112)

Baby-cut Carrots

Sunflower Soda Bread (page 213)

Ripe Bananas

Low-fat Milk

FOR SPECIAL COMPANY

Impress important guests with this elegant three-course dinner for six to eight—it even concludes with a luscious cheesecake! With a ¹/₂-cup serving of asparagus, the calorie total per serving (without wine) is 928 (grams of total fat: 23).

Red & Green Salad (page 95)

Pork Tenderloin with Rum Chutney (page 130)

Pine Nut Pilaf (page 182)

Steamed Asparagus

Chocolate-Orange Cheesecake (page 226)

Merlot or Zinfandel (optional)

Espresso Coffee

DINNER FROM THE OVEN FOR SIX

You can use the same oven to bake a crusty quick bread and bright bell peppers filled with ground lamb and spicy rice. Peas seasoned with green onions cook quickly in a skillet on the range top when the main dish is almost done. Offer crisp apples for dessert. With a medium-size apple, calories per serving total 731 (grams of total fat: 16).

Lamb-stuffed Bell Peppers (page 135)

Petite Peas with Browned Butter (page 202)

Irish Brown Bread (page 213)

Crisp Apple Wedges

Hot Tea

CLAMS WITH AN ITALIAN ACCENT

Steamed clams are a good choice for heart-healthy dining at home or away. In this supper for four, they're teamed with fresh fennel and cooked in a tomato-wine broth to make a generous one-bowl entrée. We suggest steamed broccoli as a side dish, with crisp breadsticks for crunch. With a 1/2-cup serving of broccoli, two breadsticks, one tangerine, and two cookies per person, calories per serving total 681 (grams of total fat: 9).

Clams & Fennel in Tomato Broth (page 171)

Steamed Broccoli

Sesame Breadsticks

Tangerines

Spiced Biscotti (page 228)

Italian Roast Coffee

LEAN & LIVELY THAI-STYLE TURKEY PASTA

You'll please enthusiasts of spicy Thai flavors and pasta lovers alike with this quick supper for four. Cool palates with a dessert of chilled peach soup made with frozen peaches. Make the salad using a total of two oranges and one large grapefruit, and allow a 1-cup serving of bok choy for each diner—and the caloric total per serving will be 692 (grams of total fat: 7).

Orange & Grapefruit Salad on Watercress

Thai Turkey & Pasta (page 150)

Steamed Baby Bok Choy

Frosty Peach Soup (page 123)

SEAFOOD IN A SNAP

As dramatic as it is easy to cook, this menu for four features fresh halibut fillets. Prepare just a half-recipe of the green beans to serve alongside the main dish. With a 1/2-cup serving each of sorbet and berries, the calorie total per serving (not including wine) is 517 (grams of total fat: 7).

Halibut with Horseradish Mashed Potatoes & Chard (page 160)

Green Beans with Garlic Crumbs (page 193)

Lemon Sorbet with Fresh Raspberries

Sauvignon Blanc (optional)

A GOOD NIGHT FOR CHILI

It's a healthful habit to turn to meatless recipes at least once a week. The mild chili that stars in this menu for four is also quick to make, requiring little more than half an hour to prepare and cook. Allow one pear per person and about 2 tablespoons of chocolate sauce to dip it in, and the calorie total per serving (not including beer) will be 774 (grams of total fat: 13).

Black Bean Chili (page 188)

Yogurt Cornbread (page 214)

Comice Pears with Warm Chocolate Sauce

Beer or Iced Tea

SPRING VEGETABLE CELEBRATION FOR FOUR

Colorful with spring produce, this pasta will please your vegetarian friends—or anyone who just loves vegetables. Round out the repast with a handsome loaf of homemade yeast bread (if time is short, you can purchase similar breads at a bakery). For dessert, top frozen yogurt with fresh strawberries. With a 1/2-cup serving each of yogurt and berries, calories per serving total 624 (grams of total fat: 14).

Bow Tie Pasta Primavera (page 179)

Dried Tomato Basil Bread (page 211)

Vanilla Low-fat Frozen Yogurt with Sliced Strawberries

Sparkling Mineral Water with Lemon Twists

Healthy Heart

Menus

A nutritious breakfast helps make you feel good all day. And there are so many healthful foods to choose! Energy-rich whole-grain cereals and breads, luscious fresh fruits and juices all through the year, and fat-free and reduced-fat dairy products offer both good nutrition and endless variety in taste and texture. In the pages ahead, you'll find ideas for hurried weekday breakfasts as well as menus for more leisurely meals to savor on relaxed weekends or holidays.

One important part of a heart-healthy diet is fruit or real fruit juice—at least three servings every day. Fruits are cholesterol free, generally high in vitamins, minerals, potassium, and fiber, and typically low in fat, calories, and sodium—all good reasons to give them a prominent place in your meals. And because fruits taste so refreshing in the morning, breakfast is a natural time to enjoy them.

Breakfasts & Brunche

Fit for the Day Breakfast

MENU

Gingersnap Granola with Fresh Raspberries and Fat-free Milk

Banana-Walnut Muffins (page 218)

Hot Spiced Tea

For a quick, good-tasting breakfast that starts the day with a nutritious boost, you can't beat granola. This one is really lean, because it's held together by an egg white meringue rather than with butter or other fat.

The muffins are exceptionally low in fat as well. Their secret ingredient is prune purée; you can use prune baby food or a puréed prune-apple product made to substitute for shortening in baking (look for this in the baking ingredients section of your supermarket). The recipe makes a generous two dozen muffins, so you can bake and freeze them ahead, then reheat in oven or microwave.

Gingersnap Granola

Crisp chunks of oats and gingersnaps combine with dried apples and crystallized ginger in a lightened-up granola. The recipe is an abundant one, yielding enough for snacks as well as breakfast.

PREPARATION TIME: *About 20 minutes*
BAKING TIME: *About 40 minutes*

- 5 cups regular rolled oats
- 3 cups (about 8 oz.) gingersnaps, broken into almond-size pieces
- 2 cups spoon-size shredded wheat cereal
- ½ cup toasted wheat germ
- 1 teaspoon ground cinnamon
- 3 large egg whites (about 6 tablespoons)
- ¼ teaspoon cream of tartar
- ⅓ cup sugar
  Vegetable oil cooking spray
- 2 cups (about 6 oz.) chopped dried apples
- ⅓ cup chopped crystallized ginger
  Fat-free milk
  Fresh raspberries or sliced fresh strawberries

1. In a large bowl, combine oats, gingersnap pieces, shredded wheat cereal, wheat germ, and cinnamon. Stir until well combined; set aside.

2. In another large bowl, beat egg whites and cream of tartar with an electric mixer on high speed until soft peaks form. Add sugar, 1 tablespoon at a time, beating after each addition until sugar is completely dissolved. Fold egg whites into oat mixture, pressing ingredients together with your hands until all dry ingredients are well coated.

3. Coat two 10- by 15-inch baking pans with cooking spray. Press oat mixture into pans, dividing it evenly. Bake in a 300° oven until mixture is golden brown and sticks together (about 40 minutes).

4. Add half the apples and half the ginger to one of the pans; add remaining apples and ginger to second pan. Stir until granola breaks into large chunks. Let cool completely in pans on racks.

5. Package cooled granola airtight. Store at room temperature for up to 1 month. Serve with milk and berries.

MAKES ABOUT 12 CUPS

Per ½ cup: 169 calories (12% calories from fat), 2 g total fat, 0 g saturated fat, 0 mg cholesterol, 78 mg sodium, 33 g carbohydrates, 3 g fiber, 5 g protein, 22 mg calcium, 2 mg iron

Sunday Breakfast

A leisurely Sunday morning repast is one of the weekend's great pleasures. Crisp, fragrant waffles are ideal for such relaxed breakfasts or brunches, sure to bring smiles all around the table. While you wait for the waffles to bake, make an occasion of the meal with a pitcher of sparkling Citrus Spritzers to sip. Or delight in the luxury of fresh-squeezed orange juice or a citrus blend, such as orange juice combined with tangerine or pink grapefruit juice. This menu is designed for four to six.

Citrus Spritzers

The juice and aromatic peel of oranges and limes give this drink its refreshing tingle. It's delightful at cocktail time, too.

PREPARATION TIME: *About 15 minutes*

3 medium-size oranges (about 1½ lbs. *total*)

2 large limes (about 8 oz. *total*)

2 cups white grape juice

Ice cubes

About 2 cups sparkling mineral water or club soda

1. With a vegetable peeler or citrus zester, cut 3 strips zest (orange part of peel only) from 1 orange. Cut 2 strips zest (green part of peel only) from 1 lime. Place orange and lime zests in a pitcher and bruise with a wooden spoon.

2. Squeeze juice from oranges. From 1 lime, cut 6 thin slices and reserve. Squeeze remaining limes to make juice. Add orange juice, lime juice, and grape juice to pitcher; stir to blend. (At this point, you may cover and refrigerate juice blend and lime slices separately for up to 1 day.)

3. For each serving, fill a tall glass with ice, juice blend, and sparkling water, using about 2 parts juice blend to 1 part water. Garnish with lime slices.

MAKES 4 TO 6 SERVINGS

Per serving: 115 calories (2% calories from fat), .20 g total fat, 0 g saturated fat, 0 mg cholesterol, 10 mg sodium, 30 g carbohydrates, 0 g fiber, 1 g protein, 21 mg calcium, 0 mg iron

Belgian Waffles

Topped with fresh berries and a dusting of powdered sugar, these crisp waffles are a special treat. Use a mild-flavored monounsaturated vegetable oil, such as canola oil.

PREPARATION TIME: *About 10 minutes*
BAKING TIME: *4 to 5 minutes per waffle*

- 2 cups all-purpose flour
- 4 teaspoons baking powder
- ¼ teaspoon salt
- 1 tablespoon granulated sugar
- 1½ cups fat-free milk
- 1 large egg
- 2 large egg whites (about ¼ cup)
- 3 tablespoons vegetable oil
- ½ teaspoon vanilla
- Vegetable oil cooking spray
- 2 tablespoons powdered sugar
- Sliced fresh strawberries or whole raspberries (optional)
- Mint sprigs (optional)

1. In a medium-size bowl, stir together flour, baking powder, salt, and granulated sugar. Set aside.

2. In a large bowl, combine milk, egg, egg whites, oil, and vanilla. Beat with an electric mixer on medium speed until well combined. Gradually add flour mixture, beating on low speed until blended.

3. Preheat a Belgian waffle iron according to manufacturer's directions. Coat with cooking spray. For each waffle, fill iron with about ¼ cup batter; bake until waffle is well browned and crisp and stops steaming (4 to 5 minutes). Remove to a rack and keep warm in a 200° oven while you bake remaining waffles.

4. Sprinkle with powdered sugar; serve with berries and garnish with mint sprigs, if desired.

MAKES 4 TO 6 SERVINGS (TWELVE 4-INCH-SQUARE WAFFLES TOTAL)

Per waffle: 138 calories (28% calories from fat), 4 g total fat, 1 g saturated fat, 18 mg cholesterol, 241 mg sodium, 20 g carbohydrates, 1 g fiber, 4 g protein, 133 mg calcium, 1 mg iron

Hurry-up Breakfast

Inevitably, some days begin in a whirl of activity that leaves no time for a sit-down breakfast. For such times, here's a menu for four to eat either at home or en route to school or work. You can even save the oatmeal squares for later; enjoy them as a midmorning snack with fat-free milk, wherever you may be.

Breakfast Pocket Sandwiches

Fresh vegetables season the lightened-up scrambled egg filling for whole wheat pita breads.

PREPARATION TIME: *About 20 minutes*
COOKING TIME: *6 to 8 minutes*

- 2 **whole wheat pita breads (each** 6 to 7 inches in diameter)
- 2 **large eggs**
- 4 **large egg whites (about ½ cup)**
- ⅓ **cup low-fat (2%) cottage cheese**
- ¼ **teaspoon black pepper**
  Vegetable oil cooking spray
- 1 **cup thinly sliced mushrooms**
- ¼ **cup finely chopped onion**
- ⅓ **cup finely chopped red bell** pepper
- ⅓ **cup shredded reduced-fat** Cheddar cheese

1. Cut pita breads in half crosswise. Stack, wrap in foil, and place in a 350° oven while preparing filling.

2. In a medium-size bowl, combine eggs, egg whites, cottage cheese, and black pepper; whisk until well combined. Set aside.

3. Coat a wide nonstick frying pan with cooking spray. Place over medium-high heat. When pan is hot, add mushrooms, onion, and bell pepper. Cook, stirring often, until mushrooms are lightly browned (3 to 4 minutes).

4. Reduce heat to low. Pour in egg mixture and cook, gently lifting cooked portions with a wide spatula to let uncooked eggs flow underneath, until eggs are softly set. Remove from heat and stir in Cheddar cheese; spoon mixture evenly into warm pita bread halves.

MAKES 4 SERVINGS

Per serving: 195 calories (26% calories from fat), 6 g total fat, 2 g saturated fat, 114 mg cholesterol, 406 mg sodium, 21 g carbohydrates, 3 g fiber, 16 g protein, 118 mg calcium, 1 mg iron

The Main Squeeze

This smooth pink combination of fruits and fresh-squeezed orange juice is low in fat, quick to prepare—and portable, if you're really pressed for time.

PREPARATION TIME: *About 7 minutes (15 minutes if you squeeze the oranges yourself)*

- 1½ **cups fresh ripe strawberries,** hulled and sliced
- 1 **cup fresh or frozen raspberries**
- 1 **medium-size banana (about** 6 oz.), peeled and sliced
- 1 **cup chilled orange juice (prefer-** ably freshly squeezed)

1. In blender, combine strawberries, raspberries, banana, and orange juice; whirl until smooth.

2. To serve, pour into tall glasses.

MAKES 4 SERVINGS (ABOUT 3½ CUPS TOTAL)

Per serving: 85 calories (6% calories from fat), 1 g total fat, 0 g saturated fat, 0 mg cholesterol, 1 mg sodium, 20 g carbohydrates, 3 g fiber, 1 g protein, 23 mg calcium, 1 mg iron

Oatmeal Date Squares

Here's an unexpected way to enjoy your morning oatmeal—as a husky bar cookie with a luscious cooked date filling. Bake the bars in advance, ready to munch at a moment's notice.

PREPARATION TIME: *About 25 minutes*
BAKING TIME: *26 to 28 minutes*

1½ cups chopped pitted dates
¾ cup water
2½ tablespoons lemon juice
    Vegetable oil cooking spray
1 cup regular rolled oats
¾ cup all-purpose flour
¼ cup whole wheat flour
½ teaspoon baking soda
⅛ teaspoon salt
⅓ cup butter or margarine, at room temperature
⅔ cup firmly packed brown sugar
1 teaspoon vanilla

1. In a 1½- to 2-quart pan, combine dates, water, and lemon juice. Bring to a boil over medium-high heat; then reduce heat and cook, stirring often, until mixture is thickened (about 5 minutes). Remove from heat and set aside.

2. Coat a 9-inch-square baking pan with cooking spray.

3. In a medium-size bowl, stir together oats, flours, baking soda, and salt. In a large bowl, beat butter, brown sugar, and vanilla until fluffy. Then add oat mixture, mixing until well blended (dough will be crumbly).

4. Press 2 cups of the dough firmly over bottom of baking pan; set remaining dough aside. Bake crust in a 375° oven until it looks puffy (6 to 8 minutes).

5. Remove pan from oven. Gently spread crust with date filling. Spoon remaining dough evenly over top. Return to oven and bake until topping is golden brown (about 20 minutes).

6. Remove from oven and let cool in pan on a rack. Cut into 2¼-inch squares. If made ahead, cover airtight and store at room temperature for up to 3 days.

MAKES 16 SQUARES

Per square: 163 calories (23% calories from fat), 4 g total fat, 2 g saturated fat, 10 mg cholesterol, 101 mg sodium, 31 g carbohydrates, 2 g fiber, 2 g protein, 19 mg calcium, 1 mg iron

Patio Brunch

A sun-dappled patio is the perfect setting for a spring or summer brunch—and this elegant menu for eight is the perfect way to welcome guests and celebrate a lovely late morning. To save time, you can prepare the crêpes up to a day in advance, then cover and refrigerate them until you're ready to add the filling. Serve the melon medley as a first course; or offer it alongside the crêpes, in individual butter lettuce cups.

Gingered Triple Melon Medley

Finely chopped crystallized ginger adds a subtle zip to this colorful fruit cocktail.

PREPARATION TIME: *About 20 minutes, plus at least 1 hour to chill*

2 tablespoons lime juice

2 tablespoons honey

2 tablespoons finely chopped crystallized ginger

2 cups seeded cantaloupe balls

3 cups seeded watermelon balls

3 cups seeded honeydew melon balls

Lime slices (optional)

1. In a large bowl, stir together lime juice and honey until honey is dissolved. Mix in ginger.

2. Add cantaloupe, watermelon, and honeydew melon balls, mixing lightly.

3. To blend flavors, cover and refrigerate for at least 1 hour (or for up to 3 hours). Garnish with lime slices at serving time, if desired.

MAKES 8 SERVINGS

Per serving: 86 calories (4% calories from fat), .40 g total fat, 0 g saturated fat, 0 mg cholesterol, 15 mg sodium, 21 g carbohydrates, 1 g fiber, 1 g protein, 16 mg calcium, 0 mg iron

Lemon-Blueberry Muffins

These tart-sweet, fruit-filled muffins are made with fat-free buttermilk and brushed with a lemon glaze during their last few minutes in the oven.

PREPARATION TIME: *About 15 minutes*
BAKING TIME: *23 to 25 minutes*

- 2 cups all-purpose flour
- ⅔ cup sugar
- 2 teaspoons baking powder
- ½ teaspoon baking soda
- ¼ teaspoon salt
- 1 large egg
- ¼ cup vegetable oil
- ⅔ cup fat-free buttermilk
- ½ teaspoon vanilla
- 2 teaspoons grated lemon peel
- 1 cup fresh or frozen blueberries
   Lemon Glaze (recipe follows)

1. In a large bowl, stir together flour, sugar, baking powder, baking soda, and salt. In a small bowl, beat egg with oil until blended; then stir in buttermilk, vanilla, and lemon peel.

2. Add egg mixture to flour mixture and stir just until dry ingredients are evenly moistened (batter will be stiff). Gently fold blueberries into batter.

3. Divide batter evenly among 12 paper-lined 2½-inch muffin cups (or coat cups with vegetable oil cooking spray before filling). Bake in a 375° oven for 15 minutes. Meanwhile, prepare Lemon Glaze.

4. After muffins have baked for 15 minutes, remove pan from oven and brush hot muffins with Lemon Glaze. Return to oven and continue to bake until muffins are golden brown (8 to 10 more minutes). Remove from pan and serve warm.

MAKES 1 DOZEN MUFFINS

Lemon Glaze. In a small bowl, combine 2 tablespoons **sugar** and 1 tablespoon **lemon juice.** Stir until sugar is dissolved.

Per muffin: 187 calories (25% calories from fat), 5 g total fat, 1 g saturated fat, 18 mg cholesterol, 204 mg sodium, 32 g carbohydrates, 1 g fiber, 3 g protein, 68 mg calcium, 1 mg iron

Crab & Green Onion Crêpes

A thin, eggy batter gives these famous pancakes their sturdy yet delicate texture. Here, the batter is made with egg whites and just a single egg, producing lower-fat crêpes. Filled with sweet crab in a savory, herb-flecked sauce, they're a good choice for a light supper as well as a brunch entrée.

PREPARATION TIME: *About 30 minutes, plus 1 hour for crêpe batter to stand*
COOKING TIME: *45 minutes to 1 hour*

- 16 Light Crêpes (recipe follows)
- 2 teaspoons vegetable oil
- 6 ounces mushrooms, thinly sliced
- 1 cup thinly sliced green onions
- 1 tablespoon chopped fresh thyme or 1 teaspoon dried thyme
- 1 tablespoon all-purpose flour
- ¼ teaspoon salt
- ½ teaspoon dry mustard
- ⅛ teaspoon ground red pepper (cayenne)
- 1 cup low-fat (1%) milk
- 1 pound cooked crabmeat
- 2 tablespoons chopped parsley
- 2 teaspoons lemon juice
  Vegetable oil cooking spray
  Thyme sprigs (optional)

1. Prepare Light Crêpes; set aside.

2. Heat oil in a wide nonstick frying pan over medium-high heat. Add mushrooms, onions, and chopped thyme; cook, stirring often, until mushrooms begin to brown (3 to 5 minutes). Reduce heat to medium; then stir in flour, salt, mustard, and red pepper. Cook, stirring constantly, until bubbly. Remove from heat and gradually stir in milk; return to heat and continue to cook, stirring, until sauce boils and thickens (about 3 minutes). Remove from heat and add crab, parsley, and lemon juice; mix to distribute crab well.

3. Coat two 8- by 11-inch or 9- by 13-inch baking pans with cooking spray. Spoon about 3 tablespoons of the crab mixture down center of each crêpe; roll to enclose. Arrange crêpes, seam side down, in pans.

4. Cover pans with foil and bake in a 350° oven until crêpes are heated through (18 to 20 minutes). Uncover and broil about 6 inches below heat until tops of crêpes feel dry when lightly touched (1 to 2 minutes).

5. To serve, place 2 crêpes on each plate; garnish with thyme sprigs, if desired.

MAKES 8 SERVINGS

Light Crêpes. In a blender or food processor, combine 1 **large egg,** 3 **large egg whites** (about 6 tablespoons), ⅔ cup **all-purpose flour,** 1½ teaspoons **vegetable oil,** and 1¼ cups **low-fat (1%) milk;** whirl until smoothly blended. Cover and refrigerate batter for at least 1 hour or up to 8 hours.

Heat a 6- to 7-inch nonstick crêpe pan or other flat-bottomed frying pan over medium heat. Coat with **vegetable oil cooking spray.** Stir batter and pour about 2 tablespoons into pan, quickly tilting pan so batter coats pan bottom in a thin layer. Cook until surface of crêpe feels dry and edges are lightly browned. Turn with a spatula and cook until browned on other side. Turn out onto a plate. Repeat with remaining batter, stacking crêpes as made. Makes 16 to 20 crêpes.

Per serving: 181 calories (29% calories from fat), 6 g total fat, 1 g saturated fat, 86 mg cholesterol, 296 mg sodium, 14 g carbohydrates, 1 g fiber, 18 g protein, 162 mg calcium, 2 mg iron

When you invite close friends to share a casual lunch or supper, there's no need to spend hours in the kitchen. Innumerable healthful alternatives go together quickly—and taste much fresher and better than the fat-laden entrées and desserts so often served to company.

One of the keys to vivid flavor is using spices and fresh herbs inventively. Chili Turkey Wraps, the centerpiece for a casual Sunday night supper, are made with chili-flavored tortillas and a cilantro-accented filling. The Yogurt Pesto Pasta that stars in our impromptu pasta fest sparkles with basil. Paprika and white pepper add a savory tingle to the coating for crisp baked fish you can serve in half an hour or less on a busy Friday night (or any night). And chili powder, green chiles, and fresh garlic bring a South-western piquancy to a festive baked chicken dinner for six.

Quick Casual Dinner

Summer Sunday Night

MENU

Chili Turkey Wraps

Red & Yellow Cherry Tomatoes

Sliced Peaches

Berry Pink Lemonade

On warm evenings when you're not up to more complicated cooking, sandwiches are a convenient choice. These are made without bread; instead, creamy turkey and refreshing salad ingredients are wrapped up in flavored tortillas. The filling tastes wonderful when made with cold turkey or chicken roasted on a rotisserie or in a covered barbecue earlier in the week.

For best results, use freshly purchased tortillas; if you keep them in the fridge, let them warm to room temperature so they'll be more flexible and less likely to crack when rolled. Chili-flavored tortillas make colorful wrappers, but if they're not available, you can simulate their flavor by mixing $\frac{1}{2}$ teaspoon chili powder into the cheese mixture used in the filling.

This menu is designed to serve four—but because the rosy lemonade is so refreshing on a sultry evening, we've provided a generous recipe (enough for six to eight). You can prepare and refrigerate it up to a day in advance. Wait to add the ice until serving time, the better to keep the flavor bright.

Chili Turkey Wraps

Delicious as they are with turkey or chicken, these versatile sandwiches can also be made with other cooked meats. For variety, try very thinly sliced rare lean beef (such as top round) or medium-rare leg of lamb.

PREPARATION TIME: *About 25 minutes*

- 1 large package (about 8 oz.) nonfat cream cheese, at room temperature
- 3 to 4 tablespoons tomato-based chili sauce
- 4 large chili-flavored or plain low-fat flour tortillas (*each* about 10 inches in diameter), at room temperature
- 2 cups finely slivered romaine lettuce
- 3 to 4 cups shredded cooked turkey or chicken
- ½ cup thinly sliced green onions
- ¼ cup chopped cilantro
- 1 can (about 2¼ oz.) sliced ripe olives, drained
- Cilantro sprigs

1. In a small bowl, combine cream cheese and chili sauce; mix until smooth. Spread a fourth of the cheese mixture evenly over one side of each tortilla.

2. Down center of each tortilla, spoon a fourth each of the lettuce, turkey, onions, chopped cilantro, and olives.

3. Roll tortillas snugly to enclose filling, then cut each roll in half crosswise. If desired, stand rolls upright on cut ends. Garnish with cilantro sprigs.

MAKES 4 SERVINGS

Per serving: 461 calories (16% calories from fat), 8 g total fat, 2 g saturated fat, 101 mg cholesterol, 1,165 mg sodium, 43 g carbohydrates, 4 g fiber, 52 g protein, 288 mg calcium, 5 mg iron

Berry Pink Lemonade

Revitalize wilting spirits with a long, cool sip of this refreshing raspberry-lemon drink.

PREPARATION TIME: *About 15 minutes, plus at least 1 hour to chill*

- ¾ cup sugar
- 6 cups cold water
- 1 cup fresh lemon juice
- 1 cup fresh or frozen raspberries
- Ice cubes
- Thin lemon slices (optional)

1. In a 2½- to 3-quart pitcher or refrigerator container, combine sugar, cold water, and lemon juice; stir until sugar is dissolved.

2. In a blender or food processor, whirl raspberries until puréed. Press purée through a fine wire strainer over a bowl; discard seeds. Add purée to lemonade.

3. Cover and refrigerate until lemonade is cold (at least 1 hour) or for up to 1 day. Before serving, stir well; then pour into glasses or a larger pitcher. Add ice cubes to taste. Garnish with lemon slices, if desired.

MAKES 6 TO 8 SERVINGS (ABOUT 8 CUPS TOTAL)

Per cup: 88 calories (1% calories from fat), 1 g total fat, 0 g saturated fat, 0 mg cholesterol, 0 mg sodium, 23 g carbohydrates, 1 g fiber, 0 g protein, 6 mg calcium, 0 mg iron

Impromptu Pasta Fest

Every cook cherishes the recipe that can be put together at a moment's notice with foods usually kept on hand in the refrigerator, freezer, and pantry. This saucy pasta is just such a recipe. Good at any time of year, it will serve six to eight friends and family members for a spontaneous party in less than an hour.

The dessert is a country-style, custardlike treat of French origin. Like the pasta, it's adaptable to every season. In late summer, prepare it with fresh prune plums; when they're not available, use moist dried prunes.

Yogurt Pesto Pasta

Just ⅔ cup of ham adds a mildly smoky flavor to the tangy sauce for this vermicelli dish. If you like, choose turkey ham to trim fat a bit more. To speed preparation, start preparing the sauce as the water for the pasta is coming to a boil.

PREPARATION TIME: *About 30 minutes*
COOKING TIME: *About 15 minutes*

- 2 teaspoons olive oil
- 1 medium-size onion, chopped
- 3 cloves garlic, peeled and thinly sliced
- 6 ounces mushrooms, thinly sliced
- ⅔ cup chopped cooked ham
- 1 large can (about 15 oz.) tomato sauce
- ⅓ cup (about 3 oz.) prepared pesto; or 2 tablespoons dried basil
- 1 package (about 10 oz.) frozen chopped spinach, thawed and squeezed dry
- 1 pound dried vermicelli
- 2 cups plain nonfat yogurt
- 4 teaspoons cornstarch
- Salt and pepper
- Italian parsley sprigs (optional)

1. Heat oil in a wide frying pan over high heat. Add onion, garlic, and mushrooms. Cook, stirring often, until onion is soft (about 5 minutes). Add ham and continue to cook, stirring often, until mushrooms are lightly browned (about 5 more minutes).

2. Stir in tomato sauce and pesto; reduce heat to low. Mix in spinach and heat through.

3. Meanwhile, in a 6- to 8-quart pan, bring about 4 quarts water to a boil over high heat; stir in pasta and cook, uncovered, until just tender to bite (7 to 9 minutes). Or cook pasta according to package directions. Drain and keep warm.

4. In a medium-size bowl, smoothly mix yogurt and cornstarch. Stir yogurt mixture into sauce; increase heat to high and stir until sauce is bubbly (about 3 minutes). Season to taste with salt and pepper.

5. Pour sauce over pasta. Mix lightly, using 2 spoons, until pasta is well coated with sauce. Garnish with parsley sprigs, if desired.

MAKES 6 TO 8 SERVINGS

Per serving: 428 calories (21% calories from fat), 10 g total fat, 2 g saturated fat, 11 mg cholesterol, 746 mg sodium, 65 g carbohydrates, 4 g fiber, 19 g protein, 235 mg calcium, 5 mg iron

Plum or Prune Clafouti

If you place it in the oven before dinner, this vanilla-scented fruit dessert will be ready as you're finishing the main course.

PREPARATION TIME: *About 10 minutes*
BAKING TIME: *About 35 minutes*

- Vegetable oil cooking spray
- ½ cup granulated sugar
- 2 cups (about 12 oz.) fresh prune plums, halved and pitted; or 1 cup (about 9 oz.) quartered pitted prunes
- 2 large eggs
- 1 tablespoon vanilla
- 2 tablespoons all-purpose flour
- 1 cup reduced-fat (2%) milk
- 1 teaspoon grated lemon peel
- ⅛ teaspoon ground nutmeg
- Powdered sugar (optional)

1. Coat a 9-inch-round ceramic or glass pie dish with cooking spray. Sprinkle 2 tablespoons of the granulated sugar over bottom and sides of pan; scatter plum halves or prune pieces over sugar.

2. In blender or food processor, combine eggs, vanilla, and remaining 6 tablespoons granulated sugar; whirl until smooth. Add flour and whirl again until smooth. Then add milk and lemon peel; whirl until smooth. Pour mixture over plums or prunes; sprinkle with nutmeg.

3. Bake in a 375° oven until pudding is golden brown and feels set when lightly pressed (about 35 minutes). Let cool on a rack for about 10 minutes; then dust with powdered sugar, if desired. Serve warm.

MAKES 6 TO 8 SERVINGS

Per serving: 143 calories (15% calories from fat), 2 g total fat, 1 g saturated fat, 63 mg cholesterol, 36 mg sodium, 27 g carbohydrates, 0 g fiber, 4 g protein, 56 mg calcium, 1 mg iron

Friday Night Fish Bake

In many parts of the United States, fried fish is a Friday night favorite. If you want to cook with less fat, though, baked fish makes much more sense. And as this menu for four proves, the time-tested accompaniments for a fried fish dinner—tartar sauce, coleslaw, cornbread—taste just as good with baked fillets.

Many kinds of fish take well to baking. Catfish and white-fleshed fish such as orange roughy or rockfish are closest to the sorts usually chosen for frying, but fillets of halibut and even salmon also are excellent selections for baking in a seasoned cornmeal coating.

Cornmeal-crusted Fish with Tartar Sauce

Golden cornmeal gives fish fillets a crisp, crunchy coating. Mix up the tartar sauce while the fish is in the oven.

PREPARATION TIME: *About 15 minutes*
BAKING TIME: *5 to 7 minutes*

- ½ cup yellow cornmeal
- ¼ teaspoon paprika
- ¼ teaspoon white pepper
- ¼ teaspoon salt
- 1 large egg white (about 2 tablespoons)
- 1 tablespoon fat-free milk or water
- 1 pound boneless, skinless white-fleshed fish fillets, such as orange roughy, catfish, or rockfish (*each* about ½ inch thick)
  Vegetable oil cooking spray
- ¼ cup fat-free mayonnaise
- 1 tablespoon sweet pickle relish
- 1 tablespoon finely chopped onion
- 1 tablespoon white wine vinegar
  Liquid hot pepper seasoning

1. Place a 10- by 15-inch nonstick baking pan in a 500° oven until pan is hot (about 5 minutes).

2. Meanwhile, on a plate, mix cornmeal, paprika, pepper, and salt. In a shallow bowl, beat egg white and milk to blend.

3. Rinse fish fillets, pat dry, and cut into serving-size pieces. Dip fish into egg white mixture to coat; then roll in cornmeal mixture to coat. Set aside in a single layer.

4. When baking pan is hot, coat lightly with cooking spray. Quickly arrange fish pieces well apart in pan. Bake until browned on bottom (3 to 4 minutes). Then turn fish over and continue to bake until golden on top and just opaque but still moist in thickest part; cut to test (2 to 3 more minutes).

5. Meanwhile, make tartar sauce by stirring together mayonnaise, pickle relish, onion, and vinegar in a small bowl.

6. With a wide spatula, transfer fish to individual plates. Serve with tartar sauce and hot pepper seasoning.

MAKES 4 SERVINGS

Per serving: 166 calories (8% calories from fat), 1 g total fat, 0 g saturated fat, 23 mg cholesterol, 363 mg sodium, 17 g carbohydrates, 1 g fiber, 19 g protein, 42 mg calcium, 1 mg iron

Classic Coleslaw

Coleslaw is one of those simple, old-fashioned side dishes that never falls from favor. This recipe cuts the fat-filled ingredients from the traditional dressing without losing any of the flavor. To save time, purchase a coleslaw mix from the market; or, if you'd rather make your coleslaw from scratch, just shred enough cabbage and carrots to make 6 cups.

PREPARATION TIME: *About 5 minutes*

- ⅔ cup plain nonfat yogurt or fat-free mayonnaise
- 2 tablespoons Dijon mustard
- 2 tablespoons white wine vinegar
- 6 cups coleslaw mix
- ¼ cup thinly sliced green onions
  Salt and pepper

1. In a large bowl, combine yogurt, mustard, and vinegar; stir until smooth.

2. Add coleslaw mix and onions; mix lightly to coat with dressing. Season to taste with salt and pepper.

MAKES 6 SERVINGS

Per serving: 67 calories (6% calories from fat), .50 g total fat, 0 g saturated fat, 1 mg cholesterol, 173 mg sodium, 12 g carbohydrates, 1 g fiber, 4 g protein, 130 mg calcium, 1 mg iron

A Taste of the Southwest

Favorite Southwestern flavors mingle in this informal menu for six. Baked chicken breasts stuffed with jack cheese and mild green chiles play the starring role; complement them with a colorful hominy casserole. Look for a no-salt-added salsa to accent the chicken. With the meal, sip sangria, a fruited red wine punch. You can make it with alcohol-free wine, if you wish, adding fresh orange juice, sparkling water, and orange and lime slices to taste. For an easy dessert, offer fresh fruit and anise-scented cookies.

Chicken, Cheese & Chile Rolls

For a milder, more colorful dish, substitute roasted red bell peppers for the green chiles.

PREPARATION TIME: *About 30 minutes*
BAKING TIME: *About 30 minutes*

- 6 small boneless, skinless chicken breast halves (about 5 oz. *each*)
- 3 canned whole green chiles, halved and seeded
- 2 ounces reduced-fat jack cheese, cut into 6 strips
- ⅓ cup fine dry bread crumbs
- 1 clove garlic, minced or pressed
- 1 tablespoon chili powder
- 1½ teaspoons ground cumin
- ¼ cup evaporated fat-free milk
  Vegetable oil cooking spray
- 3 cups shredded iceberg lettuce
  Slivered jalapeño chiles (optional)
  Green chile salsa
  Fat-free sour cream

1. Rinse chicken and pat dry. Place each chicken piece between 2 sheets of plastic wrap. With a heavy, flat-surfaced mallet, pound chicken firmly but gently all over to a thickness of ¼ inch.

2. At one end of each pounded chicken piece, place a green chile half and a cheese strip. Roll up securely, tucking edges in; fasten with a small metal poultry fastener or a wooden pick.

3. In a shallow bowl, mix bread crumbs, garlic, chili powder, and cumin. Pour milk into another shallow bowl. Dip each chicken roll in milk to coat; then roll in crumb mixture to coat.

4. Lightly coat a 9- by 13-inch baking pan with cooking spray; arrange chicken rolls in pan, seam side down. Bake in a 400° oven until meat is no longer pink and filling is hot in center; cut to test (about 30 minutes).

5. Divide lettuce among 6 individual plates. Slice chicken rolls, if desired, and arrange over lettuce. Garnish with jalapeño chiles, if desired. Serve with salsa and sour cream to add to taste.

MAKES 6 SERVINGS

Per serving: 236 calories (17% calories from fat), 4 g total fat, 2 g saturated fat, 89 mg cholesterol, 468 mg sodium, 10 g carbohydrates, 1 g fiber, 38 g protein, 174 mg calcium, 2 mg iron

Southwestern Hominy

Hominy is a favorite ingredient in the Southwest, where it's often called posole or pozole. Thanks to its mild corn flavor, it's a perfect foil for vivid seasonings.

PREPARATION TIME: *About 25 minutes*
BAKING TIME: *About 30 minutes*

  Vegetable oil cooking spray
- 2 large tomatoes (about 1 lb. *total*), peeled, seeded, and chopped
- 1 large onion, finely chopped
- 1 clove garlic, minced or pressed
- 1 can (about 15½ oz.) golden hominy, drained
- ½ teaspoon chili powder
  Salt and pepper
- ⅓ cup shredded reduced-fat jack cheese

1. Coat a wide frying pan with cooking spray. Place over medium-high heat. When pan is hot, add tomatoes, onion, and garlic. Cook, stirring often, until onion is soft (about 5 minutes). Stir in hominy and chili powder; season to taste with salt and pepper.

2. Coat a 1½-quart baking dish with cooking spray. Add hominy mixture. Bake in a 350° oven for 25 minutes. Sprinkle with cheese; bake until cheese is melted (about 5 more minutes).

MAKES 6 SERVINGS

Per serving: 102 calories (19% calories from fat), 2 g total fat, 1 g saturated fat, 4 mg cholesterol, 212 mg sodium, 17 g carbohydrates, 3 g fiber, 4 g protein, 75 mg calcium, 1 mg iron

Throughout the year, the changing seasons yield a colorful procession of fresh produce to delight the palate. Nothing says "springtime" more clearly than a lamb dinner with artichokes, lemon, fresh mint, and asparagus—especially when the meal ends with the year's first blushing strawberries. To celebrate summer, serve barbecued Pacific salmon that shares the grill with corn roasted in its husks. And what better dessert can the season offer than golden ripe peaches and juicy raspberries?

For autumn harvest time, bake meaty portabella mushrooms stuffed with crab and cheese, then follow them with a spicy fresh banana cake. And banishing the chill of winter is no problem with a lean beef stew accented with sherry and almonds and teamed with bright, cinnamon-glazed baby carrots.

Each of these menus illustrates the importance of fresh vegetables and fruits in a light, healthful eating plan. Not only are they good for you—they're delicious, too.

The Season's Best

Spring Lamb Dinner

Though lamb is no longer exclusively a springtime treat, it's still just right for a lovely spring weekend. In this marvelous menu for four, thick lamb chops are served with a savory risotto accented with the traditional mint. To start the meal, offer fresh artichokes with a piquant sauce; accompany the main course with steamed asparagus. Conclude the repast with the very essence of spring: a basket or bowl of plump strawberries to dip in fat-free or light sour cream flavored with fresh lemon peel and juice and a little powdered sugar.

Lamb Chops with Mint Risotto

If the risotto is ready before the lamb, it can be kept warm over very low heat for a few minutes.

PREPARATION TIME: *About 20 minutes*
COOKING TIME: *20 to 25 minutes*

- 2 teaspoons butter or margarine
- ¼ cup chopped shallots
- 1½ cups arborio or other short-grain white rice
- 1½ teaspoons grated lemon peel
  About 4¼ cups fat-free reduced-sodium chicken broth
- 4 double-bone lamb rib chops (*each* about 1¾ inches thick; about 1½ lbs. *total*), trimmed of fat
- 1 teaspoon minced garlic
- ¼ cup balsamic vinegar
- 1 teaspoon sugar
- 1 cup lightly packed slivered fresh mint
- 3 tablespoons lemon juice
  Mint sprigs and lemon slices (optional)

1. In a 3- to 4-quart pan, combine butter and shallots; cook over medium heat, stirring, until shallots are limp (about 1 minute). Add rice and stir until some of the grains are opaque (about 2 more minutes).

2. Add lemon peel and 4 cups of the broth to rice; bring to a boil. Then reduce heat and simmer, uncovered, stirring often, until rice is just tender to bite but not starchy tasting (about 15 more minutes).

3. Meanwhile, place a wide ovenproof frying pan over high heat. Rub fatty side of chops in pan to oil it lightly; then lay chops in pan and cook, turning as needed, until browned on all sides (about 5 minutes).

4. Transfer pan with chops to a 400° oven. Bake until meat in thickest part is medium-rare (pink) to medium (only slightly pink); cut to test (15 to 20 minutes). Skim and discard fat from pan; then return pan with chops to high heat. Add garlic, vinegar, and sugar. Shake pan, stirring to loosen browned bits; then stir in ¼ cup of the slivered mint. Remove pan from heat.

5. If rice is cooked before lamb is ready, turn heat to very low and stir in about ¼ cup more broth. When lamb is ready, stir lemon juice and most of the remaining ¾ cup slivered mint into rice; if you want a creamier texture, add a little more broth. Sprinkle lamb and rice with remaining slivered mint; garnish with mint sprigs and lemon slices, if desired. Serve with pan juices.

MAKES 4 SERVINGS

Per serving: 426 calories (24% calories from fat), 11 g total fat, 4 g saturated fat, 58 mg cholesterol, 711 mg sodium, 56 g carbohydrates, 6 g fiber, 25 g protein, 66 mg calcium, 8 mg iron

Summer Salmon Barbecue

To celebrate summer, take your cue from the Northwest. For centuries, salmon was the centerpiece at native Indian potlatches–lavish celebrations with day after day of feasting and gift giving. This barbecue is a somewhat less ambitious affair, but you'll still need to prepare ahead by ordering a whole salmon fillet to serve six. You'll also need to obtain a suitable untreated wood plank for cooking the fish. Aromatic cedar is the traditional choice, but it's expensive; clear fir isn't as pricey, and it also works well. A 1 by 8 plank 18 to 19 inches long is big enough to hold the salmon and fits on a 20- to 22-inch-wide round barbecue.

Pinot-Plank Salmon Fillet

Soaked in Pinot Noir, this salmon takes on a rich, aromatic flavor as it grills in a covered barbecue. Corn in the husks cooks alongside, charring lightly over the hot coals. Serve small boiled red potatoes along with the fish and corn; plan on having them ready when the fish comes off the barbecue (they'll take about 20 minutes to cook).

PREPARATION TIME: *About 45 minutes, plus at least 4 hours to soak corn (plank, fish, and wood chips also soak during this time)*
COOKING TIME: *25 to 30 minutes*

- 6 large ears corn (12 oz. *each*)
- 1 bottle (750 ml.) Gewürztraminer
- 2 to 4 cups Pinot Noir
  Wood plank (see menu introduction on page 62)
- 2 cups alder or mesquite chips
- 1 whole salmon fillet with skin (2¼ to 2½ lbs.), about 18 inches long
- 6 *each* rosemary, marjoram, and thyme sprigs
- 12 to 18 hot boiled small red thin-skinned potatoes (*each* 1½ to 2 inches in diameter)
  Lemon wedges
  Salt and pepper

Grilling with Indirect Heat

When you grill with indirect heat, the hot coals or flames are on opposite sides of the food rather than directly beneath it, and the barbecue is covered.

If you're using charcoal briquets, mound and ignite 60 briquets on the fire grate of a barbecue with a lid; open vents. When briquets are dotted with gray ash (15 to 25 minutes), push half of them to each side of the fire grate. Add 5 more briquets to each mound.

If you use a gas barbecue, it must have a control to regulate heat in the center of the grill. To heat the barbecue, cover it; turn heat to high for 10 minutes. Then turn off heat in center of barbecue, but leave heat on sides on high.

1. Pull back corn husks, but don't remove them. Discard corn silk; pull husks back in place. In an 8- to 10-quart pan, combine Gewürztraminer and 1 gallon water. Add ears of corn and set a plate on top of them to keep them immersed. Soak corn for at least 4 hours at room temperature or for up to 1 day in the refrigerator.

2. In a container just wide and long enough to hold the plank (such as a sink, pan, or heavy-duty plastic food-storage bag), combine Pinot Noir with twice that amount of water (4 to 8 cups water, depending on how much wine you use). Rinse plank; immerse in Pinot Noir mixture for at least 1 hour or up to 1 day.

3. About 30 minutes before cooking, measure 2 to 3 cups of the Pinot Noir mixture into another container; add wood chips. Also rinse fish, then immerse in Pinot Noir mixture with plank.

4. Prepare barbecue for grilling with indirect heat (see box at left). Drain wood chips and sprinkle them over hot coals. Or, if using a gas barbecue, put chips in a smoke box or foil pan directly on heat in a corner as barbecue heats.

5. Lift fish and plank from liquid. Lay fish on plank, skin side down, and top with 3 sprigs each of rosemary, marjoram, and thyme.

6. Put barbecue grill in place. Set plank and fish on grill between coals (or in center of gas barbecue). Cover barbecue, open vents, and cook for 10 minutes (if plank chars, spritz or mop dark areas with water).

7. Drain corn and lay on grill directly over heat; cover barbecue. Turn corn as husks scorch. Cook until fish is just opaque but still moist in thickest part; cut to test (15 to 20 more minutes).

8. Transfer corn and plank with fish to the table. Discard scorched herb sprigs; replace with remaining rosemary, marjoram, and thyme sprigs. Arrange potatoes on plank; garnish with lemon wedges. To serve, cut fish into pieces and lift from skin with a spatula. Pull off corn husks. Season foods to taste with salt, pepper, and lemon.

MAKES 6 SERVINGS

Per serving: 508 calories (22% calories from fat), 12 g total fat, 2 g saturated fat, 81 mg cholesterol, 114 mg sodium, 51 g carbohydrates, 6 g fiber, 46 g protein, 69 mg calcium, 3 mg iron

Shrimp & Green Onion Quesadillas

Serve these tempting filled tortilla triangles while the salmon and corn are cooking.

PREPARATION TIME: *About 10 minutes*
BAKING TIME: *6 to 8 minutes*

- 4 ounces small cooked shrimp
- ⅔ cup shredded reduced-fat jack cheese
- ½ cup sliced green onions
- ¼ cup green chile salsa
- Vegetable oil cooking spray
- 8 low-fat flour tortillas (*each* 7 to 9 inches in diameter)
- Cilantro sprigs
- Cherry tomatoes

1. In a bowl, mix shrimp, cheese, onions, and salsa.

2. Coat 2 baking sheets with cooking spray. Place 2 tortillas on each sheet. Top tortillas with shrimp mixture, covering to within ¾ inch of edges. Top each tortilla with one of the remaining tortillas.

3. Bake in a 450° oven until tortillas are lightly browned (6 to 8 minutes), switching positions of baking sheets halfway through baking.

4. Slide quesadillas onto a serving board; cut each into 6 wedges. Garnish with cilantro sprigs and cherry tomatoes.

MAKES 6 SERVINGS

Per serving: 155 calories (17% calories from fat), 3 g total fat, 2 g saturated fat, 46 mg cholesterol, 442 mg sodium, 25 g carbohydrates, 6 g fiber, 11 g protein, 205 mg calcium, 2 mg iron

Peach & Raspberry Cloud Cake

The soft-baked meringue base of this cake is as velvety as cream, and it's drenched with fresh peaches and raspberries.

PREPARATION TIME: *About 25 minutes, plus 20 minutes for meringue to cool*
BAKING TIME: *1¼ to 1½ hours*

- Vegetable oil cooking spray
- All-purpose flour
- 5 large egg whites (about ⅔ cup)
- ½ teaspoon cream of tartar
- 1 cup plus 3 tablespoons sugar
- 1 teaspoon vanilla
- 1 teaspoon anise seeds, crushed
- 3 medium-size firm-ripe peaches (about 1 lb. *total*)
- 1½ cups fresh raspberries
- ½ teaspoon grated lemon peel
- 3 tablespoons lemon juice

1. Coat an 8-inch springform pan with cooking spray; dust with flour, tapping to remove excess. Set aside.

2. In a deep bowl, beat egg whites and cream of tartar with an electric mixer on high speed until frothy. Gradually add 1 cup of the sugar; continue to beat until stiff peaks form. Beat in vanilla and anise seeds.

3. Spread meringue evenly in pan. Bake in a 275° oven until pale golden (1¼ to 1½ hours). Run a thin-bladed knife between meringue and pan rim. Place on a rack and let cool for 20 minutes.

4. Meanwhile, peel and thinly slice peaches. In a bowl, lightly mix 2 cups of the peaches with ½ cup of the raspberries, 1 tablespoon of the sugar, lemon peel, and 1 tablespoon of the lemon juice. Set aside.

5. In a blender or food processor, combine remaining peaches with remaining 1 cup raspberries, 2 tablespoons sugar, and 2 tablespoons lemon juice; whirl until smooth. Rub purée through a fine strainer into a bowl; discard residue.

6. Remove pan rim and set meringue on a plate. Spoon sliced peach mixture onto cake and drizzle with about 2 tablespoons of the fruit purée. Cut cake into wedges; offer remaining purée to add to taste.

MAKES 6 TO 8 SERVINGS

Per serving: 190 calories (2% calories from fat), 1 g total fat, 0 g saturated fat, 0 mg cholesterol, 41 mg sodium, 45 g carbohydrates, 2 g fiber, 3 g protein, 13 mg calcium, 0 mg iron

Cozy Autumn Supper

Big portabella mushrooms filled with a savory crab stuffing are the centerpiece of this fall feast for four. Begin the meal with a quick, tart broccoli soup; conclude it with a spicy banana cake.

Broccoli & Buttermilk Soup

Deceptively creamy, this wholesome soup is made with reduced-fat butter-milk smoothed with a little cornstarch. Lemon and a touch of curry powder enhance the tangy flavor.

PREPARATION TIME: *About 10 minutes*
COOKING TIME: *About 10 minutes*

- 1 package (about 10 oz.) frozen chopped broccoli
- 4 cups fat-free reduced-sodium chicken broth
- 1 tablespoon grated lemon peel
- 2 tablespoons cornstarch
- ¼ teaspoon curry powder
- 1½ cups reduced-fat (1½%) buttermilk
   Salt and pepper

1. In a 3- to 4-quart pan, combine broccoli and 2 cups of the broth. Bring to a boil over high heat, using a spoon to break broccoli apart. As soon as broccoli is separated, pour broth-broccoli mixture into a food processor or blender. Add lemon peel, then whirl until smoothly puréed.

2. In pan, stir together remaining 2 cups broth with cornstarch until smooth. Stir in curry powder, then broccoli mixture. Bring to a boil over high heat, stirring often.

3. Stir in buttermilk, season to taste with salt and pepper, and serve at once. (Do not heat soup after adding buttermilk; the color will change for the worse.) To serve, ladle soup into 4 individual bowls or large mugs.

MAKES 4 SERVINGS

Per serving: 95 calories (16% calories from fat), 2 g total fat, 1 g saturated fat, 6 mg cholesterol, 626 mg sodium, 12 g carbohydrates, 1 g fiber, 8 g protein, 155 mg calcium, 1 mg iron

Crab-filled Portabella Mushrooms

Stuffed mushrooms are familiar as a party appetizer—but when the mushrooms are hefty portabellas, the dish makes a satisfying entrée. Accompany with a salad of tender baby greens in your favorite nonfat vinaigrette.

PREPARATION TIME: *About 15 minutes*
BAKING TIME: *20 to 25 minutes*

- 4 large portabella mushrooms (*each* about 4 inches in diameter; about 12 oz. *total*)
- 1 large egg white (about 2 tablespoons)
- 1 cup soft bread crumbs
- 8 ounces cooked crabmeat
- ¾ cup shredded reduced-fat jack cheese
- ¾ cup thinly sliced green onions
- 2 teaspoons Worcestershire
   Vegetable oil cooking spray
   Lemon wedges

1. Rinse mushrooms and pat dry. Remove and chop stems.

2. In a large bowl, lightly beat egg white; mix in bread crumbs, chopped mushroom stems, crab, cheese, onions, and Worcestershire.

3. Coat a 9- by 13-inch baking pan with cooking spray. Arrange mushrooms, cup side up, in pan. Spoon crab mixture on top of mushrooms, pressing it together lightly.

4. Bake in a 350° oven until cheese is melted and filling is lightly browned (20 to 25 minutes). Serve hot, with lemon wedges.

MAKES 4 SERVINGS

Per serving: 184 calories (28% calories from fat), 6 g total fat, 3 g saturated fat, 72 mg cholesterol, 427 mg sodium, 12 g carbohydrates, 2 g fiber, 22 g protein, 276 mg calcium, 2 mg iron

Winter Fireside Feast for Six

Count on a comforting stew to take the chill off a wintry evening! This one simmers unattended while you steam rice, poach baby carrots, and bake spicy cookies to serve with apples for dessert. For an especially cozy evening, serve dinner on a tray table at hearthside.

Beef Stew with Almonds & Olives

Cut into cubes, lean top round cooks to fork-tenderness thanks to "sweating," a technique that not only cuts fat, but also spares you the troublesome task of sautéing the meat to brown it. Serve the saucy dish with currant-sprinkled steamed brown rice.

PREPARATION TIME: *About 20 minutes*
COOKING TIME: *About 2 hours*

- 2 **pounds boneless beef top round, trimmed of fat and cut into 1-inch cubes**
- 1 **large onion, chopped**
- 2 **cloves garlic, minced or pressed**
- 2 **dried bay leaves**
- 2 **cups beef broth, skimmed of fat**
- 2/3 **cup dry sherry**
- 1/3 **cup slivered almonds**
- 12 **calamata olives, pitted**
- 1 **teaspoon cornstarch**
- 3 **cups hot cooked brown rice**
- 2 **tablespoons dried currants**
- 2 **tablespoons chopped parsley**

1. In a 5- to 6-quart pan, combine beef, onion, garlic, bay leaves, and 1/3 cup water. Bring to a boil over high heat; then reduce heat to medium, cover, and boil for 20 minutes. Uncover and continue to boil, stirring often, until liquid has evaporated and a dark brown film forms on pan bottom (about 15 minutes).

2. Add broth, 1/3 cup of the sherry, and almonds; stir to scrape browned bits free. Return to a boil; then reduce heat, cover, and simmer for 1 hour. Add olives, cover, and continue to simmer until beef is tender when pierced (10 to 15 more minutes).

3. If liquid in stew exceeds 1 cup, increase heat to high and boil, uncovered, until reduced to about 1 cup. (If there is less than 1 cup liquid, add water to make this amount.) In a small bowl, mix cornstarch and remaining 1/3 cup sherry. Stir sherry mixture into stew; stir until sauce is boiling and thickened.

4. Spoon rice around edge of a wide bowl; sprinkle with currants. Spoon stew into center of bowl; sprinkle with parsley.

MAKES 6 SERVINGS

Per serving: 418 calories (28% calories from fat), 13 g total fat, 3 g saturated fat, 86 mg cholesterol, 322 mg sodium, 33 g carbohydrates, 3 g fiber, 41 g protein, 53 mg calcium, 4 mg iron

Cinnamon-poached Baby Carrots

Give baby-cut carrots the elegant treatment: poach them with a cinnamon stick in a fruity white wine such as Sauvignon Blanc, Chenin Blanc, Gewürztraminer, Johannisberg Riesling, or white Zinfandel.

PREPARATION TIME: *About 5 minutes*
COOKING TIME: *About 25 minutes*

- 1 cup slightly sweet, fruity white wine
- ⅔ cup fat-free reduced-sodium chicken broth
- 1 cinnamon stick (about 2 inches long)
- 1 teaspoon butter or margarine
- 1 package (about 1 lb.) fresh baby-cut carrots
- Freshly ground pepper and nutmeg

1. In a wide frying pan, combine wine, broth, cinnamon stick, and butter. Bring to a boil over high heat. Add carrots; reduce heat, cover, and simmer, shaking pan occasionally, until carrots are tender when pierced (10 to 12 minutes).

2. Uncover pan; bring cooking liquid to a boil over high heat. Then boil, uncovered, shaking pan often, until almost all liquid has evaporated and carrots begin to brown (8 to 10 minutes).

3. Season carrots to taste with pepper and nutmeg; garnish with the cinnamon stick used for seasoning, if desired.

MAKES 6 SERVINGS

Per serving: 42 calories (16% calories from fat), 1 g total fat, 0 g saturated fat, 2 mg cholesterol, 98 mg sodium, 8 g carbohydrates, 2 g fiber, 1 g protein, 26 mg calcium, 1 mg iron

Mega-ginger Cookies

Nippy with bits of crystallized ginger, these soft, chewy molasses cookies are easily mixed up in your food processor.

PREPARATION TIME: *About 15 minutes, plus 1 hour to chill dough*
BAKING TIME: *11 to 12 minutes*

- ½ cup chopped crystallized ginger
- ¾ cup sugar
- 6 tablespoons butter or margarine, at room temperature
- ¼ cup molasses
- 1 large egg
- 2 cups all-purpose flour
- 2 teaspoons baking soda
- ¾ teaspoon ground cinnamon
- ½ teaspoon ground nutmeg

1. In a food processor, whirl ginger and ⅓ cup of the sugar until ginger is finely ground. Pour out of processor and set aside.

2. To processor, add butter and ⅓ cup more sugar; whirl until fluffy. Add ginger mixture, molasses, and egg; whirl until combined.

3. In a large bowl, stir together flour, baking soda, cinnamon, and nutmeg. Add flour mixture to butter mixture; whirl until well blended. Then cover dough and refrigerate until it is firm to the touch (about 1 hour).

4. Shape dough into 1-inch balls; roll in remaining sugar to coat. Place balls about 2 inches apart on nonstick or oiled regular baking sheets.

5. Bake in a 350° oven until cookies are a darker brown (11 to 12 minutes). Transfer cookies to racks and let cool. If made ahead, store airtight at room temperature for up to 1 week; freeze for longer storage.

MAKES ABOUT 4 DOZEN COOKIES

Per cookie: 59 calories (24% calories from fat), 2 g total fat, 1 g saturated fat, 8 mg cholesterol, 71 mg sodium, 11 g carbohydrates, 0 g fiber, 1 g protein, 7 mg calcium, 0 mg iron

Celebrate special occasions all year round with meals that are great tasting and easy on the waistline, too. You'll win thanks from those who have learned to dread the consequences of the usual overabundant holiday repasts.

Start with an intimate Valentine's Day dinner centered on poached chicken breasts in a luscious dried fruit sauce. The menu includes a chocolate dessert, of course—a must for Valentine's Day! In June, mark Father's Day with a traditional barbecue. The customary steak, potato salad, and pie are all given a lightened-up treatment that's worth taking to heart.

When Independence Day rolls around, a potluck picnic is in order. Our menu forgoes the usual hamburgers and hotdogs for a zesty oversized chicken sandwich, ready to take to a gathering at park or beach.

Even Thanksgiving, the year's most lavish feast, can be brought within heart-healthy boundaries. Our savory cornbread-stuffed turkey breast with all the usual trimmings provides the proof.

Holiday Entertaining

Valentine's Day Dinner for Four

MENU

Sparkling Wine

Jeweled Chicken

Spiced Couscous

Steamed Sugar Snap Peas with Lemon

Warm Raspberry-Fudge Brownies with Frozen Vanilla Yogurt

Here's an enticing dinner to share with a few close friends. Boneless chicken breasts are poached in an orange sauce dappled with dried cranberries and apricots, then served with fluffy spiced couscous and tender-crisp sugar snap peas. The dessert of warm, raspberry-marbled brownies topped with frozen yogurt is appropriately luxurious—but despite its lavish taste, it's judiciously low in fat.

Jeweled Chicken

Made with frozen boneless chicken breasts, this dish is as quick to cook as it is elegant.

PREPARATION TIME: *About 15 minutes*
COOKING TIME: *25 to 30 minutes*

1¼ cups fat-free reduced-sodium chicken broth

1 teaspoon grated orange peel

1 cup orange juice

¼ cup dry white wine

½ cup slivered dried apricots

⅓ cup dried cranberries

4 frozen boneless, skinless chicken breast halves (6 to 8 oz. *each*)

2 teaspoons cornstarch blended with 2 tablespoons water

Salt

2 green onions, thinly sliced

Slivered orange peel (optional)

1. In a wide frying pan, combine broth, grated orange peel, orange juice, wine, apricots, and cranberries. Add chicken to broth mixture, cover, and bring to a boil over high heat. Reduce heat and simmer until meat in thickest part is no longer pink; cut to test (15 to 20 minutes). Transfer chicken to a platter and keep warm.

2. Bring cooking liquid to a boil over high heat; boil, uncovered, until reduced to about 1 cup (3 to 4 minutes). Stir in cornstarch mixture and return to a boil, stirring until sauce is thickened. Season to taste with salt.

3. Spoon some of the sauce over chicken; pour remaining sauce into a bowl. Sprinkle chicken with onions and slivered orange peel, if desired. Offer remaining sauce to add to taste.

MAKES 4 SERVINGS

Per serving: 328 calories (8% calories from fat), 3 g total fat, 1 g saturated fat, 115 mg cholesterol, 309 mg sodium, 26 g carbohydrates, 2 g fiber, 48 g protein, 42 mg calcium, 2 mg iron

Spiced Couscous

Assertive curry-inspired seasonings accent this golden couscous.

PREPARATION TIME: *About 10 minutes*
COOKING TIME: *12 to 15 minutes*

- 2 teaspoons olive oil
- 1 small onion, finely chopped
- ¼ cup sliced almonds
- ⅓ cup golden raisins
- 1 teaspoon ground cumin
- ¼ teaspoon ground turmeric
- ¼ teaspoon ground cinnamon
- 2½ cups fat-free reduced-sodium chicken broth
- 2 teaspoons butter or margarine
- 1½ cups couscous

1. Heat oil in a wide nonstick frying pan over medium-high heat; add onion and cook, stirring, until onion is tinged with brown (about 3 minutes). Add almonds and raisins; stir for 1 more minute. Mix in cumin, turmeric, and cinnamon; continue to cook, stirring, until almonds are just toasted (about 1 more minute).

2. Add broth and butter; increase heat to high and bring mixture to a boil. Stir in couscous, cover, and remove from heat. Let stand until liquid has been absorbed (about 5 minutes). Fluff with a fork before serving.

MAKES 4 SERVINGS

Per serving: 390 calories (18% calories from fat), 8 g total fat, 2 g saturated fat, 5 mg cholesterol, 381 mg sodium, 67 g carbohydrates, 4 g fiber, 13 g protein, 51 mg calcium, 2 mg iron

Raspberry Fudge Brownies

To streamline these rich, dark brownies, we've substituted egg whites for some of the whole eggs a traditional batter would contain. You drizzle the batter with raspberry jam before baking; to make this step easier, microwave the jam briefly to melt it slightly. The brownies are wonderful served warm with frozen yogurt (be sure you choose the low-fat kind).

PREPARATION TIME: *About 15 minutes*
BAKING TIME: *About 35 minutes*

- 7 tablespoons butter or margarine
- ¾ cup unsweetened cocoa
- 2 cups sugar
- 1½ teaspoons vanilla
- 1 large egg
- 5 large egg whites (about ⅔ cup)
- 1 cup all-purpose flour
  Vegetable oil cooking spray
- ¼ cup seedless red raspberry jam

1. In a 2- to 3-quart pan, combine butter and cocoa. Stir over medium-low heat until butter is melted and mixture is well blended. Remove from heat and stir in sugar and vanilla.

2. Add egg and egg whites; beat with an electric mixer until blended. Then gradually add flour, beating until mixture is smooth.

3. Coat a 9-inch-square baking pan with cooking spray. Spread batter in pan. Drizzle jam evenly over top. Bake in a 325° oven until brownies feel dry on top and only a few moist crumbs cling to a wooden pick inserted in center (about 35 minutes).

4. Let cool in pan on a rack for about 15 minutes; then cut into 2¼-inch squares. Serve warm or at room temperature.

MAKES 16 BROWNIES

Per brownie: 202 calories (25% calories from fat), 6 g total fat, 4 g saturated fat, 27 mg cholesterol, 76 mg sodium, 37 g carbohydrates, 1 g fiber, 3 g protein, 11 mg calcium, 1 mg iron

Father's Day Barbecue

Barbecued beef and tried-and-true accompaniments such as potato salad, French bread, and a summer fruit pie add up to a June feast all dads will enjoy. The menu serves six.

Mushroom & Dried Tomato Crostini

Crunchy toasts topped with a savory spread are known as crostini in Italy. This version is easy on the olive oil but rich in good flavor.

PREPARATION TIME: *About 15 minutes, plus 15 to 20 minutes to soak tomatoes*
COOKING TIME: *About 15 minutes*

- ¼ cup dried tomatoes (not oil-packed)
- 1 tablespoon olive oil
- 1 pound mushrooms, chopped
- ¾ cup chopped shallots
- 2 cloves garlic, minced or pressed
  Salt and white pepper
- 18 slices crusty Italian or French bread (*each* about 3½ inches wide, 5 inches long, and ½ inch thick)
  Chopped parsley

1. Place tomatoes in a small bowl and cover with boiling water; soak until soft (15 to 20 minutes). Drain; squeeze out excess liquid. Finely chop tomatoes and set aside.

2. Meanwhile, heat oil in a wide frying pan over medium-high heat. Add mushrooms, shallots, and garlic. Cook, stirring often, until liquid has evaporated and mushrooms are browned (about 10 minutes). Transfer mixture to a food processor or blender and whirl until puréed. Transfer to a bowl, then stir in tomatoes. Season to taste with salt and pepper.

3. Place bread in a single layer on a baking sheet. Broil about 5 inches below heat, turning once, until golden on both sides (about 4 minutes total).

4. To serve, spread toast with mushroom mixture. Serve at room temperature; sprinkle lightly with parsley before serving.

MAKES 1½ DOZEN APPETIZERS

Per appetizer: 98 calories (17% calories from fat), 2 g total fat, 0 g saturated fat, 0 mg cholesterol, 169 mg sodium, 17 g carbohydrates, 1 g fiber, 3 g protein, 26 mg calcium, 1 mg iron

Seed-spiced Potato Salad

Toasted cumin and mustard seeds give this potato-and-carrot salad its out-of-the-ordinary flavor. Nonfat yogurt replaces the usual mayonnaise in the dressing, cutting fat and lending piquant flavor.

PREPARATION TIME: *About 20 minutes, plus at least 30 minutes to chill*
COOKING TIME: *About 10 minutes*

- 1½ pounds thin-skinned potatoes, peeled and cut into ¾-inch chunks
- 12 ounces carrots, peeled and cut into ¾-inch chunks
- 2 teaspoons vegetable oil
- 1 teaspoon black or yellow mustard seeds
- 1 teaspoon cumin seeds
- 2 cloves garlic, minced or pressed
- ¼ teaspoon pepper
- 1 cup plain nonfat yogurt
- ¼ cup chopped parsley
  Salt

1. Place potatoes and carrots on a rack above boiling water in a 5- to 6-quart pan. Cover and steam until vegetables are tender when pierced (about 10 minutes). Lift from pan and let stand until cool (or, to cool quickly, immerse vegetables in cold water). When vegetables are cool, drain well.

2. Heat oil in a small frying pan over high heat. Stir in mustard seeds and cumin seeds. Cover pan, remove from heat, and shake (holding lid on) until popping subsides (about 40 seconds). Then add garlic and pepper.

3. In a wide bowl, combine seed mixture, yogurt, potatoes, carrots, and parsley; mix gently to coat well. Season to taste with salt. Before serving, cover and refrigerate for at least 30 minutes or up to 6 hours.

MAKES 6 SERVINGS

Per serving: 144 calories (12% calories from fat), 2 g total fat, 0 g saturated fat, 1 mg cholesterol, 54 mg sodium, 27 g carbohydrates, 4 g fiber, 5 g protein, 108 mg calcium, 2 mg iron

Cabernet-Soy Tri-tip

Tri-tip, a boneless cut of beef from the bottom sirloin, is a favorite choice for the barbecue in certain parts of California. A robust marinade of red wine, soy, and ginger makes the lean meat especially flavorful.

PREPARATION TIME: *About 10 minutes, plus at least 30 minutes to marinate*
COOKING TIME: *25 to 35 minutes*

½ **cup Cabernet Sauvignon**
⅓ **cup sugar**
¼ **cup reduced-sodium soy sauce**
3 **quarter-size slices fresh ginger**
2 **cloves garlic, peeled**
1 **beef tri-tip roast (about 2 lbs.), trimmed of fat**

1. In a large heavy-duty plastic food-storage bag (at least 1-gallon size), combine wine, sugar, and soy sauce. With the flat side of a knife, crush ginger and garlic; add to wine mixture.

2. Wipe beef with a damp paper towel; add to bag. Seal bag; turn and shake to coat beef with marinade. Set bag in a pan and refrigerate, turning occasionally, for at least 30 minutes or up to 1 day.

3. Lift beef from bag, reserving marinade. Place beef on a lightly oiled grill 4 to 6 inches above a solid bed of medium coals or over medium heat on a gas grill (you can hold your hand at grill level for 4 to 5 seconds). Close lid on gas grill. Cook beef, turning as needed to brown evenly, until a meat thermometer inserted in thickest part registers 135°F for rare (20 to 30 minutes).

4. Transfer beef to a carving board, cover lightly, and let rest for 5 to 10 minutes. Meanwhile, pour reserved marinade into a 1- to 2-quart pan. Bring to a boil over high heat; then boil until reduced to about ½ cup (about 5 minutes). Using a slotted spoon, lift out and discard ginger and garlic. Pour reduced marinade into a bowl; add juices that have accumulated around beef.

5. To serve, slice beef thinly across the grain. Offer reduced marinade to add to taste.

MAKES 6 SERVINGS

Per serving: 257 calories (20% calories from fat), 6 g total fat, 2 g saturated fat, 95 mg cholesterol, 471 mg sodium, 13 g carbohydrates, 0 g fiber, 37 g protein, 13 mg calcium, 4 mg iron

Fourth of July Potluck Picnic

This portable menu is expandable, depending on the number of people involved. The main dishes are an ample chicken salad stuffed into a hollowed-out sourdough loaf and a spicy shrimp salad. (If you include the shrimp salad, transport the salad itself and the cantaloupe halves that hold it separately; assemble at serving time.) Add appetizers, vegetable crudités, cookies, and your choice of fresh summer fruit to suit all tastes.

Pinto Bean Pâté

Piquant braised-deglazed onions enrich this creamy dip. Serve it with crisp vegetables.

PREPARATION TIME: *About 20 minutes*
COOKING TIME: *About 15 minutes*

- 1 medium-size red onion (about 8 oz.), finely chopped
- 2 cloves garlic, minced or pressed
- 1 teaspoon chili powder
- ½ teaspoon ground cumin
- ½ to ¾ cup fat-free reduced-sodium chicken broth
- 3 tablespoons white wine vinegar
- 1 can (about 15 oz.) pinto beans, rinsed and drained
  Salt and pepper
  Red bell pepper strips and baby-cut carrots

1. In a wide nonstick frying pan, combine onion, garlic, chili powder, cumin, and ¼ cup of the broth. Cook over medium-high heat, stirring often, until liquid evaporates and onion begins to brown (about 8 minutes). To deglaze, add vinegar and stir to loosen browned bits.

2. Continue to cook, stirring occasionally, until mixture begins to brown again. Add 2 tablespoons broth; stir to scrape browned bits free. Repeat browning and deglazing steps 1 or 2 more times, using 2 tablespoons broth each time; onion should be richly browned.

3. Add beans to onion mixture, remove from heat, and mash with a wooden spoon; or transfer mixture to a food processor and whirl until coarsely puréed. If necessary, add a little more broth to give beans the texture of mashed potatoes. Season to taste with salt and pepper. Mound in a bowl. If made ahead, cover and refrigerate for up to 3 days. Serve with pepper strips and baby-cut carrots.

MAKES ABOUT 1½ CUPS

Per tablespoon: 15 calories (5% calories from fat), .09 g total fat, 0 g saturated fat, 0 mg cholesterol, 45 mg sodium, 3 g carbohydrates, 1 g fiber, 1 g protein, 7 mg calcium, 0 mg iron

Sourdough Chili Chicken Salad

An edible sourdough bread bowl conveniently transports this bold chicken salad to your picnic site. En route to the picnic in a cooler, the bread soaks up flavor from the dressing.

PREPARATION TIME: *About 35 minutes, plus at least 1 hour to chill*

- 2 oblong sourdough loaves (about 1 lb. *each*) or 1 large round sourdough loaf (about 1½ lbs.)
  Chili Dressing (recipe follows)
- 1 large yellow bell pepper (about 8 oz.), seeded and chopped
- ½ cup sliced radishes
- 1 can (about 4 oz.) diced green chiles, drained
- 1 cup (about 4 oz.) matchstick pieces reduced-fat jack cheese
- 2 medium-size carrots, shredded
- ¼ cup thinly sliced green onions
- 2 cups diced cooked chicken breast

1. Cut a ½- to ¾-inch-thick slice from top crust of each loaf to form a lid; set aside. Pull out bread from center of loaves to form a shell about ⅜ inch thick. (Reserve bread from center for other uses.)

2. Prepare Chili Dressing. In a large bowl, combine bell pepper, radishes, chiles, cheese, carrots, onions, and chicken. Add all but 1 tablespoon of the dressing; mix lightly. Spoon salad mixture into bread shells. Brush reserved 1 tablespoon dressing over cut sides of lids; then place lids on loaves. Wrap in foil and refrigerate for at least 1 hour or up to 4 hours.

3. To serve, cut long loaves into slices; cut round loaf into wedges.

MAKES 6 TO 8 SERVINGS

Chili Dressing. In a small bowl, mix 2 tablespoons **vegetable oil;** ¼ cup **seasoned rice vinegar;** 1 teaspoon **chili powder;** ¼ teaspoon **ground cumin;** a dash of **ground red pepper (cayenne);** 1 small clove **garlic,** minced or pressed; and ⅓ cup chopped **cilantro.**

Per serving: 312 calories (29% calories from fat), 10 g total fat, 3 g saturated fat, 46 mg cholesterol, 735 mg sodium, 33 g carbohydrates, 3 g fiber, 23 g protein, 202 mg calcium, 2 mg iron

Light & Easy Thanksgiving Dinner

The ideal heart-healthy Thanksgiving dinner would include all the flavors of a traditional feast, yet omit much of the fat. Here's a menu for eight that meets those specifications. It only tastes extravagant: just 11 percent of the meal's calories come from fat. To save time on the day, you can make many of the dishes entirely or partially in advance.

Streusel-topped Sweet Potato Casserole

Fluffy, orange-accented sweet potatoes bake beneath a tempting spiced topping with pecans and chopped fresh apples.

PREPARATION TIME: *About 25 minutes*
COOKING TIME: *About 1 hour*

  2 pounds sweet potatoes
⅓ cup plus 2 teaspoons orange juice
  2 tablespoons brandy
½ teaspoon grated orange peel
¼ teaspoon ground ginger
  2 large egg whites (about ¼ cup)
⅓ cup firmly packed brown sugar
     Vegetable oil cooking spray
¼ cup chopped pecans
  2 tablespoons all-purpose flour
½ teaspoon ground cinnamon
½ Rome Beauty apple, cored and finely chopped

1. Place unpeeled potatoes in a 5- to 6-quart pan and add enough water to cover. Bring to a boil over high heat; then reduce heat, partially cover, and boil gently until potatoes are tender when pierced (about 30 minutes). Drain; let stand until cool enough to touch.

2. Peel potatoes and mash until smooth, mixing in ⅓ cup of the orange juice. Add brandy, orange peel, and ginger; mix well.

3. In a medium-size bowl, beat egg whites with an electric mixer on high speed until soft peaks form. Gradually add 3 tablespoons of the brown sugar, beating until stiff peaks form. Stir a fourth of the whites into potatoes; then fold in remaining whites. Spray a 2-quart baking dish with cooking spray. Spoon in potatoes; set aside.

4. In a small bowl, combine remaining brown sugar with pecans, flour, and cinnamon. Mix in apple and remaining 2 teaspoons orange juice; sprinkle evenly over potatoes. Bake in a 350° oven until potatoes are puffy and topping is lightly browned (about 30 minutes).

MAKES 8 SERVINGS

Per serving: 175 calories (14% calories from fat), 3 g total fat, 0 g saturated fat, 0 mg cholesterol, 28 mg sodium, 34 g carbohydrates, 3 g fiber, 3 g protein, 31 mg calcium, 1 mg iron

Baby Leeks in Wine Sauce

You can make this first course up to a day ahead, then cover the leeks and their sauce separately and refrigerate. Bring to room temperature or reheat to serve, spooning the sauce over the leeks at the last.

PREPARATION TIME: *About 25 minutes*
COOKING TIME: *About 20 minutes*

24 baby leeks (*each* about ½ inch wide; about 1¾ lbs. *total*)
¾ cup chopped onion
  1 clove garlic, finely chopped
¾ cup dry white wine
¾ cup fat-free reduced-sodium chicken broth
½ lemon, thinly sliced
  2 pear-shaped (Roma-type) tomatoes, seeded and chopped
  8 to 10 parsley sprigs
     Thin strands of lemon peel

1. Trim and discard root ends and tops of leeks so that each leek is about 6 inches long. Rinse leeks thoroughly.

2. In a wide nonstick frying pan, combine onion and garlic. Cook over medium-high heat, stirring often, until onion is soft but not brown (4 to 5 minutes). Add wine, broth, lemon slices, tomatoes, and parsley sprigs; then arrange leeks in wine mixture. Increase heat to high, cover, and bring to a boil. Reduce heat to low and simmer until leeks are just tender when pierced (about 10 minutes).

3. Using a slotted spoon, lift leeks from pan and arrange in a shallow rimmed dish; set aside. Discard lemon slices and parsley sprigs from cooking liquid. Bring liquid to a boil over high heat; boil until reduced to about 1 cup (3 to 5 minutes). Pour sauce over leeks.

4. Garnish with lemon peel. Serve warm or at room temperature.

MAKES 8 SERVINGS

Per serving: 53 calories (4% calories from fat), .20 g total fat, 0 g saturated fat, 0 mg cholesterol, 64 mg sodium, 9 g carbohydrates, 1 g fiber, 1 g protein, 37 mg calcium, 1 mg iron

Turkey Breast with Cornbread Stuffing

Bake the cornbread for the stuffing ahead to save time on the day of the feast. If you wish, you can also prepare and refrigerate the stuffing a day in advance.

PREPARATION TIME: *About 1 hour*

BAKING TIME: *About 2 hours for turkey, plus 20 to 25 minutes to bake cornbread*

Yogurt Cornbread (page 214)
Vegetable oil cooking spray
2 teaspoons vegetable oil
1½ cups finely chopped mushrooms
1 medium-size onion, finely chopped
2 cloves garlic, minced or pressed
¼ teaspoon dried thyme
¼ cup finely chopped parsley
3 tablespoons dried currants
2 tablespoons chopped pecans
Salt and pepper
1 boneless, skinless turkey breast half (about 3 lbs.), trimmed of fat
½ cup apple juice
2 tablespoons honey
Thyme sprigs (optional)

1. Prepare cornbread and set aside to cool.

2. Meanwhile, coat a wide nonstick frying pan with cooking spray; add oil. Place over medium-high heat. When oil is hot, add mushrooms, onion, half the garlic, and half the dried thyme. Cook, stirring, until onion is tender to bite (about 5 minutes). Remove from heat.

3. Crumble about a fourth of the cornbread to make 2 cups. Add crumbled cornbread to mushroom mixture along with parsley, currants, and pecans; season to taste with salt and pepper. Set stuffing aside. (At this point, you may transfer stuffing to a bowl, cover, and refrigerate for up to 1 day.)

4. Rinse turkey and pat dry; then place, boned side up, on heavy plastic wrap. Starting at center, slice horizontally through thickest part of each side of breast almost to outer edge; flip each cut piece over to increase width of meat. Cover with another piece of plastic wrap. Then, using a heavy, flat-surfaced mallet, pound turkey firmly but gently all over to a thickness of about ½ inch (meat will form a rectangle about 10 by 14 inches). Remove top piece of plastic wrap.

5. Spoon stuffing evenly over turkey, leaving a 2-inch margin on all sides. Starting at a short side, roll up turkey jelly-roll fashion. Using white cotton string, tie turkey roll securely at 1½-inch intervals.

6. In a small bowl, stir together apple juice, honey, remaining garlic, and remaining dried thyme.

7. Coat a rack and a 9- by 13-inch roasting pan with cooking spray. Place turkey on rack in pan. Brush with apple juice mixture, then cover loosely with foil. Roast in a 325° oven for 1 hour, basting 2 or 3 times with remaining apple juice mixture. Then uncover and continue to roast until a meat thermometer inserted in thickest part registers 165°F (about 1 more hour). As turkey roasts, brush it with pan drippings once or twice.

8. Lift turkey to a board or platter, cover lightly, and let stand for 10 minutes. Then remove and discard strings. Garnish with thyme sprigs, if desired. To serve, slice about ¼ inch thick.

MAKES 10 TO 12 SERVINGS

Per serving: 320 calories (12% calories from fat), 4 g total fat, 1 g saturated fat, 117 mg cholesterol, 367 mg sodium, 33 g carbohydrates, 2 g fiber, 36 g protein, 71 mg calcium, 3 mg iron

Holiday Cranberry Relish

This crunchy uncooked relish must be chilled for at least 8 hours before serving, so it's a good candidate for making a day or two ahead.

PREPARATION TIME: *About 15 minutes, plus at least 8 hours to chill*

- 1 small orange (about 6 oz.), cut into quarters
- 2 cups fresh cranberries
- 1 large Red Delicious apple (about 8 oz.), cored and finely chopped
- 1 can (about 8 oz.) crushed pineapple in unsweetened juice, drained
- ⅓ cup sugar
- Fresh spinach leaves, rinsed and crisped (optional)

1. Whirl orange in food processor until finely chopped; transfer to a glass bowl and set aside.

2. Add cranberries to processor and whirl until coarsely ground. Add cranberries to orange; then add apple, pineapple, and sugar. Mix well. Cover and refrigerate for at least 8 hours or up to 3 days. Serve atop spinach leaves, if desired.

MAKES ABOUT 4 CUPS

Per ⅓ cup: 57 calories (2% calories from fat), .15 g total fat, 0 g saturated fat, 0 mg cholesterol, 1 mg sodium, 16 g carbohydrates, 1 g fiber, 0 g protein, 15 mg calcium, 0 mg iron

Baked Cardamom Pears & Apricots

You can make this tempting dessert one day ahead. Prepare the oat topping, let it cool, and package airtight; set aside at room temperature. Bake and cool the fruit, then cover and refrigerate. At serving time, reheat the fruit mixture in the microwave; or add ¼ cup apple juice, cover, and bake in a 325° oven until hot (30 to 35 minutes).

PREPARATION TIME: *About 25 minutes*
BAKING TIME: *45 to 55 minutes*

- 1½ tablespoons butter or margarine, cut into small pieces
- ⅓ cup regular or quick-cooking rolled oats
- ⅓ cup toasted wheat germ
- ⅓ cup firmly packed brown sugar
- 2 tablespoons chopped almonds
- ¼ cup honey
- 1½ tablespoons lemon juice
- ½ teaspoon vanilla
- ½ teaspoon almond extract
- ½ teaspoon ground cardamom
- 1 cup (about 6 oz.) dried apricots
- 2 tablespoons water
- 4 large firm-ripe pears, such as Bosc or Comice (2 to 2¼ lbs. *total*)
- 1 quart vanilla nonfat frozen yogurt

1. In an 8- or 9-inch-square baking pan, mix butter, oats, wheat germ, brown sugar, and almonds. Bake in a 350° oven, stirring several times, until mixture is crisp and lightly browned (10 to 15 minutes). Let cool in pan on a rack.

2. Meanwhile, in a 2-quart pan, combine honey, lemon juice, vanilla, almond extract, cardamom, apricots, and water. Bring to a boil over medium-high heat; remove from heat and set aside.

3. Peel, halve, and core pears. Place pear halves, cut side down, in a shallow 2- to 2½-quart casserole. Spoon honey-apricot mixture over pears. Cover casserole tightly and bake in a 350° oven until pears are tender when pierced (35 to 40 minutes).

4. Spoon warm pears and apricot sauce into wide bowls. Add scoops of frozen yogurt to each serving; sprinkle with oat topping.

MAKES 8 SERVINGS

Per serving: 347 calories (11% calories from fat), 4 g total fat, 2 g saturated fat, 9 mg cholesterol, 109 mg sodium, 71 g carbohydrates, 5 g fiber, 9 g protein, 208 mg calcium, 2 mg iron

Healthy Heart

Recipes

Appetizers

Carrot Hummus

Cooked, mashed baby-cut carrots add bright color and extra sweetness to this lean version of the popular Middle Eastern spread. Seasoned simply with a handful of fresh dill and plenty of garlic and lemon, it's delicious with toasted pita wedges or baguette slices.

PREPARATION TIME: *About 10 minutes*
COOKING TIME: *20 to 25 minutes*

1 package (about 1 lb.) fresh baby-cut carrots

2 cans (about 15 oz. *each*) garbanzo beans, rinsed and drained

¾ cup (or to taste) coarsely chopped fresh dill or parsley

5 tablespoons (or to taste) lemon juice

1 tablespoon Asian sesame oil

1 to 3 cloves garlic, peeled

Salt

Dill or parsley sprigs

About 36 pita bread wedges (from six 6- to 7-inch-diameter pita breads), toasted; or 36 baguette slices, toasted

1. In a 2- to 3-quart pan, combine carrots and 3 cups water. Bring to a boil over high heat; then reduce heat, cover, and simmer, stirring occasionally, until carrots mash easily (15 to 20 minutes). Drain well.

2. In a food processor or blender, whirl carrots, garbanzos, chopped dill, lemon juice, oil, and garlic until smoothly puréed. Season to taste with salt.

3. Mound dip in a bowl and garnish with dill sprigs. Serve with pita wedges.

MAKES ABOUT 12 SERVINGS (ABOUT 3½ CUPS DIP TOTAL)

Per serving, including pita wedges: 161 calories (15% calories from fat), 3 g total fat, 0 g saturated fat, 0 mg cholesterol, 257 mg sodium, 29 g carbohydrates, 4 g fiber, 6 g protein, 54 mg calcium, 2 mg iron

Garbanzo Guacamole

Nutty-tasting garbanzos and juicy, sweet-tart oranges complement the traditional avocado in this unusual guacamole. Serve it with baked tortilla chips and crisp jicama sticks.

PREPARATION TIME: *About 15 minutes*

2 cans (about 15 oz. *each*) garbanzo beans, rinsed and drained

3 medium-size oranges (about 1½ lbs. *total*)

1 large firm-ripe avocado (about 10 oz.)

2 tablespoons lime juice

½ cup sliced green onions

½ cup chopped cilantro

Crushed red pepper flakes

Salt

6 cups baked tortilla chips

About 4 cups peeled jicama sticks

1. Place garbanzos in a large bowl and coarsely mash with a fork. Set aside.

2. Cut peel and all white membrane from oranges. Thinly slice 2 of the oranges crosswise; use to line a small serving bowl. Set aside. Cut between membranes of remaining orange to release segments; cut segments into ½-inch chunks and transfer to bowl with garbanzos.

3. Pit and peel avocado; cut into ½-inch chunks and mix lightly with garbanzos and orange chunks. Mix in lime juice, onions, and cilantro. Season to taste with red pepper flakes and salt.

4. Spoon guacamole into orange-lined bowl. Offer chips and jicama for dipping.

MAKES 10 TO 12 SERVINGS (ABOUT 3 CUPS DIP TOTAL)

Per serving, including chips and jicama: 195 calories (20% calories from fat), 4 g total fat, 1 g saturated fat, 0 mg cholesterol, 25 mg sodium, 37 g carbohydrates, 6 g fiber, 4 g protein, 75 mg calcium, 1 mg iron

Chipotle-Corn Cheese Dip

Boldly seasoned with smoky chipotle chiles, this dip can also be served as a spread for sliced, toasted cocktail-size bagels. Look for chipotles in adobado sauce in Latino markets or the international foods section of your supermarket.

PREPARATION TIME: *About 15 minutes*

- 1 large package (about 8 oz.) fat-free cream cheese, at room temperature
- 1 large package (about 8 oz.) Neufchâtel cheese, at room temperature
- 3 tablespoons lime juice
- 1 to 2 tablespoons minced chipotle chiles in adobado sauce
- 1 can (about 15 oz.) corn kernels, rinsed and drained
- 6 to 8 cups baked tortilla chips

1. In a large bowl, beat fat-free cream cheese and Neufchâtel cheese with an electric mixer until smooth. Add lime juice and chiles; beat until well mixed. Stir in corn; then spoon dip into a serving bowl. If made ahead, cover and refrigerate for up to 1 day.

2. Serve with chips for dipping.

MAKES 8 SERVINGS (ABOUT 2½ CUPS DIP TOTAL)

Per serving, including chips: 286 calories (24% calories from fat), 8 g total fat, 4 g saturated fat, 23 mg cholesterol, 644 mg sodium, 44 g carbohydrates, 4 g fiber, 11 g protein, 161 mg calcium, 1 mg iron

Layered Black Bean Dip

Bring out an assortment of raw vegetables or a big basket of baked tortilla chips to dunk into this zesty multicolored dip.

PREPARATION TIME: *About 30 minutes*
COOKING TIME: *About 10 minutes*

- 2 teaspoons olive oil or vegetable oil
- 1 cup finely chopped onion
- 1 clove garlic, minced or pressed
- 2 tablespoons purchased mole paste or 1 tablespoon chili powder
- About ½ cup fat-free reduced-sodium chicken broth
- 2 cans (about 15 oz. *each*) black beans, rinsed and drained
- 2 cups lightly packed cilantro leaves
- 1 can (about 4 oz.) diced green chiles
- ¼ cup green chile salsa or green taco sauce
- ⅓ cup crumbled feta cheese
- 5 to 6 cups raw vegetables, such as baby-cut carrots, cauliflower and broccoli flowerets, and celery sticks

1. In a wide nonstick frying pan, combine oil, onion, and garlic. Cook over medium-high heat, stirring often, until onion is tinged with brown (about 4 minutes). Add mole paste and ½ cup of the broth. Stir to incorporate mole; then cook, stirring, until almost all liquid has evaporated (about 4 minutes). Remove from heat.

2. Add beans to pan, mashing about half of them to thicken the mixture. If mixture is too thick for dipping easily, stir in more broth, 1 tablespoon at a time, until mixture has the desired consistency. Spread bean mixture ¾ inch thick on a platter; set aside. (At this point, you may cover and refrigerate for up to 1 day.)

3. In a food processor or blender, combine cilantro, chiles, and salsa. Whirl until mixture forms a paste as thick as pesto; occasionally scrape down paste from sides of container.

4. Spoon chile mixture over center of beans; sprinkle cheese over chile mixture. Surround with vegetables for dipping.

MAKES ABOUT 10 SERVINGS (ABOUT 4 CUPS DIP TOTAL)

Per serving, including vegetables: 109 calories (21% calories from fat), 3 g total fat, 1 g saturated fat, 4 mg cholesterol, 472 mg sodium, 17 g carbohydrates, 5 g fiber, 6 g protein, 75 mg calcium, 2 mg iron

Stuffed Jalapeño Chiles

Here's a super-simple appetizer: nothing but pickled jalapeños filled with cubes of prosciutto-wrapped cream cheese. If you don't care for spicy heat, you might substitute red or orange bell pepper strips (or even dried apricot halves) for the chiles; just top each with a prosciutto-wrapped cheese cube and secure with a wooden pick. For easiest assembly, be sure the cheese is very cold.

PREPARATION TIME: *About 20 minutes*

- 2 jars (about 1 lb. *each*) whole jalapeño chiles, drained
- 1 large package (about 8 oz.) fat-free cream cheese or Neufchâtel cheese
- 2 ounces thinly sliced prosciutto, cut into 1½-inch squares

1. Cut off and discard stem ends of chiles. With a small spoon, scoop out and discard seeds.

2. Cut cream cheese into ½-inch cubes; wrap each cube in a piece of prosciutto. Stuff wrapped cheese cubes into chiles and serve.

MAKES 12 SERVINGS

Per serving: 46 calories (21% calories from fat), 1 g total fat, 0 g saturated fat, 6 mg cholesterol, 1,284 mg sodium, 5 g carbohydrates, 0 g fiber, 5 g protein, 73 mg calcium, 2 mg iron

Rice-filled Grape Leaves

Neatly rolled grape leaves surround currant-dotted rice seasoned with mint and garlic in these bite-size appetizers. Serve them with a dry, fruity Sauvignon Blanc.

PREPARATION TIME: *About 50 minutes*
COOKING TIME: *55 to 70 minutes*

- 2 tablespoons olive oil
- 1 cup chopped onion
- ¾ cup long-grain white rice
- 1 cup dry white wine
- ⅓ cup canned tomato sauce
- ¼ cup chopped fresh mint or cilantro
- ¼ cup currants
- 1 clove garlic, minced or pressed
- ½ teaspoon dried basil
- ¼ teaspoon pepper
- 1 jar (about 8 oz.) grape leaves
- 2 tablespoons lemon juice

1. Heat oil in a 2- to 3-quart pan over medium-high heat. Add onion and cook, stirring often, until soft (about 7 minutes). Add rice and stir for 1 to 2 more minutes. Add ¼ cup water, wine, tomato sauce, mint, currants, garlic, basil, and pepper; stir to mix. Bring to a boil; then reduce heat, cover, and simmer, stirring occasionally, until rice is almost tender to bite (12 to 15 minutes). Remove from heat, uncover, and let cool for at least 20 minutes.

2. Meanwhile, rinse grape leaves, drain, and pat dry. Line bottom of a 9- by 13-inch baking dish with 5 or 6 leaves; reserve 5 or 6 additional leaves.

3. With scissors, trim stems from remaining leaves. To fill each leaf, place it with underside up and stem end toward you. Shape 1 tablespoon of the rice mixture into a 2-inch log across stem end of leaf; fold sides of leaf over filling and roll up snugly. Fit filled leaves, seam side down, in a single layer in leaf-lined dish. Cover with reserved whole leaves. In a small bowl, mix 1 cup water with lemon juice; pour mixture over filled leaves.

4. Cover dish tightly and bake in a 350° oven until liquid has been absorbed (30 to 45 minutes). Serve warm or cool. If made ahead, let cool; then cover and refrigerate for up to 1 day.

MAKES 2½ TO 3 DOZEN APPETIZERS

Per appetizer: 36 calories (26% calories from fat), 1 g total fat, 0 g saturated fat, 0 mg cholesterol, 295 mg sodium, 5 g carbohydrates, 0 g fiber, 0 g protein, 34 mg calcium, 0 mg iron

Artichokes with Lemonnaise

On its own, an artichoke is innocent of fat; it's the accompanying dip or sauce that often causes trouble. This rich-flavored dunking sauce, made with silken-style tofu, is a guilt-free replacement for the usual melted butter or mayonnaise—and it gives you a little extra protein, too.

PREPARATION TIME: *About 15 minutes*
COOKING TIME: *35 to 40 minutes*

3 tablespoons distilled white vinegar

1 teaspoon black peppercorns

4 artichokes (*each* about 4 inches in diameter; about 3 lbs. *total*)

½ cup drained extra-firm, firm, or soft silken-style tofu

2 tablespoons lemon juice

2 teaspoons extra-virgin olive oil

½ teaspoon dry mustard

Salt and freshly ground pepper

1. Half-fill a 6- to 8-quart pan with water. Add vinegar and peppercorns; bring to a boil over high heat.

2. Meanwhile, slice off and discard top 1 inch of each artichoke. Trim stems flush with bottoms. With scissors, cut thorny tips from remaining outer leaves.

3. Add artichokes to boiling water; cover and simmer until artichoke bottoms are tender when pierced (30 to 35 minutes). Drain.

4. While artichokes are cooking, make lemonnaise. In a blender or food processor (a blender produces the best results), whirl tofu, lemon juice, oil, and mustard until smooth. Season to taste with salt and pepper. Cover and refrigerate until ready to use.

5. Serve artichokes with lemonnaise for dipping.

MAKES 4 SERVINGS

Per serving: 107 calories (25% calories from fat), 3 g total fat, 0 g saturated fat, 0 mg cholesterol, 152 mg sodium, 16 g carbohydrates, 7 g fiber, 7 g protein, 73 mg calcium, 2 mg iron

Grilled Onion Quesadillas

Pan-grilled red onion, refried beans, and jarlsberg cheese fill these crisp morsels; serve them hot from the oven, with toppings of shredded cabbage and your favorite salsa. They're good with fresh lemonade or cold beer.

PREPARATION TIME: *About 10 minutes*
COOKING TIME: *15 to 20 minutes*

1 medium-size red onion (about 8 oz.), cut crosswise into ⅓-inch-thick slices

4 large low-fat flour tortillas (*each* about 10 inches in diameter)

1 can (about 1 lb.) nonfat refried beans

5 ounces reduced-fat jarlsberg cheese, thinly sliced

2 cups salsa

4 cups finely shredded cabbage; or 4 cups coleslaw mix

1. Place a wide frying pan over high heat. Lay onion slices in pan; cook, turning occasionally, until browned (7 to 10 minutes). If onion begins to scorch or stick, add water, 1 tablespoon at a time.

2. Lightly brush tortillas on both sides with water. Spread beans over half of each tortilla. Separate onion slices into rings; arrange over beans. Top with cheese. Fold each tortilla in half to cover filling.

3. Place filled tortillas slightly apart on 2 large baking sheets. Bake in a 500° oven until tortillas are crisp and golden (6 to 8 minutes), switching positions of baking sheets halfway through baking.

4. Meanwhile, in a medium-size serving bowl, mix 1 cup of the salsa with cabbage. Place remaining salsa in a small serving bowl.

5. To serve, cut each quesadilla into 3 wedges; arrange wedges on a platter. Offer cabbage mixture and salsa to top individual servings.

MAKES 12 SERVINGS

Per serving: 143 calories (11% calories from fat), 2 g total fat, 1 g saturated fat, 4 mg cholesterol, 763 mg sodium, 23 g carbohydrates, 4 g fiber, 8 g protein, 140 mg calcium, 2 mg iron

ARTICHOKES WITH LEMONNAISE

Provençal Pizza

With a thin, crisp crust and just a sprinkling of cheese, this pizza offers flavors typical of the south of France—mixed herbs, garlic, plenty of slivered onions, a robust tomato sauce, and tiny Niçoise olives.

PREPARATION TIME: *20 to 25 minutes*
COOKING TIME: *35 to 45 minutes*

1¾ cups thinly slivered red onions

3 large cloves garlic, peeled and thinly sliced

1 teaspoon olive oil

1 can (about 6 oz.) no-salt-added tomato paste

1½ teaspoons herbes de Provence

1 loaf (about 1 lb.) frozen bread dough, thawed

⅔ cup freshly shredded Parmesan cheese

9 canned anchovy fillets, drained, patted dry, and halved lengthwise

¼ cup Niçoise olives

1. Place a 14- by 16-inch baking stone or 14- by 17-inch baking sheet (not nonstick) on bottom rack of a 500° oven. Heat for at least 30 minutes.

2. Meanwhile, combine onions, garlic, oil, and ¼ cup water in a wide nonstick frying pan. Cover; cook over medium-low heat until water has evaporated (10 to 12 minutes). Stir in ¼ cup more water. Cover and cook, stirring occasionally, until water has evaporated again and onions are very soft (15 to 20 more minutes). If onions begin to scorch or stick, add water, 1 tablespoon at a time. Remove from heat.

3. In a small bowl, stir together tomato paste, herbes de Provence, and ½ cup water. Set aside.

4. On a floured board, knead bread dough briefly to expel air. Gather dough into a smooth ball, then roll out to make a 14-inch circle. Drape circle over rolling pin; transfer to a very well floured baking

PROVENÇAL PIZZA

sheet or a piece of cardboard at least 14 inches in diameter. Smooth dough circle. Shake pan or cardboard gently; if dough sticks, lift and dust underneath with more flour.

5. Spread dough with tomato paste mixture. Scatter evenly with cooked onions, then with cheese. Crisscross pairs of anchovy pieces in evenly spaced "X" shapes over pizza. Distribute olives evenly over pizza; press into dough.

6. Slide pizza onto preheated baking stone or sheet. Bake until bottom of crust is browned and crisp (9 to 12 minutes). Slide a baking sheet under pizza and lift to a board. To serve, cut into wedges; watch for olive pits as you eat.

MAKES 8 TO 10 SERVINGS

Per serving: 231 calories (27% calories from fat), 7 g total fat, 2 g saturated fat, 10 mg cholesterol, 586 mg sodium, 33 g carbohydrates, 3 g fiber, 10 g protein, 153 mg calcium, 2 mg iron

Double-decker Focaccia

Frozen bread dough streamlines the process of making this savory focaccia, filled with feta cheese and fresh herbs. Cut the warm bread into small rectangles to accompany a before-dinner glass of wine or other apéritif.

PREPARATION TIME: *About 15 minutes*
RISING TIME: *45 to 60 minutes*
BAKING TIME: *About 45 minutes*

- ¼ cup yellow cornmeal
- 2 loaves (about 1 lb. *each*) frozen white bread dough, thawed
- 8 ounces feta cheese
- 1 tablespoon minced fresh rosemary or 1½ teaspoons dried rosemary
- 1 tablespoon minced fresh oregano or 1½ teaspoons dried oregano

  Cracked pepper

  About 2 teaspoons olive oil

1. Sprinkle cornmeal over bottom of a well-oiled 9- by 13-inch baking pan. Place half the bread dough in pan; press and stretch dough with your fingers to fill pan evenly. (If dough is too elastic, let it rest for a few minutes, then stretch it again; repeat as needed to fill pan.)

2. Crumble cheese in chunks evenly over dough. Sprinkle with half the rosemary and half the oregano; then sprinkle with pepper.

3. On a floured board, roll out (or stretch and pat) remaining dough to make a rectangle roughly 9 by 13 inches. Place this rectangle atop cheese-topped dough in pan; then carefully stretch top layer of dough to cover bottom layer completely. Cover lightly with plastic wrap; let rise in a warm place until almost doubled (45 to 60 minutes).

4. Brush dough with oil. With your fingers, gently press dough all over, forming dimples in surface. Sprinkle with remaining rosemary and oregano. Bake in a 400° oven until focaccia is well browned on edges and bottom, about 45 minutes; lift with a spatula to check. (If top starts to brown too much, cover bread lightly with foil.) Loosen edges from pan sides and bottom. Turn focaccia out onto a rack; invert again to turn upright. Let cool slightly before serving. To serve, cut into about 1½- by 2-inch rectangles.

MAKES 36 APPETIZERS

Per appetizer: 90 calories (29% calories from fat), 3 g total fat, 1 g saturated fat, 7 mg cholesterol, 192 mg sodium, 13 g carbohydrates, 1 g fiber, 3 g protein, 41 mg calcium, 1 mg iron

White Bean & Olive Pesto Bruschetta

Traditional Italian bruschetta is nothing more than thickly sliced country bread that's grilled over charcoal and rubbed with garlic and olive oil. Sometimes it features tomatoes or other seasonings, though—as in this rather lavish version, where crisp-toasted crusty bread is topped first with a mustard-accented white bean pâté, then with ripe tomato slices and a tangy pesto based on ripe olives.

PREPARATION TIME: *About 20 minutes*
COOKING TIME: *About 5 minutes*

- 1 can (about 15 oz.) cannellini (white kidney beans), rinsed and drained
- 2 tablespoons fat-free mayonnaise
- 1 tablespoon Dijon mustard
- ½ teaspoon dried thyme
- ½ cup pitted ripe olives
- 2 tablespoons drained capers
- 2 teaspoons lemon juice
- 2 teaspoons honey
- 1 teaspoon Asian sesame oil
- 1 clove garlic, peeled
- 2 tablespoons chopped fresh basil
- 2 tablespoons grated Parmesan cheese
- 8 slices crusty bread, such as Italian ciabatta or French bread (*each about ½ inch thick; about 8 oz. total*)
- 2 large tomatoes (about 1 lb. *total*), thinly sliced and drained

1. In a small bowl, combine beans, mayonnaise, 2 teaspoons of the mustard, and thyme. Mash beans with a fork, mixing until ingredients are well blended; set aside.

2. In a food processor or blender, combine olives, capers, lemon juice, honey, remaining 1 teaspoon mustard, oil, and garlic; whirl until coarsely puréed, scraping sides of container as needed. With a spoon, stir in basil and cheese; set aside.

3. Cut bread slices in half and arrange slightly apart in a large, shallow baking pan. Broil about 6 inches below heat, turning once, until golden on both sides (about 5 minutes). Let cool on a rack.

4. Top toast slices equally with bean mixture. Arrange tomatoes over bean mixture; top with olive pesto.

MAKES 8 SERVINGS

Per serving: 197 calories (17% calories from fat), 4 g total fat, 1 g saturated fat, 1 mg cholesterol, 566 mg sodium, 32 g carbohydrates, 6 g fiber, 9 g protein, 78 mg calcium, 3 mg iron

Chicken Fingers

Bake tender strips of chicken breast in a spicy, herb-seasoned cornmeal coating, then offer a creamy mustard sauce for dunking. Perfectly suited to the role of appetizer, the crunchy morsels also make a satisfying light meal when teamed with a green salad or a bowl of Gazpacho (page 116).

PREPARATION TIME: *About 20 minutes*
BAKING TIME: *About 20 minutes*

- 2 pounds boneless, skinless chicken breasts
- ⅔ cup all-purpose flour
- 3 tablespoons yellow cornmeal
- 1 teaspoon chili powder
- ½ teaspoon salt
- ½ teaspoon dried thyme
- ½ teaspoon dried oregano

1. Rinse chicken and pat dry; then cut crosswise into strips about 1 inch wide and 3 inches long (some pieces may be shorter). Set aside.

2. In a shallow pan, stir together flour, cornmeal, chili powder, salt, thyme, oregano, and cheese. Pour buttermilk into a shallow bowl; stir in garlic.

3. Dip chicken strips, a few at a time, into buttermilk mixture; drain briefly. Then coat with flour mixture, pressing chicken lightly into mixture to make coating adhere; shake off excess. Set chicken aside.

4. Cut butter into chunks and place in a 10- by 15-inch baking pan;

- **2** tablespoons grated Parmesan cheese
- **2/3** cup low-fat (1%) buttermilk
- **2** cloves garlic, minced or pressed
- **3** tablespoons butter or margarine
  Mustard Sauce (recipe follows)

set pan in a 450° oven until butter is melted. Turn chicken strips in butter to coat lightly, then arrange evenly in pan (strips can overlap slightly, if necessary). Bake, turning as needed, until chicken is golden brown on outside and no longer pink in center; cut to test (about 20 minutes). If any pieces begin to overbrown before remaining chicken is done, remove them from oven and keep warm.

5. While chicken is baking, prepare Mustard Sauce. Serve hot chicken strips with sauce.

MAKES 8 SERVINGS

Mustard Sauce. In a small bowl, stir together 1 cup **fat-free sour cream,** ½ cup **honey mustard,** and 2 to 4 tablespoons minced **cilantro** or parsley. Garnish with **cilantro sprigs** or parsley sprigs.

Per serving, including sauce: 296 calories (21% calories from fat), 6 g total fat, 3 g saturated fat, 83 mg cholesterol, 344 mg sodium, 24 g carbohydrates, 1 g fiber, 31 g protein, 108 mg calcium, 2 mg iron

CHICKEN FINGERS

Salads

Creamy Caesar Salad

Like traditional Caesar salad, this one features romaine lettuce tossed with crisp, garlicky croutons and Parmesan cheese. The piquant egg dressing isn't entirely typical, though—it's creamy in texture, thanks to a generous helping of fat-free sour cream and mayonnaise.

PREPARATION TIME: *About 20 minutes*
COOKING TIME: *About 10 minutes*

- 5 slices sourdough sandwich bread (about 5 oz. *total*)
- 1 tablespoon olive oil
- 4 cloves garlic, minced or pressed
- 1 large egg
- 2 tablespoons lemon juice
- ²/₃ cup fat-free sour cream
- ½ cup fat-free mayonnaise
- 6 canned anchovy fillets, drained, patted dry, and finely chopped
- 1 teaspoon Worcestershire
- 8 cups lightly packed bite-size pieces of rinsed, crisped romaine lettuce
- ⅓ cup grated Parmesan cheese

1. Tear or cut bread into 1-inch chunks. Heat oil in a wide nonstick frying pan over medium-high heat. Add half the garlic, then bread. Cook, stirring often, until croutons are lightly browned (about 10 minutes). Remove from pan and set aside.

2. In a large bowl, beat egg and lemon juice until well blended. Stir in sour cream, mayonnaise, anchovies, Worcestershire, and remaining garlic; beat to blend smoothly.

3. Add lettuce to bowl with dressing; mix gently but thoroughly. Sprinkle with croutons, then with cheese. Toss lightly and serve.

MAKES 4 TO 6 SERVINGS

Per serving: 231 calories (27% calories from fat), 7 g total fat, 2 g saturated fat, 53 mg cholesterol, 678 mg sodium, 29 g carbohydrates, 3 g fiber, 12 g protein, 206 mg calcium, 3 mg iron

Red & Green Salad

Red bell pepper, red onion, and dried cranberries add festive touches to a simple leaf lettuce salad.

PREPARATION TIME: *About 20 minutes*

- ¼ cup white wine vinegar
- 1 tablespoon olive oil
- ½ teaspoon minced fresh tarragon or ¼ teaspoon dried tarragon
- 1 teaspoon honey
- 1 clove garlic, minced or pressed
- 1 small head *each* red leaf and green leaf lettuce (about 1 lb. *total*), rinsed, crisped, and finely shredded
- 1 large red bell pepper (about 8 oz.), seeded and slivered
- 1 cup firmly packed cilantro leaves, minced
- ¾ cup dried cranberries
- ¼ cup chopped red onion
- 8 large green leaf lettuce leaves, rinsed and crisped
- 4 large tomatoes (about 2 lbs. *total*), thinly sliced

1. In a large bowl, stir together vinegar, oil, tarragon, honey, and garlic. Add shredded red and green lettuce, bell pepper, cilantro, cranberries, and onion; mix gently but thoroughly.

2. To serve, line 6 to 8 individual plates with lettuce leaves; arrange tomatoes atop lettuce. Top with salad.

MAKES 6 TO 8 SERVINGS

Per serving: 109 calories (21% calories from fat), 3 g total fat, 0 g saturated fat, 0 mg cholesterol, 21 mg sodium, 21 g carbohydrates, 4 g fiber, 2 g protein, 69 mg calcium, 2 mg iron

Red Slaw

This tangy slaw is a colorful companion for grilled turkey burgers or low-fat sausages. A cumin-scented blend of olive oil and fruity balsamic vinegar seasons shredded red cabbage, chopped pickled beets, and kidney beans.

PREPARATION TIME: *About 15 minutes*

- 3 tablespoons balsamic vinegar
- 3 tablespoons olive oil
- ½ teaspoon cumin seeds
- 1 can (about 15 oz.) pickled beets, drained and coarsely chopped
- 1 small can (about 8¾ oz.) red kidney beans, rinsed and drained
- 1 cup dried cranberries or raisins
- ½ cup thinly sliced green onions
- 6 cups very finely shredded red cabbage
- Salt and pepper

1. In a large bowl, stir together vinegar, oil, and cumin seeds. Stir in beets, beans, cranberries, and onions.

2. Add cabbage to bowl; mix gently. Season to taste with salt and pepper.

MAKES 6 TO 8 SERVINGS

Per serving: 186 calories (30% calories from fat), 6 g total fat, 1 g saturated fat, 0 mg cholesterol, 209 mg sodium, 31 g carbohydrates, 4 g fiber, 3 g protein, 53 mg calcium, 1 mg iron

Papaya, Orange & Berry Salad

A cooling combination of papaya wedges, summer berries, and orange segments tames the heat of a spicy jalapeño dressing in this refreshing first course. It's a fine prelude to an entrée of grilled tuna or salmon.

PREPARATION TIME: *About 25 minutes*

- ¼ cup lime juice
- 1 tablespoon minced cilantro
- 1 or 2 fresh red or green jalapeño chiles, seeded and minced
- 1 teaspoon sugar
- 2 large oranges (about 1¼ lbs. *total*)
- 1 cup fresh raspberries
- 1 cup fresh blueberries
- 1 large papaya (about 1¼ lbs.)
- 12 to 16 large butter lettuce leaves, rinsed and crisped

1. In a small bowl, stir together lime juice, cilantro, chiles, and sugar.

2. Cut peel and all white membrane from oranges; cut between membranes to release segments. Place orange segments in a large bowl and add raspberries and blueberries. Add lime juice mixture and stir gently until fruit is evenly coated (be careful not to crush raspberries).

3. Peel and halve papaya; scoop out and discard seeds. Cut papaya halves lengthwise into ½-inch-thick slices.

4. To serve, line 4 individual plates with lettuce leaves. Arrange papaya slices attractively atop lettuce. Spoon berry mixture over papaya slices.

MAKES 4 SERVINGS

Per serving: 117 calories (4% calories from fat), 1 g total fat, 0 g saturated fat, 0 mg cholesterol, 8 mg sodium, 29 g carbohydrates, 5 g fiber, 2 g protein, 67 mg calcium, 0 mg iron

PAPAYA, ORANGE & BERRY SALAD

Fruit Salad with Lemon–Poppy Seed Dressing

Wonderful at a summer lunch or supper, this combination of ripe mangoes and fresh blueberries is topped with a luscious, velvety blend of vanilla yogurt and lemon curd.

PREPARATION TIME: *About 15 minutes*

- 1 cup vanilla nonfat or low-fat yogurt
- 3 tablespoons purchased lemon curd
- ½ teaspoon grated lemon peel
- ½ teaspoon poppy seeds
- 2 large firm-ripe mangoes (about 2½ lbs. *total*)
- 1 cup fresh blueberries
- 1 tablespoon chopped fresh mint
- 12 to 16 large butter lettuce leaves, rinsed and crisped
- Mint sprigs

1. In a small bowl, stir together yogurt, lemon curd, lemon peel, and poppy seeds. Set aside.

2. Peel mangoes; cut fruit from pits in ½-inch chunks and place in a large bowl. Add blueberries and chopped mint; mix gently.

3. To serve, line 4 individual plates with lettuce leaves; top with fruit salad. Spoon dressing evenly over salads; garnish with mint sprigs.

MAKES 4 SERVINGS

Per serving: 238 calories (6% calories from fat), 2 g total fat, 0 g saturated fat, 2 mg cholesterol, 58 mg sodium, 57 g carbohydrates, 3 g fiber, 5 g protein, 114 mg calcium, 1 mg iron

Fruit & Feta Salad

For all its nutrients, spinach salad is often undone by a rich dressing— but that's not the case here! The deep green leaves are tossed with nothing more than honey-sweetened balsamic vinegar, making a lean base for a medley of mangoes, pears, and avocado.

PREPARATION TIME: *About 20 minutes*

- ½ cup balsamic vinegar
- 3 tablespoons honey
- 8 ounces fresh baby spinach leaves, rinsed and crisped
- 2 large firm-ripe mangoes (about 2½ lbs. *total*)
- 2 large firm-ripe pears (about 1 lb. *total*), peeled, cored, and cut into ½-inch-thick slices
- 1 large avocado (about 8 oz.), peeled, pitted, and cut into ½-inch-thick slices
- About ¾ cup crumbled feta cheese
- Freshly ground pepper

1. In a small bowl, whisk together vinegar and honey until well blended. Place spinach in a large bowl; pour ¼ cup of the vinegar mixture over it and toss to mix. Arrange spinach on a platter or on 4 to 6 individual plates.

2. Peel mangoes and cut fruit from pits in ½-inch-thick slices. Decoratively arrange mangoes, pears, avocado, and cheese over spinach. Season to taste with pepper and remaining vinegar mixture.

MAKES 4 TO 6 SERVINGS

Per serving: 302 calories (26% calories from fat), 10 g total fat, 4 g saturated fat, 15 mg cholesterol, 234 mg sodium, 55 g carbohydrates, 6 g fiber, 6 g protein, 158 mg calcium, 2 mg iron

Crunchy Corn Salad

Savor the sweetness of fresh-picked corn in this simple, sage-scented salad. Cut the kernels from the cobs (be sure to get all the juice, too) and toss them with cucumber and tiny peas; then pour on a few spoonfuls of hot browned butter and serve. What better partner for a simple broiled sea bass or swordfish fillet?

PREPARATION TIME: *About 20 minutes*
COOKING TIME: *About 4 minutes*

  4   medium-size ears corn (*each about 8 inches long; about 2 lbs. total*), husks and silks removed
  1   cup finely chopped European cucumber
  ⅔   cup frozen tiny peas, thawed and drained
  ½   teaspoon grated lime peel
  1   tablespoon lime juice
  1   tablespoon finely shredded fresh sage
  1   tablespoon butter or margarine
  12 to 16 large butter lettuce leaves, rinsed and crisped
      Sage sprigs

1. In a large, shallow bowl, hold one ear of corn upright and, with a sharp knife, cut kernels from cob. Then, using blunt edge of knife, scrape juice from cob into bowl. Repeat with remaining ears of corn. Discard cobs.

2. Add cucumber, peas, lime peel, lime juice, and shredded sage to bowl. Mix gently but thoroughly; set aside.

3. Melt butter in a small nonstick frying pan over medium heat. Heat until butter just begins to brown; do not scorch (about 4 minutes). Working quickly, pour butter over corn salad and blend well.

4. To serve, line 4 individual plates with lettuce leaves; top with corn salad. Garnish with sage sprigs.

MAKES 4 SERVINGS

Per serving: 129 calories (25% calories from fat), 4 g total fat, 2 g saturated fat, 8 mg cholesterol, 86 mg sodium, 22 g carbohydrates, 5 g fiber, 5 g protein, 11 mg calcium, 1 mg iron

Creamy Cucumber Salad

Cucumber salad is a summer classic; this one features a tart, creamy dressing of yogurt, garlic, mint, and dill. Try it as a cooling counterpoint to spicy barbecued chicken or Teriyaki Sea Bass (page 159). For the best flavor, chill the salad for at least 3 hours before serving.

PREPARATION TIME: *About 20 minutes, plus at least 3 hours to chill*

- 3 large cucumbers (about 2 lbs. *total*)
- ½ teaspoon salt
- 2 cups plain nonfat yogurt
- 3 cloves garlic, minced or pressed
- 2 tablespoons lemon juice
- 1 tablespoon minced fresh dill or 1½ teaspoons dried dill weed
- 1 tablespoon minced fresh mint or 1½ teaspoons dried mint
  About 2 teaspoons olive oil
- 12 to 16 large butter lettuce leaves, rinsed and crisped
  Fresh mint leaves (optional)

1. Peel and halve cucumbers; scrape out and discard seeds. Thinly slice cucumbers, place in a colander, and mix in salt. Let drain for 15 minutes.

2. In a large bowl, combine drained cucumbers, yogurt, garlic, lemon juice, and dill. Cover and refrigerate for at least 3 hours or up to 8 hours.

3. To serve, sprinkle cucumber mixture with minced mint, then drizzle with 2 teaspoons oil. Mix gently. Line a serving bowl with lettuce leaves; spoon in salad and drizzle with a few more drops of oil. Garnish with mint leaves, if desired.

MAKES 8 SERVINGS

Per serving: 60 calories (20% calories from fat), 1 g total fat, 0 g saturated fat, 1 mg cholesterol, 161 mg sodium, 8 g carbohydrates, 1 g fiber, 4 g protein, 133 mg calcium, 0 mg iron

Potato Salad with Peppers & Feta

Whirled until smooth in your blender, roasted red peppers and nonfat cottage cheese make a tangy dressing for chunks of red potatoes in this rosy, herb-flecked salad.

PREPARATION TIME: *About 20 minutes*
COOKING TIME: *35 to 40 minutes*

2½ pounds red thin-skinned potatoes (*each* 2½ to 3 inches in diameter), scrubbed

½ cup thinly sliced green onions

1½ cups (about 6 oz.) crumbled feta cheese

¼ cup minced fresh basil

1½ cups bottled roasted red peppers (not oil-packed), drained

½ cup nonfat cottage cheese

½ cup fat-free reduced-sodium chicken broth

2 tablespoons lemon juice
About ¼ teaspoon black pepper

1. In a 5- to 6-quart pan, bring about 3 quarts water to a boil over high heat. Add potatoes; reduce heat, cover, and simmer until just tender when pierced (30 to 35 minutes). Drain, immerse in cold water until cool, and drain again.

2. Cut cooled potatoes into quarters or eighths; place in a large bowl and mix in onions, feta cheese, and basil.

3. In a blender, whirl red peppers, cottage cheese, broth, lemon juice, and ¼ teaspoon of the black pepper until smooth. Pour over potato mixture and mix gently but thoroughly. Season to taste with additional black pepper. If made ahead, cover and refrigerate for up to 1 day.

MAKES 6 SERVINGS

Per serving: 268 calories (25% calories from fat), 8 g total fat, 5 g saturated fat, 0 mg cholesterol, 551 mg sodium, 39 g carbohydrates, 4 g fiber, 11 g protein, 195 mg calcium, 2 mg iron

Caesar Potato Salad

Light, fresh ingredients—among them red potatoes, garlic, lemon juice, and parsley—bring plenty of flavor to this salad. A purée made from a little of the cooked potatoes is the basis for the smooth, oil-free dressing.

PREPARATION TIME: *About 15 minutes*
COOKING TIME: *40 to 50 minutes*

2½ pounds red thin-skinned potatoes (*each* 2½ to 3 inches in diameter), scrubbed

2 cloves garlic, minced or pressed

1 teaspoon Worcestershire

2 teaspoons Dijon mustard

3 tablespoons lemon juice

1 tablespoon red wine vinegar

9 canned anchovy fillets, drained and patted dry

¼ cup grated Parmesan cheese
Salt and pepper

1 tablespoon minced parsley

1. Cook potatoes as directed above for Potato Salad with Peppers & Feta. Remove all but one potato from cooking water; immerse in cold water until cool, then drain and set aside.

2. Meanwhile, continue to cook remaining potato until it is very soft and skin has begun to peel away (5 to 10 more minutes). Remove potato from pan, reserving cooking water, and cut in half.

3. Cut cooled whole potatoes and one soft-cooked potato half into ½-inch-thick slices; place in a large bowl. Peel remaining potato half, cut into chunks, and place in a blender with ½ cup of the cooking water. Whirl until smooth. Spoon purée into a small bowl; let cool.

4. In a medium-size bowl, combine garlic, Worcestershire, mustard, lemon juice, and vinegar. Mince 4 of the anchovy fillets; add to bowl. Then stir in ⅔ cup of the cooled potato purée. Pour dressing over potatoes; add cheese and gently mix to coat potatoes. Season to taste with salt and pepper. Garnish with parsley and remaining 5 anchovy fillets. If made ahead, cover and refrigerate for up to 1 day.

MAKES 6 SERVINGS

Per serving: 184 calories (9% calories from fat), 2 g total fat, 1 g saturated fat, 5 mg cholesterol, 300 mg sodium, 35 g carbohydrates, 3 g fiber, 6 g protein, 60 mg calcium, 2 mg iron

Broccoli, Onion & Bacon Salad

Peel the stems of the broccoli that stars in this salad—it makes each thin slice a bit more tender. Then enjoy the crunchy uncooked vegetable with red onion and raisins in a sweet-and-sour dressing.

PREPARATION TIME: *10 to 15 minutes*
COOKING TIME: *5 to 7 minutes*

About 1½ pounds broccoli

1 small mild red onion (4 to 5 oz.), thinly sliced and separated into rings

⅔ cup golden raisins

6 slices bacon

¼ cup seasoned rice vinegar

2 teaspoons prepared mustard

3 tablespoons honey

2 tablespoons water

1. Rinse broccoli. Cut off and discard tough stem ends. Thinly slice flowerets; peel tender stems and thinly slice. Combine broccoli, onion, and raisins in a large bowl.

2. Cook bacon in a wide frying pan over medium heat until browned and crisp (5 to 7 minutes); lift from pan and drain on paper towels. Pour off and discard drippings, but do not rinse pan. When bacon is cool, crumble it and add to broccoli mixture.

3. To bacon cooking pan, add vinegar, mustard, honey, and water. Stir to mix, scraping browned bits free from pan bottom. Pour dressing over broccoli and mix well. Serve; or, if made ahead, cover and let stand at room temperature for up to 2 hours.

MAKES 4 TO 6 SERVINGS

Per serving: 211 calories (23% calories from fat), 6 g total fat, 2 g saturated fat, 8 mg cholesterol, 438 mg sodium, 37 g carbohydrates, 5 g fiber, 7 g protein, 80 mg calcium, 2 mg iron

Garbanzo Salad with Chutney Dressing

Mellow garbanzos, plenty of crunchy raw vegetables, and a sprinkling of sharp feta cheese add up to a hearty salad that's great alongside simply cooked entrées. Or serve it on its own at lunchtime, perhaps with a platter of sliced tomatoes and hot yeast rolls.

PREPARATION TIME: *About 20 minutes*

⅓ cup lime or lemon juice

2 tablespoons Major Grey's chutney, any large pieces chopped

1 tablespoon sugar

¾ teaspoon ground cumin

2 cans (about 15 oz. *each*) garbanzo beans, rinsed and drained

1 cup peeled, diced cucumber

1 large red bell pepper (about 8 oz.), seeded and diced

½ cup chopped red onion

2 tablespoons chopped cilantro

Salt and pepper

6 large red leaf lettuce leaves, rinsed and crisped

⅔ cup crumbled feta cheese

1. In a large bowl, stir together lime juice, chutney, sugar, and cumin. Add garbanzos, cucumber, bell pepper, onion, and cilantro. Mix lightly; then season to taste with salt and pepper.

2. To serve, line 6 individual plates with lettuce leaves; top evenly with salad and sprinkle with cheese.

MAKES 6 SERVINGS

Per serving: 185 calories (27% calories from fat), 6 g total fat, 2 g saturated fat, 13 mg cholesterol, 389 mg sodium, 26 g carbohydrates, 5 g fiber, 8 g protein, 129 mg calcium, 2 mg iron

BROCCOLI, ONION & BACON SALAD

GARBANZO TABBOULEH SALAD

Garbanzo Tabbouleh Salad

Made with couscous instead of the usual bulgur, this quick-to-assemble tabbouleh is perfect for patio dining. Lemon juice and plenty of mint give it a refreshing flavor.

PREPARATION TIME: *About 20 minutes, plus at least 30 minutes to chill*
COOKING TIME: *About 10 minutes*

1²/₃ cups couscous

1 to 1½ cups firmly packed fresh mint leaves, minced

1 can (about 15 oz.) garbanzo beans, rinsed and drained

2 tablespoons olive oil

About ½ cup lemon juice

Salt and pepper

1 cup plain nonfat yogurt

½ cup Major Grey's chutney, any large pieces chopped

6 to 8 large red leaf lettuce leaves, rinsed and crisped

2 large tomatoes (about 1 lb. *total*), thinly sliced

Mint sprigs

1. In a 3- to 4-quart pan, bring 2¼ cups water to a boil over high heat. Stir in couscous. Cover, remove from heat, and let stand until liquid has been absorbed (about 5 minutes). Transfer to a shallow bowl and let cool, fluffing occasionally with a fork.

2. Add minced mint, garbanzos, oil, and lemon juice to couscous. Mix; season to taste with salt and pepper. Cover and refrigerate until cool (at least 30 minutes) or for up to 4 hours; fluff occasionally with a fork.

3. Meanwhile, in a small bowl, stir together yogurt and chutney; cover and refrigerate until serving time.

4. To serve, line a platter with lettuce leaves. Mound salad in center; arrange tomatoes around edge or along one side. Garnish with mint sprigs. Offer chutney dressing to add to taste.

MAKES 8 SERVINGS

Per serving: 334 calories (12% calories from fat), 4 g total fat, 1 g saturated fat, 3 mg cholesterol, 289 mg sodium, 62 g carbohydrates, 8 g fiber, 125 g protein, 171 mg calcium, 7 mg iron

Pastina Salad

Great for picnics or potlucks, this basil-scented salad combines orzo and sweet corn in a fresh orange dressing. If you like, substitute another tiny pasta for the orzo; you can also use thawed frozen corn in place of fresh.

PREPARATION TIME: *About 15 minutes*
COOKING TIME: *About 20 minutes*

2 ounces thinly sliced prosciutto or bacon, cut into thin strips

1½ cups dried orzo or other tiny rice-shaped pasta

4 cups fresh corn kernels; or 4 cups frozen corn kernels, thawed

¼ cup thinly sliced green onions

1 tablespoon chopped fresh basil

¼ cup olive oil

1 teaspoon finely shredded orange peel

2 tablespoons orange juice

1 or 2 cloves garlic, minced or pressed

Pepper

1. Cook prosciutto in a wide nonstick frying pan over medium-high heat, stirring often, just until crisp (about 3 minutes). Remove from pan and set aside.

2. In a 4- to 5-quart pan, bring about 8 cups water to a boil over medium-high heat; stir in pasta and cook, uncovered, until just tender to bite (about 10 minutes). Or cook pasta according to package directions. Drain, rinse with cold water, and drain again.

3. Pour pasta into a large bowl; add corn, onions, and chopped basil. Mix gently. In a small bowl, stir together oil, orange peel, orange juice, and garlic; add to pasta mixture and mix gently but thoroughly. Season to taste with pepper and sprinkle salad with prosciutto.

MAKES 6 SERVINGS

Per serving: 352 calories (30% calories from fat), 12 g total fat, 2 g saturated fat, 8 mg cholesterol, 194 mg sodium, 52 g carbohydrates, 4 g fiber, 12 g protein, 15 mg calcium, 2 mg iron

Soba Salad

Tangy, hot, and sweet, this easy-to-make salad is a good companion for barbecued chicken. Buckwheat noodles are seasoned with lime, red pepper, garlic, and sesame oil, tossed with grated carrot and chopped peanuts, and served cool. You can make the salad a day ahead; it keeps well in the refrigerator.

PREPARATION TIME: *About 10 minutes*
COOKING TIME: *About 15 minutes*

- 6 ounces dried soba (buckwheat noodles)
- ¼ cup distilled white vinegar
- 2 tablespoons lime juice
- 2 tablespoons sugar
- 2 teaspoons Asian sesame oil
- 1 clove garlic, minced or pressed
- ¼ to ½ teaspoon crushed red pepper flakes
- ¼ teaspoon salt
- ½ cup chopped cilantro
- 1 medium-size carrot, grated
- ¼ to ½ cup chopped roasted salted peanuts

1. In a 3- to 4-quart pan, bring about 8 cups water to a boil over high heat; stir in noodles and cook, uncovered, until just tender to bite (8 to 10 minutes). Or cook noodles according to package directions. Drain, rinse with cold water, and drain again. Set aside.

2. In a large bowl, combine vinegar, lime juice, sugar, oil, garlic, red pepper flakes, and salt; stir until sugar is dissolved.

3. To dressing, add cooled noodles, cilantro, carrot, and peanuts. Mix gently but thoroughly. If made ahead, cover and refrigerate for up to 1 day.

MAKES 6 SERVINGS

Per serving: 188 calories (28% calories from fat), 6 g total fat, 1 g saturated fat, 0 mg cholesterol, 401 mg sodium, 30 g carbohydrates, 2 g fiber, 6 g protein, 21 mg calcium, 1 mg iron

Spicy Shrimp Salad

Pasta seashells mingle with ginger- and chile-seasoned tiny shrimp in a cool main-dish salad. Serve it on a bed of baby spinach.

PREPARATION TIME: *About 10 minutes*
COOKING TIME: *About 15 minutes*

- 1 cup dried small pasta shells
- ⅓ cup seasoned rice vinegar
- 1 tablespoon minced fresh ginger
- 1 tablespoon soy sauce
- 1 teaspoon Asian sesame oil
- ¼ cup sliced green onions
- ⅛ to ¼ teaspoon crushed red pepper flakes
- 8 cups fresh baby spinach leaves, rinsed and crisped
- 1 cup frozen tiny peas, thawed
- 6 ounces small cooked shrimp

1. In a 3- to 4-quart pan, bring about 6 cups water to a boil over high heat. Stir in pasta and cook, uncovered, until just tender to bite (8 to 10 minutes). Or cook pasta according to package directions. Drain pasta, rinse with cold water, and drain again.

2. In a small bowl, stir together vinegar, ginger, soy sauce, oil, onions, and red pepper flakes. Measure 3 tablespoons of this dressing into a large bowl; add spinach and mix. Mound spinach mixture equally on 4 individual plates.

3. To large bowl, add remaining dressing, pasta, peas, and shrimp; mix gently but thoroughly. Mound pasta mixture atop spinach. Drizzle salads with any dressing left in bottom of bowl.

MAKES 4 SERVINGS

Per serving: 207 calories (10% calories from fat), 2 g total fat, 0 g saturated fat, 83 mg cholesterol, 844 mg sodium, 31 g carbohydrates, 5 g fiber, 16 g protein, 78 mg calcium, 4 mg iron

SOBA SALAD

Warm Chinese Chicken Salad

A fragrant sesame dressing flavors this hearty chicken salad. You might serve it with crisp-toasted pita wedges and fresh pineapple spears.

PREPARATION TIME: *About 15 minutes*
COOKING TIME: *About 5 minutes*

- ⅓ cup seasoned rice vinegar
- 1 tablespoon soy sauce
- 1½ teaspoons sugar
- 1½ teaspoons Asian sesame oil
- 7 cups finely shredded iceberg lettuce
- 3 cups bite-size pieces radicchio
- ⅓ cup cilantro leaves
- ¼ cup sliced green onions
- 1 pound boneless, skinless chicken breasts, cut into thin strips
- 2 cloves garlic, minced or pressed
  Cilantro sprigs

1. In a small bowl, stir together vinegar, 1 tablespoon water, soy sauce, sugar, and oil. Set aside.

2. In a large serving bowl, combine lettuce, radicchio, cilantro leaves, and onions; set aside.

3. In a wide nonstick frying pan or wok, combine chicken, 1 tablespoon water, and garlic. Cook over medium-high heat, stirring often, until chicken is no longer pink in center; cut to test (3 to 4 minutes). If pan appears dry, add water, 1 tablespoon at a time. Add vinegar mixture to chicken; bring to a boil, stirring.

4. Quickly pour chicken mixture over greens; mix gently but thoroughly. Garnish with cilantro sprigs and serve at once.

MAKES 4 SERVINGS

Per serving: 183 calories (17% calories from fat), 3 g total fat, 1 g saturated fat, 66 mg cholesterol, 627 mg sodium, 10 g carbohydrates, 1 g fiber, 28 g protein, 60 mg calcium, 2 mg iron

Thai Tofu Salad

A creamy dressing of peanut butter and plum jam adds richness to a warm main-dish salad of hot, herb-seasoned tofu cubes served atop spinach leaves and fresh orange slices. Accompany with hot rice and jasmine tea.

PREPARATION TIME: *About 20 minutes*
COOKING TIME: *About 5 minutes*

- 3 tablespoons plum jam
- 2 tablespoons peanut butter
  Crushed red pepper flakes
- 6 medium-size oranges (about 3 lbs. *total*)
  About 30 large fresh spinach leaves, rinsed and crisped
- 1 package (12 to 14 oz.) firm silken-style tofu
- ¼ cup seasoned rice vinegar
- ⅓ cup firmly packed cilantro leaves
- ⅓ cup firmly packed fresh basil leaves
- ⅓ cup firmly packed fresh mint leaves
- ½ teaspoon grated orange peel

1. In a small bowl, beat together jam and peanut butter to blend smoothly. Season to taste with red pepper flakes. Set aside.

2. Cut peel and all white membrane from oranges; thinly slice oranges crosswise. Line 4 individual plates with spinach; arrange oranges atop spinach. Set aside.

3. Rinse and drain tofu; pat dry. Cut into ½-inch cubes. In a bowl, combine tofu and vinegar; set aside, gently stirring occasionally.

4. In a food processor or blender, whirl cilantro, basil, and mint until minced. Pour into a shallow bowl; stir in orange peel. With a slotted spoon, transfer tofu to herb mixture; discard vinegar. Mix tofu with herb mixture, pressing lightly to coat. Pour herb-coated tofu into a wide nonstick frying pan. Add 1 tablespoon water. Cook over medium-high heat, stirring gently, until heated through (about 4 minutes).

5. Spoon hot tofu mixture over oranges and spinach. Top each serving equally with peanut dressing. Serve at once.

MAKES 4 SERVINGS

Per serving: 382 calories (29% calories from fat), 14 g total fat, 2 g saturated fat, 0 mg cholesterol, 399 mg sodium, 52 g carbohydrates, 10 g fiber, 22 g protein, 444 mg calcium, 15 mg iron

Southwestern Crab Salad

This tostada-style salad makes a nice light lunch or supper on a warm day. To assemble each serving, you top a crisp-baked corn tortilla with shredded lettuce and a combination of crab, bell pepper, and tomato in a tart lime dressing.

PREPARATION TIME: *About 15 minutes*
BAKING TIME: *About 15 minutes*

 6 corn tortillas (*each* about 6 inches in diameter)
12 ounces cooked crabmeat
 1 medium-size tomato (about 6 oz.), chopped and drained
 1 medium-size red bell pepper (about 6 oz.), seeded and chopped
 ¼ cup chopped green onions
 2 tablespoons chopped cilantro
 2 tablespoons lime juice
 1 tablespoon white wine vinegar
 1 small clove garlic, minced or pressed
 ¼ teaspoon crushed red pepper flakes
 ⅛ teaspoon salt
1½ cups shredded green leaf lettuce

1. Place tortillas in a single layer on a large baking sheet. Bake in a 350° oven until crisp (about 15 minutes). Set aside.

2. Meanwhile, in a large bowl, combine crab, tomato, bell pepper, onions, and cilantro. Toss to mix well. In a small bowl, stir together lime juice, vinegar, garlic, red pepper flakes, and salt. Add to crab mixture and stir well.

3. To serve, place one tortilla on each of 6 individual plates. Top tortillas equally with lettuce, then with crab mixture.

MAKES 6 SERVINGS

Per serving: 130 calories (12% calories from fat), 2 g total fat, 0 g saturated fat, 57 mg cholesterol, 253 mg sodium, 15 g carbohydrates, 2 g fiber, 14 g protein, 120 mg calcium, 1 mg iron

Shrimp Salsa Salad

Elegant to look at, this fruit-and-seafood salad is surprisingly simple: cantaloupe halves are filled with a combination of melon, papaya, cucumber, and tiny shrimp. If you like, enjoy the dish as a picnic entrée; transport melon halves and filling separately, then assemble at your destination.

PREPARATION TIME: *About 15 minutes*

 3 small cantaloupes (about 4 lbs. *total*)
 1 medium-size firm-ripe papaya (about 1 lb.), peeled, seeded, and diced
 1 small cucumber (about 6 oz.), peeled, seeded, and diced
 5 ounces small cooked shrimp
   About 2 tablespoons minced fresh mint
 3 tablespoons lime juice
 1 tablespoon honey
   Mint sprigs

1. Cut 2 of the cantaloupes in half lengthwise. Scoop out and discard seeds. If any of the melon halves does not sit steadily, cut a very thin slice from base so it sits steadily. Set melon halves aside.

2. Peel, seed, and dice remaining cantaloupe. Transfer to a large bowl. Add papaya, cucumber, shrimp, minced mint, lime juice, and honey. Mix gently.

3. Set each melon half in a bowl or on a dinner plate. Spoon a fourth of the fruit mixture into each melon half. If made ahead, cover and refrigerate for up to 4 hours. Just before serving, garnish each melon half with mint sprigs.

MAKES 4 SERVINGS

Per serving: 171 calories (6% calories from fat), 1 g total fat, 0 g saturated fat, 73 mg cholesterol, 112 mg sodium, 33 g carbohydrates, 3 g fiber, 11 g protein, 71 mg calcium, 2 mg iron

Soups

SPRING GREEN MINESTRONE

110

Spring Green Minestrone

Nourishing white beans and fresh vegetables, simmered until tender in vegetable or chicken broth, make a delicate yet satisfying soup. For an April evening supper, swirl a dollop of basil-and-mint pesto into each bowlful, and offer a loaf of crusty whole-grain bread.

PREPARATION TIME: *25 to 30 minutes*
COOKING TIME: *About 15 minutes*

Basil-Mint Pesto (recipe follows)

8 **cups vegetable broth or fat-free reduced-sodium chicken broth**

2 **large leeks (about 1¼ lbs. *total*)**

⅔ **cup dried orzo or other tiny rice-shaped pasta**

1 **pound thin asparagus, tough ends snapped off**

1 **can (about 15 oz.) cannellini (white kidney beans), rinsed and drained**

8 **ounces Chinese pea pods (snow or sugar peas) or sugar snap peas, ends trimmed**

4 **ounces fresh baby spinach leaves, rinsed and drained**

¼ **cup grated Parmesan cheese**

Salt and pepper

1. Prepare Basil-Mint Pesto; set aside.

2. In a 5- to 6-quart pan, bring broth to a boil over high heat. Meanwhile, trim and discard root ends and at least 1 to 2 inches from tops of leeks. Cut leeks in half lengthwise and rinse well; then thinly slice leek halves crosswise. Set aside.

3. Add pasta to boiling broth; cover and boil for 5 minutes. Meanwhile, cut asparagus spears into 2-inch lengths.

4. Add leeks, asparagus, beans, and pea pods to pasta-broth mixture; cover and cook until pasta is tender to bite (4 to 5 more minutes). Then add spinach and cook just until wilted (about 1 minute).

5. To serve, ladle soup into 6 individual bowls. Offer pesto, cheese, salt, and pepper to season individual servings.

MAKES 6 SERVINGS

Basil-Mint Pesto. In a blender, combine 1 clove **garlic**, peeled; 3 tablespoons **extra-virgin olive oil**; 3 tablespoons grated **Parmesan cheese**; 2 tablespoons **water**; 1 cup lightly packed **fresh basil leaves**; and ⅓ cup **fresh mint leaves.** Whirl until smooth. Season to taste with **salt**.

Per serving, including pesto: 294 calories (15% calories from fat), 10 g total fat, 2 g saturated fat, 5 mg cholesterol, 558 mg sodium, 38 g carbohydrates, 6 g fiber, 15 g protein, 183 mg calcium, 4 mg iron

Lentil & Kale Soup

Just right for lunch on a cold winter day, this sturdy soup features lentils cooked with vitamin-rich kale, potatoes, and whole-kernel corn in a chile-accented tomato broth. Accompany it with Yogurt Cornbread (page 214) or Sunflower Soda Bread (page 213).

PREPARATION TIME: *About 15 minutes*
COOKING TIME: *About 1 hour*

- 1 tablespoon olive oil
- 2 large onions, diced
- 3 cloves garlic, minced or pressed
- 1 tablespoon chili powder
- ½ teaspoon ground cumin
- 2 dried bay leaves
- 8 cups fat-free reduced-sodium chicken broth
- ¾ cup lentils, sorted and rinsed
- 1 can (about 14½ oz.) diced tomatoes
- 1 pound kale
- 1 pound thin-skinned potatoes
- 1 cup frozen corn kernels, thawed
- 2 tablespoons tamari or soy sauce

1. Heat oil in a 6- to 8-quart pan over medium-high heat. Add onions and garlic; cook, stirring often, until onions are soft and pale golden (about 12 minutes). If pan appears dry, add water, 1 tablespoon at a time. Add chili powder, cumin, and bay leaves; stir for 1 more minute.

2. Add broth, lentils, and tomatoes. Bring to a boil; then reduce heat, cover, and simmer until lentils are just tender to bite (about 25 minutes). Meanwhile, trim and discard tough stems from kale; chop leaves and tender stems. Scrub potatoes and cut into ½-inch cubes.

3. Add kale and potatoes to pan; adjust heat to bring soup to a gentle boil. Cover and cook until potatoes are tender to bite (about 15 minutes). Add corn and tamari; cook just until corn is heated through (about 1 minute).

4. To serve, ladle soup into 8 individual bowls.

MAKES 8 SERVINGS

Per serving: 223 calories (11% calories from fat), 3 g total fat, 0 g saturated fat, 0 mg cholesterol, 939 mg sodium, 39 g carbohydrates, 6 g fiber, 13 g protein, 120 mg calcium, 4 mg iron

Pumpkin Soup

Here's an elegant first-course soup with harvest flavors. The recipe yields a generous eight servings, making it an ideal starter for an autumn dinner party. You can refrigerate it for up to a day, then reheat before serving.

PREPARATION TIME: *About 10 minutes*
COOKING TIME: *About 15 minutes*

- 1 large onion, chopped
- 2 cloves garlic, minced or pressed
- 1 teaspoon pumpkin pie spice
- ⅛ teaspoon ground red pepper (cayenne)
- 3¾ cups fat-free reduced-sodium chicken broth
- 1 can (about 15 oz.) solid-pack pumpkin
- 1 tablespoon honey
- 1 cup reduced-fat (2%) milk
- 4 teaspoons cornstarch
- 1 tablespoon lemon juice
- ½ cup fat-free sour cream
  Lemon slices

1. In a 4- to 5-quart pan, combine onion, garlic, pumpkin pie spice, red pepper, and ¼ cup of the broth. Cook over high heat, stirring often, until broth has evaporated and onion is almost tender to bite (4 to 5 minutes). Pour onion mixture into a blender or food processor; whirl until smoothly puréed, adding a little more broth, if needed.

2. Return purée to pan; add remaining broth (about 3½ cups), pumpkin, and honey. Smoothly mix milk and cornstarch; stir into soup. Bring to a boil over high heat, stirring. Stir in lemon juice; remove from heat. (At this point, you may let cool, then cover and refrigerate until next day. Reheat until steaming before serving.)

3. To serve, ladle soup into 6 to 8 shallow individual bowls. Top with sour cream; garnish with lemon slices.

MAKES 6 TO 8 SERVINGS

Per serving: 83 calories (10% calories from fat), 1 g total fat, 0 g saturated fat, 3 mg cholesterol, 327 mg sodium, 15 g carbohydrates, 2 g fiber, 4 g protein, 75 mg calcium, 1 mg iron

PUMPKIN SOUP

Tomato-Bread Soup

Made with fresh, ripe red or orange tomatoes, this soup captures late summer's most enticing flavors in each big, basil-dotted bowlful. The golden-toasted sourdough slices that underlie the soup can be prepared up to a day in advance, then stored in a sealed plastic bag until you are ready to use them.

PREPARATION TIME: *About 15 minutes*
COOKING TIME: *About 40 minutes*

- 5 ounces sourdough bread (about one-third of a 1-lb. loaf), cut into six ¾-inch-thick slices
- 2 tablespoons olive oil
- 2 large onions, chopped
- 3 cloves garlic, minced or pressed
- 3 pounds ripe red or orange tomatoes, peeled and coarsely chopped
- 3 cups fat-free reduced-sodium chicken broth
- ½ cup dry red wine
- 1 cup firmly packed fresh basil leaves, slivered

    Basil sprigs (optional)

1. Brush bread slices on both sides with 1 tablespoon of the oil. Arrange in a single layer on a baking sheet. Broil about 5 inches below heat until golden (about 2 minutes). Turn bread over; broil until golden on other side (about 2 more minutes). Let cool on a rack.

2. In a 5- to 6-quart pan, combine remaining 1 tablespoon oil, onions, and garlic. Cook over medium-high heat, stirring often, until onions are golden brown and sweet tasting (about 15 minutes). If pan appears dry, add water, 1 tablespoon at a time. Add tomatoes, broth, and wine. Bring to a boil; then reduce heat and simmer, uncovered, until reduced to about 8 cups (about 15 minutes).

3. Stir slivered basil into soup. Place one toast slice in each of 6 individual bowls. Ladle soup over toast; garnish with basil sprigs. (Or, if desired, ladle soup into bowls first; then top each serving with a slice of toast and a basil sprig.)

MAKES 6 SERVINGS

Per serving: 216 calories (27% calories from fat), 6 g total fat, 1 g saturated fat, 0 mg cholesterol, 456 mg sodium, 32 g carbohydrates, 6 g fiber, 8 g protein, 114 mg calcium, 3 mg iron

Porcini Mushroom Soup

A purée of cooked mushrooms and russet potatoes gives this soup a smooth richness you wouldn't expect from a dish with so little fat. Soft goat cheese whirled into the soup—and spread over toasted baguette slices to accompany it—rounds out the flavor. With a leafy salad alongside, it's all you need for a light yet satisfying meal.

PREPARATION TIME: *About 30 minutes*
COOKING TIME: *About 45 minutes*

- ¾ cup (about 1 oz.) dried porcini mushrooms
- 5 cups fat-free reduced-sodium chicken broth, heated
- 1¼ pounds fresh mushrooms, sliced
- 1 cup chopped onion
- ½ cup dry white wine
- 2 cups peeled, chopped russet potatoes
- ¼ cup chopped parsley
- ¼ teaspoon ground nutmeg
- 2½ cups low-fat (1%) milk or fat-free milk
- 4 ounces seeded or plain slender baguette (about 2 inches in diameter), cut into ⅓-inch-thick slices
- 3 ounces chive-flavored or plain soft fresh goat cheese
- Parsley sprigs

1. In a medium-size bowl, soak porcini in hot broth until pliable (about 15 minutes). Swish porcini to loosen any grit, then lift out and set aside. Reserve broth.

2. In a 5- to 6-quart pan, combine soaked porcini, fresh mushrooms, onion, and ¼ cup of the wine. Cook over high heat, stirring often, until liquid has evaporated and a deep brown film forms on pan bottom (about 10 minutes). Stir in remaining ¼ cup wine; continue to cook, stirring often, until pan liquid evaporates and brown film forms again (2 to 3 more minutes). Remove 8 to 12 mushroom slices from pan and set aside to use for garnish.

3. Carefully pour mushroom-soaking broth into pan (do not add any grit from bottom of bowl). Add potatoes, 3 tablespoons of the chopped parsley, and nutmeg. Bring to a boil; then reduce heat, cover, and simmer until porcini are very tender when pierced (about 20 minutes). Add milk; stir until steaming (about 4 minutes).

4. Meanwhile, place bread in a 10- by 15-inch baking pan; broil about 5 inches below heat until golden (about 2 minutes). Turn bread over, spread with half the cheese, and broil until cheese is melted (about 2 more minutes). Sprinkle with remaining 1 tablespoon chopped parsley. Set aside.

5. In a blender, whirl soup and remaining cheese, a portion at a time, until smoothly puréed. Ladle into 4 to 6 individual bowls; garnish with reserved mushroom slices and parsley sprigs. Float cheese-topped toast on soup or serve alongside.

MAKES 4 TO 6 SERVINGS

Per serving: 283 calories (20% calories from fat), 6 g total fat, 3 g saturated fat, 23 mg cholesterol, 863 mg sodium, 40 g carbohydrates, 5 g fiber, 17 g protein, 197 mg calcium, 4 mg iron

Creamy Mushroom Bisque

Substantial enough to serve as a main course with bread and thin slices of your favorite reduced-fat cheese, this potato-mushroom purée also makes a festive starter for holiday dinners.

PREPARATION TIME: *About 15 minutes*
COOKING TIME: *About 25 minutes*

- 4 cups fat-free reduced-sodium chicken broth
- 2 large thin-skinned potatoes (about 1 lb. *total*), peeled and cut into 1-inch chunks
- 1 pound mushrooms, cut into quarters
- ¼ cup fresh tarragon leaves
- ½ cup half-and-half
  Salt and white pepper
- 4 ounces thinly sliced prosciutto or lean smoked ham, chopped
  Tarragon sprigs

1. In a 3- to 4-quart pan, combine broth, potatoes, and mushrooms. Bring to a boil over high heat; then reduce heat, cover, and simmer until potatoes are very soft when pierced (about 20 minutes).

2. In a blender or food processor, whirl potato-mushroom mixture, tarragon leaves, and half-and-half, a portion at a time, until puréed. Return soup to pan; season to taste with salt and pepper. Then stir over medium heat just until hot.

3. To serve, ladle soup into 4 individual wide, shallow bowls. Mound a fourth of the prosciutto atop each serving; garnish with tarragon sprigs.

MAKES 4 SERVINGS

Per serving: 234 calories (30% calories from fat), 8 g total fat, 3 g saturated fat, 34 mg cholesterol, 1,111 mg sodium, 26 g carbohydrates, 3 g fiber, 16 g protein, 51 mg calcium, 3 mg iron

Gazpacho

Cool and refreshing, gazpacho has been described by some of its fans as a salad in a soup bowl. This version features plenty of fresh herbs along with the usual chopped tomato, cucumber, bell pepper, and onion. With iced tea and whole wheat crackers, it's a fine light lunch.

PREPARATION TIME: *About 25 minutes, plus at least 1 hour to chill*

- 2 large cans (about 28 oz. *each*) tomatoes
- 2 tablespoons chopped fresh basil
- 1 tablespoon chopped cilantro
- 1 tablespoon balsamic vinegar
- 2 teaspoons chopped fresh marjoram
- 2 teaspoons chopped fresh oregano
- 1 teaspoon lemon juice
- 1 cup vegetable broth
- 1 small cucumber (about 6 oz.)
- 1 medium-size firm-ripe tomato (about 6 oz.)
- 1 medium-size green bell pepper (about 6 oz.)
- 1 medium-size white onion
  Salt and pepper

1. In a blender or food processor, combine canned tomatoes and their juice, basil, cilantro, vinegar, marjoram, and oregano. Whirl until smoothly puréed. Pour into a large bowl; stir in lemon juice and broth. Cover and refrigerate for at least 1 hour or for up to 1 day.

2. Peel and seed cucumber; cut into ½-inch cubes. Cut tomato into ½-inch cubes. Seed bell pepper and cut into ½-inch squares. Finely chop onion; rinse in cold water and drain well.

3. Stir cucumber, cubed tomato, bell pepper, and onion into chilled soup. Season to taste wtih salt and pepper. To serve, ladle into 6 individual bowls.

MAKES 6 SERVINGS

Per serving: 83 calories (8% calories from fat), 1 g total fat, 0 g saturated fat, 0 mg cholesterol, 480 mg sodium, 18 g carbohydrates, 3 g fiber, 4 g protein, 90 mg calcium, 2 mg iron

Polenta Soup with Gorgonzola

A bowl of this thick soup will fuel you for an afternoon of skating or shopping—or fill you up after the busy day is through. Spicy nuggets of turkey sausage stud each hearty bowlful; pungent Gorgonzola cheese is sprinkled on top.

PREPARATION TIME: *About 10 minutes*
COOKING TIME: *About 25 minutes*

- 4 ounces mild or hot turkey Italian sausage, casings removed
- 1 cup thinly sliced mushrooms
- 3½ cups fat-free reduced-sodium chicken broth
- ¾ cup polenta or yellow cornmeal
- 2 ounces Gorgonzola or other blue-veined cheese, crumbled
- Thinly sliced green onions

1. Crumble sausage into a 4- to 5-quart pan. Add mushrooms. Cook over medium heat, stirring often, until sausage is tinged with brown and mushrooms are soft (about 10 minutes); if pan appears dry, add water, 1 tablespoon at a time.

2. Add broth, 2 cups water, and polenta to pan; blend well. Bring to a rolling boil; then reduce heat so soup boils gently. Cook, stirring often, until polenta tastes creamy (7 to 10 minutes).

3. To serve, ladle soup into 4 individual bowls; sprinkle with cheese and garnish with onions.

MAKES 4 SERVINGS

Per serving: 302 calories (24% calories from fat), 8 g total fat, 4 g saturated fat, 28 mg cholesterol, 873 mg sodium, 42 g carbohydrates, 5 g fiber, 15 g protein, 90 mg calcium, 2 mg iron

Garlic Soup with White Beans

A good lead-in for a crisp roast chicken or sizzling broiled lamb chops, this soup will delight garlic lovers. Start by lightly browning an entire head of peeled, sliced garlic; then add broth, creamy-textured cannellini, and a confetti of diced fresh vegetables.

PREPARATION TIME: *About 20 minutes*
COOKING TIME: *About 30 minutes*

- 1 head garlic
- 1 teaspoon vegetable oil
- 6 cups fat-free reduced-sodium chicken broth
- 1 can (about 15 oz.) cannellini (white kidney beans), rinsed and drained
- 3 tablespoons finely chopped red bell pepper
- 3 tablespoons minced green onions
- 3 tablespoons finely chopped tomato
- ¼ teaspoon Asian sesame oil

1. Peel garlic cloves and thinly slice. Heat vegetable oil in a wide non-stick frying pan over medium-low heat. Add garlic and cook, stirring often, until golden brown (about 10 minutes; do not scorch). If pan appears dry or garlic sticks to pan, stir in water, 1 tablespoon at a time.

2. Meanwhile, in a 4- to 5-quart pan, bring broth to a boil over high heat.

3. When garlic is browned, pour about ½ cup of the hot broth into frying pan, stirring to loosen browned bits. Then pour garlic-broth mixture into large pan of broth. Reduce heat, cover, and simmer for 15 minutes; then increase heat to high and bring to a boil. Add beans, reduce heat, and boil gently just until beans are heated through (2 to 3 minutes).

4. Add bell pepper, onions, tomato, and sesame oil; simmer just until vegetables are heated through (about 2 minutes). To serve, ladle into 6 individual bowls.

MAKES 6 SERVINGS

Per serving: 87 calories (14% calories from fat), 1 g total fat, 0 g saturated fat, 0 mg cholesterol, 652 mg sodium, 11 g carbohydrates, 3 g fiber, 7 g protein, 32 mg calcium, 1 mg iron

Sausage & Spring Vegetable Soup

Tender fresh asparagus and tiny sweet peas give this easy, fennel-seasoned soup its springtime flavor. Serve it as a meal starter; or offer larger servings as a lunch or supper entrée with a satisfying salad such as Creamy Caesar Salad (page 95).

PREPARATION TIME: *About 15 minutes*
COOKING TIME: *15 to 20 minutes*

- 8 ounces mild or hot turkey Italian sausage, casings removed
- ½ teaspoon fennel seeds
- 8 cups fat-free reduced-sodium chicken broth
- 2 cups diced carrots
- 2 cups thinly sliced asparagus
- 1 package (about 10 oz.) frozen tiny peas, thawed
- ½ cup thinly sliced green onions

1. Crumble sausage into a 4- to 5-quart pan. Add fennel seeds and 1 tablespoon water. Cook over medium-high heat, stirring often, until sausage is tinged with brown (about 10 minutes); if pan appears dry, add water, 1 tablespoon at a time.

2. Add broth and carrots and bring to a boil over high heat. Reduce heat to a simmer and add asparagus and peas; cook just until vegetables are heated through (about 3 minutes). Remove pan from heat and stir in onions.

3. To serve, ladle into 8 individual bowls.

MAKES 8 SERVINGS

Per serving: 110 calories (26% calories from fat), 3 g total fat, 1 g saturated fat, 15 mg cholesterol, 805 mg sodium, 10 g carbohydrates, 4 g fiber, 11 g protein, 36 mg calcium, 2 mg iron

Lentil Soup with Lamb

Lamb meatballs flavored with chili and coriander simmer to doneness in a thick lentil soup with curry seasonings. If time is important, look for decorticated lentils when you shop; by using them, you'll cut the cooking time by 15 to 20 minutes. Round out the meal with a crusty sourdough loaf and a selection of baby greens in a citrus vinaigrette.

PREPARATION TIME: *About 25 minutes*
COOKING TIME: *50 to 55 minutes*

- 1 large onion, chopped
- 1 teaspoon cumin seeds
- 1 tablespoon minced fresh ginger
- 1 tablespoon curry powder
- 8 cups fat-free reduced-sodium chicken broth
- 1 pound (about 2¼ cups) regular lentils or decorticated red lentils, sorted and rinsed
- 1 pound lean ground lamb
- 1 teaspoon ground coriander
- 1 teaspoon chili powder
- 1 cup fat-free sour cream
- ¼ cup cilantro leaves

1. In a 4- to 5-quart pan, combine onion, cumin seeds, ginger, and ¼ cup water. Cook over high heat, stirring often, until liquid has evaporated and onion begins to stick to pan (about 5 minutes). Add 2 tablespoons water; stir to loosen onion. Then cook, stirring, until onion sticks to pan again (about 3 minutes); again add 2 tablespoons water and stir onion free. Cook, stirring, until liquid has evaporated and onion is light brown (about 3 more minutes).

2. Reduce heat to low and add curry powder; stir until fragrant (about 1 minute).

3. Add broth and lentils. Bring to a boil over high heat; then reduce heat, cover, and simmer just until lentils are almost tender to bite (25 to 30 minutes for regular lentils; about 10 minutes for decorticated lentils).

4. In a medium-size bowl, mix lamb, coriander, and chili powder. Form into 1-inch balls. Gently stir meatballs into simmering soup. Then cover and simmer, gently stirring occasionally, until meatballs are no longer pink in center; cut to test (about 10 minutes).

5. To serve, ladle into 6 individual bowls. Offer sour cream and cilantro to add to taste.

MAKES 6 SERVINGS

Per serving: 453 calories (12% calories from fat), 6 g total fat, 2 g saturated fat, 54 mg cholesterol, 849 mg sodium, 56 g carbohydrates, 10 g fiber, 43 g protein, 122 mg calcium, 9 mg iron

Tortellini Minestrone

Low in fat, high in carbohydrates, good tasting, and ready in no time: it's no wonder pasta is so widely appreciated. Here—in the form of shapely tortellini—it stars in a main-dish soup you can put together in well under 30 minutes. Choose plain or spinach tortellini (or use some of each); those with a pesto or mushroom filling are especially good in this recipe.

PREPARATION TIME: *About 5 minutes*
COOKING TIME: *About 15 minutes*

8 cups fat-free reduced-sodium chicken broth

½ cup dry white wine

½ teaspoon dried oregano

1 cup fresh baby-cut carrots, halved lengthwise

1 cup chopped red bell pepper

1 package (about 9 oz.) fresh tortellini or ravioli

12 ounces boneless, skinless chicken breasts, cut into 1-inch pieces

¼ cup chopped parsley

1. In a 5- to 6-quart pan, combine broth, wine, oregano, and carrots. Bring to a boil over high heat. Add bell pepper and tortellini; boil, uncovered, for 4 minutes.

2. Stir in chicken. Simmer until pasta is tender to bite and chicken is no longer pink in center; cut to test (about 2 minutes). Stir in parsley.

3. To serve, ladle into 4 individual bowls.

MAKES 4 SERVINGS

Per serving: 357 calories (17% calories from fat), 6 g total fat, 2 g saturated fat, 77 mg cholesterol, 1,347 mg sodium, 36 g carbohydrates, 3 g fiber, 33 g protein, 56 mg calcium, 3 mg iron

Turkey Kielbasa Soup

Enjoy this inviting soup with slices of rye toast and a fruit plate of sliced oranges, apples, and ripe pears. Abundant with vegetables and slices of sausage, the soup is especially welcome when time is short: it's ready to serve in just half an hour. Preparation goes especially quickly if you use purchased shredded cabbage, but shred your own if you prefer.

PREPARATION TIME: *About 10 minutes*
COOKING TIME: *About 20 minutes*

3½ cups fat-free reduced-sodium chicken broth

1 can (about 15 oz.) garbanzo beans, rinsed and drained

3 cups shredded green cabbage (or cabbage with shredded carrots)

1 cup diced thin-skinned potatoes

½ cup chopped onion

1 clove garlic, minced or pressed

8 ounces turkey kielbasa, cut into ¼-inch-thick slices

1 tablespoon white wine vinegar

1½ tablespoons minced parsley

Parsley sprigs

1. In a 5- to 6-quart pan, combine broth, garbanzos, cabbage, potatoes, onion, and garlic. Bring to a boil over high heat; then reduce heat, cover, and simmer until potatoes are tender to bite (about 10 minutes).

2. Add kielbasa, cover, and simmer until heated through (about 5 more minutes). Stir in vinegar and minced parsley.

3. To serve, ladle into 4 individual bowls; garnish with parsley sprigs.

MAKES 4 SERVINGS

Per serving: 223 calories (26% calories from fat), 6 g total fat, 3 g saturated fat, 30 mg cholesterol, 1,421 mg sodium, 25 g carbohydrates, 5 g fiber, 17 g protein, 54 mg calcium, 2 mg iron

Shrimp Soup with Shells

East and West combine in this first-course soup. Carrots, pasta seashells, and brilliant snow peas simmer in a broth seasoned with fresh ginger and sesame oil; at serving time, tiny shrimp mixed with cilantro and green onion are spooned into each serving. If you like, offer larger helpings as a light supper entrée.

PREPARATION TIME: *About 20 minutes*
COOKING TIME: *About 20 minutes*

- 8 cups fat-free reduced-sodium chicken broth
- 2 tablespoons minced fresh ginger
- 2 cups diced carrots
- 1 cup dried small pasta shells
- 1 package (about 10 oz.) frozen Chinese pea pods (snow or sugar peas), thawed and cut in half diagonally
- 1 package (about 10 oz.) frozen tiny peas, thawed
- ¼ teaspoon (or to taste) Asian sesame oil
- 1 pound small cooked shrimp
- ½ cup thinly sliced green onions
- ¼ cup minced cilantro

1. In a 5- to 6-quart pan, bring broth to a boil over high heat. Stir in ginger, carrots, and pasta. Then reduce heat, cover, and boil gently until carrots and pasta are just tender to bite (8 to 10 minutes).

2. Add pea pods, peas, and oil; simmer until vegetables are heated through (about 4 minutes). Remove soup from heat and keep warm.

3. In a small bowl, combine shrimp, onions, and cilantro. To serve, ladle soup into 8 individual bowls; top evenly with shrimp mixture.

MAKES 8 SERVINGS

Per serving: 181 calories (6% calories from fat), 1 g total fat, 0 g saturated fat, 111 mg cholesterol, 749 mg sodium, 21 g carbohydrates, 4 g fiber, 20 g protein, 63 mg calcium, 4 mg iron

Frosty Peach Soup

This quick dessert soup is made with frozen peaches, so you can enjoy it even in midwinter. Frozen concentrated pink lemonade intensifies the purée's color and gives it a tart-sweet flavor.

PREPARATION TIME: *About 10 minutes*

- 1 large can (about 12 oz.) frozen pink lemonade concentrate
- 2 packages (about 1 lb. *each*) frozen unsweetened sliced peaches
- 2 teaspoons lemon juice
- 1 teaspoon honey
- ¼ to ½ teaspoon ground coriander
- About 1½ cups chilled sparkling mineral water
- ½ cup fat-free sour cream
- Mint sprigs or shredded lemon peel (optional)

1. In a blender or food processor, whirl lemonade concentrate, peaches, lemon juice, honey, and coriander, a portion at a time, until smoothly puréed. Add 1½ cups of the sparkling water, or enough to thin soup to desired consistency (soup should be thick).

2. Pour soup into 6 individual bowls; top each serving with a dollop of sour cream. Garnish with mint sprigs or lemon peel, if desired.

MAKES 6 SERVINGS

Per serving: 225 calories (1% calories from fat), .30 g total fat, 0 g saturated fat, 2 mg cholesterol, 20 mg sodium, 56 g carbohydrates, 3 g fiber, 3 g protein, 40 mg calcium, 1 mg iron

Mixed Berry Soup

When fresh berries are at their peak, take advantage of the bounty to serve this bright dessert soup. It could hardly be simpler: just add your choice of mixed berries to a "broth" of white grape juice sparked with ginger and orange liqueur, then top with a dollop of sour cream.

PREPARATION TIME: *About 10 minutes*

- 2½ cups mixed fresh berries, such as blueberries, raspberries, blackberries, and thinly sliced strawberries
- 1 tablespoon lemon juice
- 2 cups chilled white grape juice
- 2 tablespoons minced crystallized ginger
- 3 tablespoons orange-flavored liqueur
- 4 to 6 tablespoons fat-free sour cream
- Mint sprigs (optional)

1. Place berries in a large bowl; drizzle with lemon juice and mix gently. (At this point, you may cover and refrigerate for up to 2 hours.)

2. In a small bowl, combine grape juice and ginger. Stir in liqueur, then pour mixture over berries.

3. To serve, ladle soup into 4 to 6 individual bowls; top each serving with a dollop of sour cream. Garnish with mint sprigs, if desired.

MAKES 4 TO 6 SERVINGS

Per serving: 161 calories (2% calories from fat), .40 g total fat, 0 g saturated fat, 2 mg cholesterol, 27 mg sodium, 35 g carbohydrates, 3 g fiber, 2 g protein, 37 mg calcium, 0 mg iron

Meats

ROAST BEEF WITH FENNEL

Roast Beef with Fennel

Treat dinner guests to tender, juicy beef roasted with red potatoes, shallots, and cubed fresh fennel and served with a rich port wine gravy. Tri-tip is a relatively lean, boneless cut that comes from the triangular end of the bottom sirloin; if you can't find it, substitute top round.

PREPARATION TIME: *About 35 minutes*
COOKING TIME: *About 1 ¼ hours*

- 2 **large heads fennel** (*each* 3½ to 4 inches in diameter; about 1½ lbs. *total*)
- 4 **teaspoons olive oil**
- 2 **pounds small red thin-skinned potatoes** (*each* about 1½ inches in diameter)
- 1 **pound shallots, cut into halves**
- 1 **cup port**
- 2 **tablespoons firmly packed brown sugar**
- 1 **tablespoon soy sauce**
- 1 **beef tri-tip or top round roast** (about 2 lbs.), trimmed of fat
- 2 **tablespoons whipping cream**
- 3 **tablespoons chopped fresh oregano or 1 tablespoon dried oregano**

1. Rinse fennel. Trim base, stems, and any bruised portions from each head; reserve feathery leaves. Cut fennel into 1-inch chunks. In a 12- by 17-inch roasting pan, combine fennel with 2 teaspoons of the oil. Bake in a 450° oven for 15 minutes. Meanwhile, scrub potatoes, cut into 1-inch chunks, and set aside.

2. To pan with fennel, add potatoes, shallots, and remaining 2 teaspoons oil; stir gently. Bake for 15 more minutes. If pan appears dry, add water, 2 tablespoons at a time.

3. Meanwhile, in a 1½- to 2-quart pan, combine port, brown sugar, and soy sauce; stir over medium heat just until sugar is dissolved. Remove from heat and let cool slightly.

4. Remove pan from oven. Push vegetables to sides of pan; set beef in center and baste with ¼ cup of the port mixture. Return pan to oven and roast until a meat thermometer inserted in thickest part of beef registers 135°F for rare (about 35 minutes). After about 15 minutes, baste beef and vegetables with ¼ cup more port mixture. After 25 minutes, check temperature every 5 minutes. If pan appears dry at any point during roasting, add water, 2 to 4 tablespoons at a time, stirring to loosen browned bits from pan; do not let drippings scorch.

5. Transfer beef to a carving board, cover lightly, and let rest for about 15 minutes. Meanwhile, to prepare gravy, bring remaining port mixture to a boil over high heat. Then reduce heat and boil gently until reduced to ½ cup. Add cream and continue to boil until gravy is thick enough to coat the back of a spoon. Remove from heat and stir in about a third of the oregano. Keep warm.

6. To serve, slice beef thinly across the grain and arrange on a platter. With a slotted spoon, ladle vegetables around beef. Garnish platter with reserved fennel leaves; sprinkle remaining oregano over beef and vegetables. Pour any drippings from roasting pan and carving board into gravy; stir gravy, then pour into a small pitcher and offer to season beef and vegetables.

MAKES 8 SERVINGS

Per serving: 347 calories (20% calories from fat), 8 g total fat, 2 g saturated fat, 70 mg cholesterol, 281 mg sodium, 38 g carbohydrates, 3 g fiber, 30 g protein, 75 mg calcium, 5 mg iron

Grilled Tri-tip
with Cilantro

Add flavor to this barbecue-roasted beef by cutting slits in the roast before grilling and stuffing them with a soy-cilantro seasoning blend.

PREPARATION TIME: *About 25 minutes, plus about 15 minutes to marinate*
COOKING TIME: *20 to 25 minutes*

- 1 **beef tri-tip or top round roast (2 to 2½ lbs.), trimmed of fat**
- ¼ **cup soy sauce**
- ¼ **cup chopped cilantro**
- 2 **tablespoons chopped fresh oregano or 2 teaspoons dried oregano**
- 3 **cloves garlic, minced or pressed**
- ½ **teaspoon pepper**

1. Cut 1-inch-long slits about ½ inch deep and 1 inch apart over top and bottom surfaces of beef. In a small bowl, stir together soy sauce, chopped cilantro, oregano, garlic, and pepper. Set beef in a rimmed dish; spoon soy mixture over it, spooning it into slits. Cover and refrigerate for about 15 minutes.

2. Lift beef from dish and drain briefly; discard marinade. Set beef on an oiled grill 4 to 6 inches above a solid bed of medium-hot coals or over medium-high heat on a gas grill (you can hold your hand at grill level for 3 to 4 seconds). Close lid on gas grill. Cook beef, turning once, until a meat thermometer inserted in thickest part registers 135°F for rare (20 to 25 minutes for a 1½- to 2-inch-thick roast).

3. Transfer beef to a carving board, cover lightly, and let rest for 5 to 10 minutes. To serve, thinly slice beef across the grain.

MAKES 6 TO 8 SERVINGS

Per serving: 157 calories (24% calories from fat), 4 g total fat, 1 g saturated fat, 69 mg cholesterol, 394 mg sodium, 2 g carbohydrates, 0 g fiber, 27 g protein, 17 mg calcium, 3 mg iron

Skewered Beef with
Cherry Glaze

Morsels of beef tenderloin stay moist and tender under a garnet-hued cherry glaze. Nestle the skewers atop a bed of fluffy couscous or rice, and offer steamed green beans or fresh spinach for color contrast.

PREPARATION TIME: *About 10 minutes*
COOKING TIME: *About 20 minutes*

- 1 **cup cherry jam**
- 1 **cup Merlot or other dry red wine**
- 3 **tablespoons raspberry or red wine vinegar**
- 2 **tablespoons minced fresh rosemary or 1 teaspoon crumbled dried rosemary**
- 1 **pound beef tenderloin, cut into 20 equal pieces**
- 8 **green onions (ends trimmed), cut crosswise into halves**
- 2¼ **cups beef broth, skimmed of fat**
- 1½ **cups couscous**

1. In a wide frying pan, stir together jam, wine, vinegar, and rosemary. Bring to a boil over high heat; then boil, stirring often, until reduced to 1 cup (10 to 12 minutes). Keep warm over very low heat.

2. While sauce is boiling, thread beef and onion pieces alternately on 4 metal skewers (at least 8 inches long).

3. Lay skewers in a broiler pan; brush evenly with about a third of the cherry sauce. Broil about 4 inches below heat until beef is browned (4 to 5 minutes). Turn skewers over, brush with half the remaining cherry sauce, and broil until browned on other side (about 4 minutes).

4. Meanwhile, in a 2- to 3-quart pan, bring broth to a boil over high heat. Stir in couscous. Cover, remove from heat, and let stand until broth has been absorbed (about 5 minutes).

5. To serve, fluff couscous; spoon onto a platter or 4 individual plates and top with skewers. Spoon remaining cherry sauce over skewers.

MAKES 4 SERVINGS

Per serving: 696 calories (13% calories from fat), 9 g total fat, 3 g saturated fat, 72 mg cholesterol, 415 mg sodium, 109 g carbohydrates, 4 g fiber, 36 g protein, 68 mg calcium, 5 mg iron

Beef Fajitas

Marinate thin-sliced beef in lime and garlic, then quick-cook it to serve in heated flour tortillas with fresh tomato relish, homemade guacamole, and sour cream. You can spoon the toppings over the beef-filled tortillas, if you like; or let guests assemble their own servings, enclosing meat as well as toppings inside the soft, warm tortillas. (To make the steak easier to slice thinly, partially freeze it before cutting.)

PREPARATION TIME: *About 30 minutes, plus at least 30 minutes to marinate*
COOKING TIME: *About 15 minutes*

- 1½ **pounds lean beef round steak, trimmed of fat and cut across the grain into ¼-inch-thick slanting slices**
- 2 **tablespoons lime juice**
- ½ **teaspoon salt**
- ⅛ **teaspoon pepper**
- 2 **cloves garlic, minced or pressed**
- 1 **cup lightly packed chopped cilantro**
- 1 **cup chopped tomatoes**
- ½ **cup chopped onion**
   Chunky Guacamole (recipe follows)
- 12 **small fat-free flour tortillas (*each about 6 inches in diameter*)**
- 1 **teaspoon vegetable oil**
- 1½ **cups shredded iceberg lettuce**
- ½ **to 1 cup fat-free sour cream**

1. In a shallow dish, combine steak, lime juice, salt, pepper, and garlic. Cover and refrigerate for at least 30 minutes or up to 8 hours, stirring occasionally.

2. In a small bowl, combine cilantro, tomatoes, and onion. Cover and refrigerate for at least 30 minutes or up to 1 hour.

3. Prepare Chunky Guacamole; cover and refrigerate.

4. Stack tortillas, wrap in foil, and heat in a 325° oven until warm (about 15 minutes). Meanwhile, heat oil in a wide nonstick frying pan over medium-high heat. Lift steak from marinade and drain briefly; discard marinade. Add steak to pan and cook, stirring often, until browned on the outside but still pink in center; cut to test (about 5 minutes). Remove steak from pan with a slotted spoon; keep warm.

5. To serve, divide steak evenly among warm tortillas; roll up tortillas to enclose filling and arrange on a platter, seam side down. Top evenly with lettuce, tomato mixture, and Chunky Guacamole. Offer sour cream to add to taste.

MAKES 6 SERVINGS

Chunky Guacamole. In a small bowl, combine ½ medium-size **avocado**, peeled and cut into ½-inch cubes, and 2 tablespoons **lime juice**; toss gently to, coat avocado with lime juice. Add ⅓ cup finely chopped **tomato**; 1 tablespoon chopped **green onion**; ½ small **fresh jalapeño chile**, seeded and finely chopped; 1 teaspoon **honey**; 1 clove **garlic**, minced or pressed; and ⅛ teaspoon **salt**. Mix gently. Cover and refrigerate for up to 1 hour; stir before serving.

Per serving, including guacamole: 362 calories (23% calories from fat), 9 g total fat, 2 g saturated fat, 69 mg cholesterol, 643 mg sodium, 37 g carbohydrates, 2 g fiber, 31 g protein, 68 mg calcium, 4 mg iron

Taco Salad

This version of ever-popular taco salad features a hot mixture of lean beef, cream-style corn, and chiles spooned over crisp lettuce and topped with beans and cheese. Offer a creamy salsa–sour cream dressing to spoon over individual servings, and serve plenty of baked tortilla chips alongside.

PREPARATION TIME: *About 25 minutes*
COOKING TIME: *About 15 minutes*

  Salsa Dressing (recipe follows)
1 **pound lean ground beef**
1 **tablespoon olive oil**
1 **teaspoon cumin seeds**
10 **cups baked tortilla chips, either nacho cheese flavored or plain**
1 **can (about 15 oz.) cream-style corn**
1 **can (about 4 oz.) diced green chiles**
2 **tablespoons chili powder**
1 **large head red leaf lettuce (about 1½ lbs.), separated into leaves, rinsed, and crisped**
1 **can (about 15 oz.) red kidney beans, rinsed and drained**
1½ **cups (about 6 oz.) shredded reduced-fat sharp Cheddar cheese**
2 **large tomatoes (about 1 lb. *total*), cut into wedges and drained**
½ **cup thinly sliced green onions**
1 **large yellow or red bell pepper (about 8 oz.), seeded and cut into thin strips**

1. Prepare Salsa Dressing; cover and refrigerate.

2. Crumble beef into a wide nonstick frying pan; add oil and cumin seeds. Cook over medium-high heat, stirring often, until beef is tinged with brown (10 to 12 minutes); if pan appears dry or beef sticks to pan, add water, 2 tablespoons at a time.

3. While beef is browning, finely crush 2 cups of the tortilla chips. Reserve remaining 8 cups chips for garnish and to serve alongside salad.

4. Add corn, chiles, and chili powder to beef in pan. Cook, stirring, just until corn is heated through. Remove from heat, stir in crushed chips, and let cool until still warm, but no longer hot.

5. To assemble salad, line a wide salad bowl or rimmed platter with large lettuce leaves; break remaining leaves into bite-size pieces and arrange atop whole leaves. Spoon beef mixture evenly over lettuce. Arrange beans, cheese, tomatoes, onions, and bell pepper over beef mixture. Garnish with a few chips, if desired; serve remaining chips on the side. Offer Salsa Dressing to add to taste.

MAKES 8 SERVINGS

Salsa Dressing. In a small bowl, stir together 1½ cups **fat-free sour cream**, ¾ cup **mild red or green chile salsa**, about ⅓ cup (or to taste) minced **cilantro**, and ¼ teaspoon **ground cumin**. If you prefer a thinner dressing, add **water**, 1 tablespoon at a time, to achieve the desired consistency. Spoon dressing into a small serving bowl; garnish with **cilantro sprigs**, if desired. Cover and refrigerate while preparing salad.

Per serving, including dressing: 630 calories (29% calories from fat), 20 g total fat, 8 g saturated fat, 62 mg cholesterol, 1,226 mg sodium, 84 g carbohydrates, 10 g fiber, 30 g protein, 423 mg calcium, 4 mg iron

TACO SALAD

Pork Tenderloin with Rum Chutney

Here's a fast, delicious way to cook lean pork tenderloin: brown it quickly, then bake and serve with a simple sauce of rum and piquant chutney. Complete a delectable menu with nutty-tasting brown rice and steamed bok choy or asparagus.

PREPARATION TIME: *About 10 minutes*
COOKING TIME: *About 20 minutes*

2 pork tenderloins (about 1 lb. *each*), trimmed of fat and silvery membranes
   About ½ teaspoon salt
   About ½ teaspoon black pepper
   Ground red pepper (cayenne)
2 teaspoons vegetable oil
¼ cup rum
1 cup Major Grey's chutney, any large pieces chopped

1. Sprinkle pork lightly with salt and black pepper; then sprinkle with as much red pepper as you like.

2. Set a wide frying pan over high heat. When pan is hot, add oil; swirl to coat pan. Add pork and cook, turning as needed, until browned on all sides (about 4 minutes). Remove pan from heat.

3. Transfer pork to a 9- by 13-inch baking pan (do not rinse frying pan). Bake in a 400° oven until a meat thermometer inserted in thickest part of pork registers 155°F (about 15 minutes). Lift pork to a platter, cover lightly, and let rest for 5 minutes.

4. Meanwhile, add rum to frying pan. Place over medium heat and stir to loosen browned bits; then pour rum mixture into baking pan. Add chutney and stir over low heat until heated through.

5. Cut pork into ½-inch-thick slanting slices. Offer with rum-chutney mixture to spoon over pork.

MAKES 6 TO 8 SERVINGS

Per serving: 346 calories (17% calories from fat), 6 g total fat, 2 g saturated fat, 84 mg cholesterol, 683 mg sodium, 37 g carbohydrates, 0 g fiber, 27 g protein, 7 mg calcium, 2 mg iron

Pork Medallions with Sweet Peppers

Succulent medallions of pork—slices of the tenderloin—are a perfect choice for heart-healthy meals. Here, the sautéed medallions are paired with a tender-crisp medley of green, red, and yellow bell peppers. Complete the meal with a crisp salad, hot rice, and a simple dessert such as fresh pineapple wheels sprinkled with crystallized ginger.

PREPARATION TIME: *About 25 minutes*
COOKING TIME: *About 15 minutes*

¼ cup orange juice
¼ cup dry vermouth
2 teaspoons cornstarch
¼ to ½ teaspoon dried sage
¼ cup all-purpose flour
¼ teaspoon dried basil
⅛ teaspoon salt
⅛ teaspoon black pepper
1 pound pork medallions
1 teaspoon vegetable oil

1. In a small bowl, stir together orange juice, vermouth, cornstarch, and sage. Set aside.

2. In a shallow bowl, stir together flour, dried basil, salt, and black pepper. Dip pork medallions in flour mixture to coat.

3. Heat ½ teaspoon of the oil in a wide nonstick pan over medium-high heat. Add pork and cook, turning as needed, until lightly browned on outside and no longer pink in center; cut to test (about 10 minutes). If pan appears dry, add water, 1 tablespoon at a time. Remove pork from pan and keep warm. Wipe pan dry with a paper towel (be careful; pan is hot).

4. Heat remaining ½ teaspoon oil in pan over medium-high heat. Add all bell peppers and shallot; cook, stirring often, until peppers are almost tender-crisp to bite (about 3 minutes).

1 *each* medium-size red, green, and yellow bell pepper (about 6 oz. *each*), seeded and cut into julienne strips

1 tablespoon minced shallot

Basil sprigs (optional)

5. Stir orange juice mixture, pour over peppers, and bring to a boil. Then reduce heat and cook, stirring, until sauce is thickened. Spoon peppers and sauce onto a large platter; arrange pork over peppers. Garnish with basil sprigs, if desired.

MAKES 4 SERVINGS

Per serving: 259 calories (28% calories from fat), 8 g total fat, 2 g saturated fat, 75 mg cholesterol, 133 mg sodium, 18 g carbohydrates, 2 g fiber, 25 g protein, 25 mg calcium, 2 mg iron

PORK MEDALLIONS WITH SWEET PEPPERS

Pork & Persimmon Risotto

Juicy, tender-crisp persimmons sweetly back up pork and blue cheese in a creamy main-dish risotto made with arborio rice. Flat, tomato-shaped Fuyu persimmons are crisp when ripe; their peak season runs from mid-October through November.

PREPARATION TIME: *About 15 minutes*
COOKING TIME: *About 25 minutes*

- 12 ounces pork tenderloin, trimmed of fat and silvery membrane
- 1 tablespoon butter, margarine, or olive oil
- 6 tablespoons minced shallots
- 1 cup arborio or other short-grain white rice
- ½ teaspoon ground allspice
- ¼ teaspoon pepper
- 1¼ cups dry white wine
  About 3 cups fat-free reduced-sodium chicken broth
- 2 Fuyu persimmons (6 to 7 oz. *each*)
- ½ cup crumbled blue-veined cheese
  Minced Italian parsley and Italian parsley sprigs

1. Cut pork across the grain into ⅛-inch-thick slices. Place a wide nonstick frying pan over medium-high heat; when pan is hot, add pork and cook, stirring often, until no longer pink (about 4 minutes). Remove from pan and keep warm.

2. Add butter and shallots to pan. Cook over medium-high heat, stirring, until shallots are soft (about 1 minute). Add rice to pan and cook, stirring often, until some of the grains are opaque (2 to 3 minutes). Stir in allspice and pepper. In a bowl, stir together wine and 3 cups of the broth; add 1 cup of this mixture to rice. Continue to cook, stirring often, until liquid has been absorbed (about 3 minutes).

3. Add remaining 3¼ cups broth mixture to rice; bring to a boil. Then reduce heat and simmer, uncovered, stirring often, until rice is just tender to bite but not starchy tasting (12 to 15 more minutes).

4. Meanwhile, cut stems from persimmons. Cut one persimmon into matchstick pieces; cut the other crosswise into thin slices (cut slices in half to form semicircles, if desired).

5. Stir pork and any accumulated juices, ¼ cup of the cheese, and matchstick persimmon pieces into rice. Stir in enough additional broth to give risotto a creamy texture, then ladle onto a platter or into 4 wide individual bowls. Garnish with sliced persimmons, parsley, and remaining ¼ cup cheese.

MAKES 4 SERVINGS

Per serving: 507 calories (22% calories from fat), 11 g total fat, 6 g saturated fat, 76 mg cholesterol, 735 mg sodium, 62 g carbohydrates, 3 g fiber, 28 g protein, 130 mg calcium, 6 mg iron

PORK & PERSIMMON RISOTTO

Stir-fried Pork & Asparagus

Keep this dish in mind for busy nights—it cooks in under 15 minutes. For added flavor, the pork strips soak briefly in a marinade of red wine and orange juice before going into the pan.

PREPARATION TIME: *About 15 minutes*
COOKING TIME: *About 10 minutes*

- ½ cup dry red wine
- ¼ cup orange juice
- 2 tablespoons seasoned rice vinegar
- ¼ cup finely chopped shallots
- 2 teaspoons chopped fresh tarragon or ½ teaspoon dried tarragon
- 1 pound pork tenderloin, trimmed of fat and silvery membrane
- 1½ pounds asparagus
- 1 teaspoon olive oil
- 4 to 6 cups hot cooked rice
- 2 medium-size oranges (about 1 lb. *total*), cut into thin wedges

1. In a large bowl, stir together wine, orange juice, vinegar, shallots, and tarragon. Cut pork into thin strips about 2 inches long; add to marinade and stir to coat. Set aside; stir occasionally.

2. Snap off and discard tough ends of asparagus; then cut spears into 3-inch lengths. Place asparagus and ½ cup water in a wide nonstick frying pan. Cover and cook over medium-high heat, stirring occasionally, until asparagus is tender-crisp to bite (4 to 5 minutes). Drain asparagus, transfer to a plate, and keep warm. Wipe pan dry (be careful; pan is hot).

3. Heat oil in pan over medium-high heat. Lift pork from marinade and drain briefly; reserve ¼ cup of the marinade. Add pork to pan and cook, stirring often, until no longer pink in center; cut to test (3 to 4 minutes). Add reserved ¼ cup marinade and bring to a boil.

4. To serve, spoon rice onto a platter or 4 individual plates. Spoon pork mixture and asparagus over rice. Arrange orange wedges alongside rice.

MAKES 4 SERVINGS

Per serving: 493 calories (11% calories from fat), 6 g total fat, 2 g saturated fat, 74 mg cholesterol, 137 mg sodium, 73 g carbohydrates, 4 g fiber, 34 g protein, 98 mg calcium, 5 mg iron

Penne with Ham & Peas

Seasoned with lemon and mint, this combination of slivered ham, chunky penne, and sweet peas makes a nice light dinner or lunch.

PREPARATION TIME: *About 15 minutes*
COOKING TIME: *About 15 minutes*

- 3 tablespoons olive oil
- 1 tablespoon lemon juice
- 1 teaspoon honey
- ⅓ cup slivered green onions
- ¼ cup chopped fresh mint
- 12 ounces dried penne
- 1 package (about 10 oz.) frozen tiny peas, thawed
- 8 ounces thinly sliced ham, cut into 1-inch strips
- Pepper
- Mint sprigs

1. In a small bowl, stir together oil, lemon juice, and honey to blend well; then stir in onions and chopped mint. Set aside.

2. In a 5- to 6-quart pan, bring about 3 quarts water to a boil over high heat; stir in pasta and cook, uncovered, until just tender to bite (8 to 10 minutes). Or cook pasta according to package directions.

3. Drain pasta well and transfer to a large serving bowl. Working quickly, add peas and three-fourths of the ham; mix well. Stir oil mixture and pour over pasta; mix well again. Season to taste with pepper, sprinkle with remaining ham, and garnish with mint sprigs.

MAKES 4 SERVINGS

Per serving: 565 calories (28% calories from fat), 18 g total fat, 4 g saturated fat, 10 mg cholesterol, 845 mg sodium, 76 g carbohydrates, 7 g fiber, 24 g protein, 49 mg calcium, 6 mg iron

Lamb-stuffed Bell Peppers

Bell peppers make attractive—and edible—containers for an aromatic lamb-and-rice stuffing. Choose red, yellow, or green bell peppers, or try a medley of all three. Alongside, you might serve Petite Peas with Browned Butter (page 202).

PREPARATION TIME: *About 15 minutes*
COOKING TIME: *45 to 55 minutes*

- ½ cup catsup
- 1 tablespoon cornstarch
- 6 medium-size bell peppers (about 2¼ lbs. *total*)
- 1 pound lean ground lamb
- 1 large onion, chopped
- 4 cloves garlic, minced or pressed
- 3 cups cooked rice
- ½ cup golden raisins
- ½ teaspoon ground cumin
- ½ teaspoon ground cinnamon
- ½ teaspoon black pepper
- Salt
- 1 large egg
- 2 large egg whites (about ¼ cup)
- ½ cup cilantro leaves (optional)
- 1 cup fat-free sour cream

1. In a small bowl, stir together catsup and cornstarch to blend smoothly; set aside.

2. Cut a thin slice from top of each bell pepper, trimming down just far enough to remove the stems. Pull out and discard seeds. Trim pepper flesh away from stems and finely chop; discard stems. Rinse and drain pepper shells; then set them, open end up, in a shallow 1½- to 2-quart casserole.

3. Crumble lamb into a wide nonstick frying pan. Cook over medium heat, stirring often, until tinged with brown (12 to 14 minutes); if pan appears dry, add water, 1 tablespoon at a time. Add onion, garlic, and chopped bell pepper; continue to cook, stirring often, until onion is soft (about 5 more minutes).

4. Remove pan from heat. Stir in catsup mixture, rice, raisins, cumin, cinnamon, and black pepper. Season to taste with salt. Add egg and egg whites; mix well.

5. Fill peppers equally with lamb mixture, packing it in lightly. Bake, uncovered, in a 375° oven until peppers are soft when pierced (30 to 40 minutes). Garnish with cilantro leaves, if desired. Offer sour cream to add to taste.

MAKES 6 SERVINGS

Per serving: 435 calories (24% calories from fat), 12 g total fat, 5 g saturated fat, 90 mg cholesterol, 349 mg sodium, 60 g carbohydrates, 4 g fiber, 23 g protein, 118 mg calcium, 3 mg iron

TURKISH LAMB SHANKS

Turkish Lamb Shanks

Oven-braising brings out the tenderness of lamb shanks cooked with onions, bell pepper, and tomatoes. Serve them on a bed of rice, couscous, or bulgur, with a salad of thinly sliced cucumbers on the side.

PREPARATION TIME: *15 minutes*
BAKING TIME: *About 2¼ hours*

- 4 lamb shanks (about 1 lb. *each*), bones cracked
- 4 large onions, cut into quarters or coarsely chopped
- 1 large bell pepper (about 8 oz.), seeded and cut into strips
- 1 can (about 14½ oz.) stewed tomatoes
- 1½ cups fat-free reduced-sodium chicken broth
- ½ teaspoon black pepper
- ½ teaspoon dried thyme
- 2 cups long-grain white rice

1. Place lamb in a 12- by 17-inch roasting pan. Bake in a 450° oven for 15 minutes. Arrange onions in pan around lamb; continue to bake until lamb is browned (about 30 more minutes). Remove pan from oven; reduce oven temperature to 400°.

2. To pan, add bell pepper, tomatoes, broth, black pepper, and thyme. Cover tightly and continue to bake until lamb pulls easily from bones (about 1½ more hours). Skim and discard fat from pan juices.

3. About 30 minutes before lamb is done, place rice and 3½ cups water in a 4- to 5-quart pan; bring to a boil over high heat. Then reduce heat, cover, and simmer until liquid has been absorbed and rice is tender to bite (about 20 minutes).

4. To serve, spoon rice into 4 individual rimmed plates or shallow bowls. Spoon lamb, vegetables, and pan juices over rice.

MAKES 4 SERVINGS

Per serving: 804 calories (25% calories from fat), 21 g total fat, 9 g saturated fat, 159 mg cholesterol, 590 mg sodium, 96 g carbohydrates, 8 g fiber, 54 g protein, 142 mg calcium, 8 mg iron

Sautéed Lamb with Maple-Mustard Pears

Fresh pears poached in cider vinegar and sauced with maple syrup and spicy mustard nicely complement chunks of lean lamb. For a pretty presentation, the sautéed meat is spooned into crimson radicchio leaves.

PREPARATION TIME: *About 20 minutes*
COOKING TIME: *About 15 minutes*

- 4 to 8 large radicchio leaves, rinsed and crisped
- 1 pound lean boneless leg of lamb, trimmed of fat and cut into ¾-inch chunks
- ¼ teaspoon salt
- ⅛ teaspoon pepper
- ⅓ cup maple syrup
- 1 tablespoon Dijon mustard
- 1 tablespoon chopped fresh thyme or 1 teaspoon dried thyme
- 3 large firm-ripe pears (about 1½ lbs. *total*), cored and cut into ¼- to ½-inch-thick slices
- ½ cup cider vinegar
- 2 teaspoons butter or margarine
- ¼ cup sliced green onions

1. Arrange 1 or 2 radicchio leaves (overlapping, if necessary) on each of 4 individual plates. Set aside.

2. In a large bowl, mix lamb, salt, and pepper; set aside. In a small bowl, stir together syrup, mustard, and chopped thyme; set aside.

3. In a wide nonstick frying pan, combine pears and vinegar; bring to a boil over high heat. Then reduce heat and simmer, uncovered, until pears are tender when pierced (about 7 minutes). Stir syrup mixture well; pour into pan and cook, stirring, just until sauce boils and thickens (about 5 minutes). Remove pear mixture from pan; keep warm. Wipe pan clean (be careful; pan is hot).

4. Melt butter in pan over medium-high heat. Add lamb and cook, stirring often, just until done to your liking; cut to test (3 to 5 minutes for medium-rare). Remove from heat and stir in onions. Spoon lamb equally into radicchio leaves; spoon pear mixture alongside.

MAKES 4 SERVINGS

Per serving: 331 calories (21% calories from fat), 8 g total fat, 3 g saturated fat, 78 mg cholesterol, 328 mg sodium, 42 g carbohydrates, 4 g fiber, 24 g protein, 48 mg calcium, 3 mg iron

Green Chile Stew

Earthy flavors mingle in this succulent stew; green chiles, cumin, and corn add Southwestern accents. Serve warm corn tortillas alongside.

PREPARATION TIME: *About 30 minutes*
COOKING TIME: *About 1¾ hours*

- 3 pounds boneless lamb stew meat (shoulder or neck), trimmed of fat and cut into 1-inch chunks
- 2 large onions, chopped
- 2 teaspoons cumin seeds
- 4 cups beef broth (skimmed of fat)
- 2 tablespoons chili powder
- 12 small thin-skinned potatoes (*each* about 2 inches in diameter), scrubbed
- 24 small carrots (*each* about 4 inches long), peeled
- 2 cups fresh or frozen corn kernels
- 3 large cans (about 7 oz. *each*) whole green chiles, torn into wide strips

1. In a 6- to 8-quart pan, combine lamb, onions, cumin seeds, and ¾ cup of the broth. Bring to a boil over high heat; then reduce heat to medium, cover, and boil for 20 minutes. Uncover and continue to boil, stirring often, until broth has evaporated and lamb starts to brown (20 to 25 minutes).

2. Stir in chili powder. Add ¼ cup more broth and stir to loosen browned bits. Then cook, stirring often, until liquid has evaporated and browned bits stick to pan (about 1 minute).

3. Pour remaining 3 cups broth into pan and stir to loosen browned bits. Add potatoes, carrots, corn, and chiles. Bring to a boil; then reduce heat, cover, and simmer until lamb is very tender when pierced (about 1 hour). To serve, ladle stew into 6 to 8 wide individual bowls.

MAKES 6 TO 8 SERVINGS

Per serving: 525 calories (25% calories from fat), 15 g total fat, 5 g saturated fat, 128 mg cholesterol, 1,086 mg sodium, 53 g carbohydrates, 9 g fiber, 46 g protein, 84 mg calcium, 6 mg iron

Lamb Pilaf

Ground meats are the basis for many a quick supper dish. This one's made with ground lamb; you brown the meat, mix in dried fruits, herbs, and green onions, and spoon the savory mixture over couscous.

PREPARATION TIME: *About 25 minutes*
COOKING TIME: *About 20 minutes*

- 1 pound lean ground lamb
- 2¾ cups beef broth, skimmed of fat
- 2 cloves garlic, minced or pressed
- ½ teaspoon ground cumin
- 1⅔ cups couscous
- 1 large tomato (about 8 oz.), diced
- ½ cup chopped dried apricots
- ¼ cup golden raisins
- 2 tablespoons apricot jam
- 1 teaspoon dried oregano
- 1 teaspoon cornstarch
- ½ cup thinly sliced green onions
- 1 to 2 cups plain nonfat yogurt

1. Crumble lamb into a wide nonstick frying pan. Cook over medium-high heat, stirring often, until tinged with brown (about 12 minutes); if pan appears dry, add water, 1 tablespoon at a time.

2. Meanwhile, combine 2½ cups of the broth, garlic, and cumin in a 2- to 3-quart pan. Bring to a boil over high heat. Stir in couscous; then cover, remove from heat, and let stand until liquid has been absorbed (about 5 minutes). Mix in tomato, fluffing couscous with a fork; keep warm.

3. To lamb, add apricots, raisins, jam, and oregano. Stir until heated through. In a small bowl, smoothly mix cornstarch and remaining ¼ cup broth; stir into lamb mixture. Stir until mixture boils and thickens. Remove from heat; stir in onions.

4. To serve, fluff couscous with a fork; then spoon onto a platter. Top with lamb mixture. Offer yogurt to add to taste.

MAKES 4 SERVINGS

Per serving: 617 calories (13% calories from fat), 9 g total fat, 3 g saturated fat, 77 mg cholesterol, 580 mg sodium, 93 g carbohydrates, 5 g fiber, 41 g protein, 297 mg calcium, 4 mg iron

Hoisin Lamb in Pita Pockets

Whole wheat pita breads make nutritious edible containers for a combination of garlic-seasoned, browned ground lamb and crisp shredded napa cabbage. Alongside, offer an assortment of raw vegetables such as baby-cut carrots, red pepper strips, and thin jicama slices to dip in low-fat ranch dressing.

PREPARATION TIME: *About 10 minutes*
COOKING TIME: *About 15 minutes*

12   ounces lean ground lamb
 1   medium-size onion, minced
 3   cloves garlic, minced or pressed
 3   tablespoons hoisin sauce
¼   cup dry sherry
¼   cup fat-free reduced-sodium chicken broth
 1   teaspoon cornstarch
¼   cup minced cilantro
 4   whole wheat pita breads (*each* 6 to 7 inches in diameter), cut in half crosswise
 3   cups finely shredded napa cabbage

1. In a wide frying pan, combine lamb, onion, and garlic. Cook over medium-high heat, stirring often, until lamb is browned (12 to 14 minutes). If pan appears dry, add water, 1 tablespoon at a time.

2. In a small bowl, stir together hoisin sauce, sherry, broth, and cornstarch until smoothly blended. Add hoisin mixture to pan along with cilantro. Bring to a boil, stirring; then reduce heat to low and keep warm.

3. Fill pita bread halves equally with cabbage, then with lamb mixture. Serve immediately.

MAKES 4 SERVINGS

Per serving: 371 calories (17% calories from fat), 7 g total fat, 2 g saturated fat, 56 mg cholesterol, 661 mg sodium, 47 g carbohydrates, 2 g fiber, 24 g protein, 122 mg calcium, 3 mg iron

Poultry

Braised Chicken with Artichokes

Trimming artichokes back to their tender centers—and discarding the fuzzy chokes—brings you to the sweetest part of this thorny vegetable. The delicate hearts provide a marvelous counterpoint to juicy chicken thighs cooked with button mushrooms. Alongside, offer soft polenta or potatoes mashed with reduced-fat buttermilk to soak up the sauce.

PREPARATION TIME: *About 20 minutes*
COOKING TIME: *About 35 minutes*

- 2 tablespoons vinegar (any kind)
- 4 artichokes (*each* about 3½ inches in diameter; about 2¾ lbs. *total*); or 1 package (about 9 oz.) frozen artichoke hearts, thawed
- 8 ounces mushrooms
- 8 skinless chicken thighs (1½ to 1¾ lbs. *total*), trimmed of fat
- 1 small onion, chopped
- 1½ cups fat-free reduced-sodium chicken broth
- 1 tablespoon balsamic vinegar
- 2 tablespoons tomato paste
- ½ teaspoon dried thyme
- ½ cup chopped parsley
  Italian parsley sprigs (optional)

1. If using fresh artichokes, combine about 8 cups water and the 2 tablespoons vinegar in a large bowl. Cut off and discard top third of each artichoke. Trim stems flush with bases. Break off and discard outer leaves, leaving tender, pale green inner leaves. Cut artichokes into quarters lengthwise. With a sharp knife, cut fuzzy chokes from artichoke hearts; discard chokes. Also pull out and discard tiny leaves with thorny tips. As artichokes are prepared, immerse them in water-vinegar mixture to keep them from darkening. Set aside.

2. Cut any large mushrooms in half; set mushrooms aside.

3. Rinse chicken, pat dry, and place in a wide nonstick frying pan over medium-high heat. Cook, turning as needed, until lightly browned on all sides (4 to 5 minutes). Remove chicken from pan and set aside.

4. To pan, add mushrooms, onion, and ½ cup of the broth. Stir to loosen browned bits. Cover and cook for 5 minutes; then uncover and continue to cook, stirring often, until mushrooms are lightly browned (about 5 more minutes). Remove pan from heat; stir in balsamic vinegar, tomato paste, thyme, and remaining 1 cup broth. Then return chicken to pan.

5. Swish fresh artichokes in water-vinegar mixture to rinse; then drain. Lay fresh or thawed frozen artichokes on top of chicken; cover and bring to a boil over high heat. Then reduce heat and simmer until artichokes are tender when pierced and chicken is no longer pink near bone; cut to test (about 15 minutes).

6. To serve, sprinkle chopped parsley over chicken mixture; then spoon onto a platter or 4 individual plates. Garnish with parsley sprigs, if desired.

MAKES 4 SERVINGS

Per serving: 248 calories (21% calories from fat), 6 g total fat, 1 g saturated fat, 112 mg cholesterol, 488 mg sodium, 18 g carbohydrates, 7 g fiber, 33 g protein, 81 mg calcium, 4 mg iron

Quick Chicken Mole

Ripe banana, crisp almonds, and raisins add to the exotic flavor of the chocolate-accented sauce for this simmered chicken. Serve a basket of warm corn tortillas alongside to dip into the sauce or enclose rice and morsels of chicken.

PREPARATION TIME: *About 15 minutes*
COOKING TIME: *About 35 minutes*

- 1 teaspoon olive oil or vegetable oil
- 1 medium-size onion, minced
- 2 cloves garlic, minced or pressed
- ¾ cup fat-free reduced-sodium chicken broth
- 1 can (about 8 oz.) tomato sauce
- 1 small ripe banana (about 4 oz.), peeled and mashed
- 1 tablespoon chili powder
- 1 tablespoon unsweetened cocoa
- 1 teaspoon ground cinnamon
- 1 teaspoon ground cumin
- ¼ teaspoon black pepper
- ¼ teaspoon ground red pepper (cayenne)
- 4 boneless, skinless chicken breast halves (about 6 oz. *each*)
  About 4 cups hot cooked rice
- ¼ cup toasted sliced almonds
- 2 tablespoons raisins
  Warm corn tortillas

1. Heat oil in a wide nonstick frying pan over medium-high heat. Add onion and garlic. Cook, stirring often, until onion is tinged with brown (5 to 7 minutes). Add 1 tablespoon of the broth and stir to loosen browned bits.

2. Add remaining broth, tomato sauce, banana, chili powder, cocoa, cinnamon, cumin, black pepper, and red pepper. Bring to a boil; then reduce heat, cover, and simmer for 10 minutes. Rinse chicken, pat dry, and add to sauce. Cover and continue to simmer until meat in thickest part is no longer pink; cut to test (about 15 more minutes).

3. To serve, divide rice among 4 individual plates. Place one piece of chicken atop rice on each plate; spoon sauce over chicken and sprinkle with almonds and raisins. Offer tortillas alongside.

MAKES 4 SERVINGS

Per serving: 467 calories (14% calories from fat), 7 g total fat, 1 g saturated fat, 68 mg cholesterol, 552 mg sodium, 65 g carbohydrates, 4 g fiber, 36 g protein, 100 mg calcium, 6 mg iron

Cornmeal-crusted Chicken

Grilling is a quick and tasty way to prepare boneless, skinless chicken breasts. These are pounded thin and rolled in a cornmeal-Parmesan coating before cooking. Top them with a combination of tomatoes and slivered arugula in a light, tart dressing.

PREPARATION TIME: *About 20 minutes*
COOKING TIME: *10 to 11 minutes*

- 6 boneless, skinless chicken breast halves (about 6 oz. *each*)
- 1¼ pounds pear-shaped (Roma-type) tomatoes, chopped
- 1 cup lightly packed finely slivered arugula
- ¼ cup minced shallots
- 2 to 3 tablespoons drained capers
- 2 tablespoons lemon juice
- 1 tablespoon olive oil

1. Rinse chicken and pat dry. Place each piece between 2 sheets of plastic wrap; with a flat-surfaced mallet, pound firmly but gently all over to a thickness of ¼ to ⅓ inch.

2. In a medium-size bowl, combine tomatoes, arugula, shallots, capers, lemon juice, oil, and honey; set aside at room temperature.

3. In a shallow bowl, beat egg with 1 tablespoon water to blend. In another shallow bowl, stir together cornmeal, cheese, black pepper, and red pepper. Dip each chicken breast half in egg mixture to coat; then dip in cornmeal mixture, turning to coat completely.

4. Place chicken on a well-oiled grill 4 to 6 inches above a solid bed of medium coals or over medium heat on a gas grill (you can hold your

1 teaspoon honey

1 large egg

¾ cup yellow cornmeal

¼ cup grated Parmesan cheese

½ teaspoon black pepper

¼ teaspoon ground red pepper (cayenne)

hand at grill level for 4 to 5 seconds). Close lid on gas grill. Cook chicken until browned on bottom (about 5 minutes). Turn chicken over and continue to cook until browned on other side and no longer pink in center; cut to test (5 to 6 more minutes).

5. To serve, arrange chicken on a platter or 6 individual plates; top with tomato-arugula mixture.

MAKES 6 SERVINGS

Per serving: 310 calories (20% calories from fat), 7 g total fat, 2 g saturated fat, 126 mg cholesterol, 373 mg sodium, 21 g carbohydrates, 2 g fiber, 40 g protein, 87 mg calcium, 3 mg iron

Chicken with Orange Salsa

Salsa keeps on moving higher on everybody's list of favorite condiments— it's made with an assortment of vegetables and fruits, comes in a range of heat levels, and has little (if any) fat. Here, it's used in a simple orange sauce for cubed, stir-fried boneless chicken breasts.

PREPARATION TIME: *About 10 minutes*
COOKING TIME: *15 to 20 minutes*

- 1 cup orange juice
- ½ cup red salsa
- 2 tablespoons firmly packed brown sugar
- ¼ teaspoon ground cumin
- ¼ teaspoon ground ginger
- 1 teaspoon vegetable oil
- 1¼ pounds boneless, skinless chicken breasts, cut into ¾-inch cubes
- 4 large oranges (about 3½ lbs. *total*), cut into slices or wedges

1. In a wide nonstick frying pan, combine orange juice, salsa, brown sugar, cumin, and ginger. Bring to a boil over medium-high heat; then boil, stirring, until reduced to 1 cup (7 to 10 minutes). Remove from pan and keep warm.

2. Wipe pan clean (be careful; pan is hot). Pour oil into pan and heat over medium-high heat. Add chicken and 1 tablespoon water. Cook, stirring often, until chicken is no longer pink in center; cut to test (about 5 minutes).

3. Transfer chicken to a platter and top with warm salsa. Arrange oranges alongside chicken.

MAKES 4 SERVINGS

Per serving: 318 calories (9% calories from fat), 3 g total fat, 1 g saturated fat, 82 mg cholesterol, 416 mg sodium, 37 g carbohydrates, 5 g fiber, 35 g protein, 109 mg calcium, 1 mg iron

Stir-fried Chicken & Chile Tacos

Warm corn tortillas enclose this stir-fry of slivered bell peppers, zesty fresh chiles, and boneless chicken breast. Garlic and fresh lime juice enhance all the flavors, so you won't need to add much (if any) salt.

PREPARATION TIME: *About 20 minutes*
COOKING TIME: *About 10 minutes*

- 12 corn tortillas (*each* about 6 inches in diameter)
- 2 medium-size red bell peppers (about 12 oz. *total*)
- 2 large fresh mild green chiles (about 8 oz. *total*)
- 4 or 5 fresh jalapeño chiles
- 1⅓ pounds boneless, skinless chicken breasts
- 1 tablespoon vegetable oil
- 1 large onion, thinly sliced
- 3 cloves garlic, minced or pressed
- 1 tablespoon cumin seeds
- ½ cup chopped cilantro
- 3 tablespoons lime juice
  Lime wedges
  Salsa and plain nonfat yogurt

1. Stack tortillas, wrap in foil, and heat in a 350° oven until hot (about 10 minutes). Meanwhile, seed bell peppers and mild chiles; cut into thin slivers about 3 inches long. Seed jalapeño chiles; cut into thin slivers. Rinse chicken, pat dry, and cut into thin strips about 3 inches long.

2. Heat 2 teaspoons of the oil in a wide nonstick frying pan over medium-high heat. Add chicken and cook, stirring often, until no longer pink in center; cut to test (4 to 5 minutes). Remove from pan.

3. To pan, add remaining 1 teaspoon oil, onion, garlic, and cumin seeds. Cook, stirring often, for 1 minute. Add bell peppers and all chiles; cook, stirring often, until peppers and chiles begin to wilt (2 to 3 minutes). Return chicken to pan; stir in cilantro and lime juice. Pour into a bowl.

4. Fill tortillas with chicken mixture. Squeeze lime over filling; add salsa and yogurt to taste. Fold to enclose and eat out of hand.

MAKES 4 TO 6 SERVINGS

Per serving: 351 calories (16% calories from fat), 6 g total fat, 1 g saturated fat, 70 mg cholesterol, 185 mg sodium, 42 g carbohydrates, 6 g fiber, 34 g protein, 158 mg calcium, 3 mg iron

Southwestern Chicken Pot Pie

This updated, streamlined version of an old-time family favorite is chunky with chicken breast, potatoes, black beans, corn, and chiles.

PREPARATION TIME: *About 40 minutes*
COOKING TIME: *About 1¼ hours*

1 cup fat-free reduced-sodium chicken broth

4 boneless, skinless chicken breast halves (about 1½ lbs. *total*), cut into ¾-inch chunks

8 ounces thin-skinned potatoes, scrubbed and diced

3 tablespoons cornstarch

1 can (about 14½ oz.) Mexican-style stewed tomatoes

1 can (about 15 oz.) black beans, rinsed and drained

1 small can (about 8¾ oz.) corn kernels, drained

1 can (about 4 oz.) diced green chiles

½ cup chopped cilantro

1 unbaked refrigerated pie crust (½ of 15-oz. package), at room temperature

1. In a wide nonstick frying pan, stir together ½ cup of the broth, chicken, and potatoes. Cover and cook over high heat, stirring occasionally, until potatoes are just barely tender when pierced and chicken is no longer pink in center; cut to test (about 5 minutes). Meanwhile, in a small bowl, stir together remaining ½ cup broth and cornstarch until smoothly blended.

2. When chicken is done, add cornstarch mixture to pan; bring to a boil, stirring. Remove from heat; stir in tomatoes, beans, corn, chiles, and cilantro. Pour into a 10-inch pie pan.

3. Unfold pastry according to package directions. Place on a lightly floured board and roll out to a 12-inch round. Place pastry over filling; fold edges under (flush with pan rim) and flute firmly against rim. Make a few decorative slits in crust.

4. Bake in a 350° oven until filling is hot in center (about 1 hour). If crust begins to overbrown before pie is done, cover pie loosely with foil. Before serving, let pie cool for 10 minutes; then spoon from dish.

MAKES 6 SERVINGS

Per serving: 417 calories (26% calories from fat), 12 g total fat, 4 g saturated fat, 75 mg cholesterol, 856 mg sodium, 44 g carbohydrates, 4 g fiber, 33 g protein, 47 mg calcium, 3 mg iron

Chicken & Feta Cheese Burritos

When time is short, try burritos filled with chicken strips, hot black beans, and crumbled feta cheese.

PREPARATION TIME: *About 15 minutes*
COOKING TIME: *About 10 minutes*

1 teaspoon ground cumin

½ teaspoon pepper

1 pound boneless, skinless chicken breasts, cut into ½- by 3-inch strips

4 large low-fat or regular flour tortillas (*each* about 10 inches in diameter)

1 can (about 15 oz.) black beans

2 teaspoons vegetable oil

½ cup crumbled feta cheese

1 to 1½ cups purchased fresh green chile salsa

1. In a shallow bowl, mix cumin and pepper. Add chicken and toss to coat. Set aside. Stack tortillas, wrap in foil, and heat in a 350° oven until hot (about 5 minutes).

2. Meanwhile, place beans and their liquid in a 1-quart pan. Cover and cook over medium-high heat, stirring occasionally, until bubbly (about 5 minutes). Also heat oil in a wide nonstick frying pan over medium-high heat. Add chicken and cook, stirring often, until no longer pink in center; cut to test (4 to 5 minutes).

3. To assemble each burrito, lay a tortilla flat. Top with a fourth each of the chicken, beans (including liquid), and cheese, arranging fillings down center of tortilla; then top with 2 tablespoons of the salsa. Fold sides of tortilla over filling; roll up tightly to enclose. Offer remaining salsa to add to taste.

MAKES 4 SERVINGS

Per serving: 472 calories (19% calories from fat), 10 g total fat, 4 g saturated fat, 85 mg cholesterol, 1,337 mg sodium, 53 g carbohydrates, 9 g fiber, 41 g protein, 219 mg calcium, 6 mg iron

SIMMERED COCONUT-CURRY CHICKEN

Simmered Coconut-Curry Chicken

Hearty whole chicken legs and diced potatoes cloaked in a creamy, spicy golden sauce make a richly satisfying entrée. To keep it lean, use light coconut milk instead of the regular kind in the sauce—you'll cut the fat by 75 percent. Offer aromatic fresh lime wedges to squeeze over each serving.

PREPARATION TIME: *About 20 minutes*
COOKING TIME: *About 45 minutes*

- 1 large onion, chopped
- 2 tablespoons minced fresh ginger
- 2 tablespoons mustard seeds
- 1 tablespoon curry powder
- 4 whole chicken legs (about 10 oz. *each*), skin removed, trimmed of fat
- 3 cups fat-free reduced-sodium chicken broth
- 1½ cups diced red thin-skinned potatoes
- 1 large red bell pepper (about 8 oz.), seeded and chopped
- 1 can (about 14 oz.) light coconut milk
- 3 tablespoons cornstarch
- 1 package (about 10 oz.) frozen tiny peas
- ¼ cup chopped cilantro
  Lime wedges

1. In a 5- to 6-quart pan, combine onion, ginger, mustard seeds, and ¼ cup water. Cook over high heat, stirring often, until onion is tinged with brown and a brown film begins to form on pan bottom (5 to 7 minutes).

2. Add curry powder, chicken, broth, potatoes, and bell pepper to pan; stir to loosen browned bits. Bring to a boil. Then reduce heat, cover, and simmer until meat near bone is no longer pink; cut to test (about 25 minutes).

3. In a small bowl, smoothly blend a little of the coconut milk with cornstarch; then stir in remaining coconut milk. Pour mixture into pan with chicken; stir to blend. Stir in peas. Bring sauce to a boil; then reduce heat and simmer, stirring often, for about 10 minutes.

4. To serve, place one piece of chicken in each of 4 individual wide, shallow bowls; top equally with sauce and sprinkle with cilantro. Season to taste with lime.

MAKES 4 SERVINGS

Per serving: 466 calories (28% calories from fat), 15 g total fat, 5 g saturated fat, 130 mg cholesterol, 825 mg sodium, 39 g carbohydrates, 8 g fiber, 44 g protein, 99 mg calcium, 5 mg iron

Chicken Chutney Burgers

Seasoned with mustard and chutney, these moist chicken burgers are broiled, then served on toasted sourdough with thin red onion rings and fresh spinach leaves.

PREPARATION TIME: *About 10 minutes*
COOKING TIME: *6 to 7 minutes*

- ⅔ cup Major Grey's chutney, any large pieces chopped
- 1½ tablespoons lemon juice
- 1 tablespoon Dijon mustard
- 12 ounces lean ground chicken
- ¼ cup sliced green onions
- ½ teaspoon ground cumin
- 8 slices sourdough French bread (*each* about 3 by 6 inches and ½ inch thick), toasted
- 4 thin slices red onion, separated into rings
- 20 small fresh spinach leaves, rinsed and crisped

1. In a large bowl, stir together chutney, lemon juice, and mustard. Measure out two-thirds of the mixture and set aside.

2. To remaining chutney mixture, add chicken, green onions, and cumin. Mix thoroughly; then shape into 4 patties, each about 4 inches wide. Place patties on an oiled rack in a broiler pan. Broil about 3 inches below heat, turning once, until well browned on both sides and no longer pink in center; cut to test (6 to 7 minutes).

3. To assemble sandwiches, spread one side of each toast slice with reserved chutney mixture. Then fill sandwiches with chicken burgers, onion rings, and spinach leaves.

MAKES 4 SERVINGS

Per serving: 426 calories (20% calories from fat), 9 g total fat, 2 g saturated fat, 71 mg cholesterol, 891 mg sodium, 62 g carbohydrates, 2 g fiber, 20 g protein, 84 mg calcium, 4 mg iron

Rosemary Roast Turkey

Provided you discard the skin, roast turkey is pleasantly low in fat. In this recipe, a mixture of fresh rosemary and garlic is slipped beneath the skin before roasting; lemon and more garlic and rosemary go into the cavity to perfume the bird while it's in the oven. Serve the sliced meat with a fragrant gravy made from the pan juices, broth, and white wine.

PREPARATION TIME: *About 15 minutes, plus 15 to 30 minutes for turkey to stand*
ROASTING TIME: *1½ to 2¼ hours*

- 1   turkey (10 to 13 lbs.)
- 1   lemon, cut in half
- 6   cloves garlic, peeled
- ¼   cup coarsely chopped fresh rosemary
- 5   to 8 rosemary sprigs (*each* 4 to 6 inches long)
      Turkey Gravy (recipe follows)

1. Pull off and discard lumps of fat from turkey; remove giblets and neck and reserve for other uses. Rinse turkey inside and out; pat dry with paper towels. Squeeze juice from one lemon half into body cavity, then place juiced half in cavity. Rub juice of remaining lemon half over turkey skin.

2. Chop 3 of the garlic cloves; mix chopped garlic with chopped rosemary. Slide your fingers under turkey skin to gently loosen it (leave skin in place, though) on breast, around outside of thighs and legs, and over back (from neck end). Push rosemary-garlic mixture under loosened skin, distributing evenly. Place remaining 3 garlic cloves and rosemary sprigs inside turkey.

3. Place turkey, breast up, on a V-shaped rack in a 12- by 17-inch roasting pan (or a pan at least 2 inches longer and wider than the bird). Roast in a 350° oven until a meat thermometer inserted through thickest part of breast to bone registers 165°F (1½ to 2¼ hours). Baste with drippings during roasting, if desired. If pan appears dry at any point during roasting, add water, ¼ cup at a time, stirring to loosen browned bits from pan.

4. Transfer turkey to a platter. Cover loosely and let stand for 15 to 30 minutes before carving. Meanwhile, skim and discard fat from pan juices; leave skimmed juices in pan and use to prepare Turkey Gravy.

5. To serve, carve turkey; serve with gravy.

MAKES 8 SERVINGS (4 OZ. OF SKINLESS MEAT EACH), PLUS LEFTOVERS

Turkey Gravy. Place ½ cup **all-purpose flour** in a wide frying pan; stir over high heat until flour is a medium brown (6 to 7 minutes). Add toasted flour to **Rosemary Roast Turkey** pan juices in roasting pan; smoothly whisk in 1½ cups **fat-free reduced-sodium chicken broth** and ½ cup **dry white wine**. Set pan over high heat and stir, scraping drippings free, until gravy boils vigorously; then reduce heat and simmer, stirring, for 4 to 5 more minutes. Season to taste with **salt** and **pepper**. Makes 8 servings.

Per serving of turkey: 191 calories (26% calories from fat), 5 g total fat, 2 g saturated fat, 87 mg cholesterol, 84 mg sodium, 0 g carbohydrates, 0 g fiber, 33 g protein, 29 mg calcium, 2 mg iron

Per serving of gravy: 64 calories (22% calories from fat), 2 g total fat, 1 g saturated fat, 3 mg cholesterol, 60 mg sodium, 7 g carbohydrates, 0 g fiber, 3 g protein, 2 mg calcium, 0 mg iron

Chicken Pinwheel Sandwiches

Great for lunch or dinner, these rolled tortilla sandwiches are filled with sliced chicken, fresh herbs, and a savory spread made from garbanzo beans, mustard, and seasoned soft cheese.

PREPARATION TIME: *About 20 minutes*

- 2 cans (about 15 oz. *each*) garbanzo beans, rinsed and drained
- 1 package (about 4 oz.) reduced-fat herb-seasoned cheese spread, such as Boursin or Rondelé
- ¼ cup fat-free mayonnaise
- 1 tablespoon Dijon mustard
- ½ cup chopped cilantro
- ½ cup chopped fresh dill
- ½ cup chopped green onions
- 8 low-fat flour tortillas (*each* 7 to 9 inches in diameter)
- 12 ounces very thinly sliced cooked chicken
- 8 to 16 large butter lettuce leaves, rinsed and crisped

1. Place beans in a large bowl and coarsely mash with a fork. Stir in cheese spread, mayonnaise, and mustard; set aside. In a small bowl, combine cilantro, chopped dill, and onions. Set aside.

2. Divide bean mixture equally among tortillas. With a spatula, spread mixture to cover tortillas evenly. Sprinkle with cilantro mixture; then top with chicken. Roll up tortillas tightly, jelly roll style. (At this point, you may cover and refrigerate for up to 3 hours.)

3. Line 8 individual plates with lettuce leaves. With a serrated knife, carefully cut each rolled tortilla diagonally into 4 equal slices (wipe knife clean between cuts, if desired); arrange on lettuce-lined plates.

MAKES 8 SERVINGS

Per serving: 265 calories (29% calories from fat), 8 g total fat, 2 g saturated fat, 43 mg cholesterol, 623 mg sodium, 25 g carbohydrates, 4 g fiber, 20 g protein, 130 mg calcium, 2 mg iron

Saffron Turkey with Rice

Rice and hearty chunks of turkey thigh bake together in a tomato-chile sauce brilliant with saffron and turmeric, making a dish that's reminiscent of paella without the seafood—all the better for a rustic entrée you can put together easily to share with friends. Round out a casual party menu with a salad of butter lettuce and sliced oranges and a basket of hot, crusty rolls.

PREPARATION TIME: *About 25 minutes*
COOKING TIME: *About 1 hour*

- 2 tablespoons olive oil
- 2 cups long-grain white rice
- 1 large onion, finely chopped
- 3 cloves garlic, minced or pressed
- 3 cups fat-free reduced-sodium chicken broth
- 3 pounds boneless, skinless turkey thighs, cut into 16 pieces
- 1 large red bell pepper (about 8 oz.), seeded and diced
- 1 can (about 8 oz.) tomato sauce
- 1 can (about 4 oz.) diced green chiles
- 1 teaspoon ground turmeric
- 1/2 teaspoon salt
- 1/2 teaspoon black pepper
- 1/4 to 1/2 teaspoon saffron threads

1. Heat oil in a 6- to 8-quart ovenproof pan over medium-high heat. Add rice, onion, and garlic; cook, stirring often, until onion and rice are pale golden (about 12 minutes).

2. Add broth, turkey pieces, bell pepper, tomato sauce, chiles, turmeric, salt, black pepper, and saffron threads; stir to blend.

3. Bake, uncovered, in a 400° oven until turkey is no longer pink in center (cut to test), all liquid has been absorbed, and rice is tender to bite (about 50 minutes).

MAKES 8 SERVINGS

Per serving: 385 calories (26% calories from fat), 11 g total fat, 3 g saturated fat, 128 mg cholesterol, 1,238 mg sodium, 31 g carbohydrates, 2 g fiber, 39 g protein, 60 mg calcium, 5 mg iron

Thai Turkey & Pasta

Speedy and spicy, this supper dish is zippy with ginger, garlic, red pepper, and lime. Prepare it with leftover turkey or purchased cooked turkey breast, cut into matchstick strips.

PREPARATION TIME: *About 10 minutes*
COOKING TIME: *About 15 minutes*

- 12 ounces fresh or dried linguine
- 3/4 cup fat-free reduced-sodium chicken broth
- 1/4 cup seasoned rice vinegar
- 2 tablespoons soy sauce
- 1 tablespoon minced fresh ginger
- 1 tablespoon minced garlic
- 1/4 teaspoon crushed red pepper flakes
- 8 ounces cooked turkey, cut into thin strips
- 1/3 cup minced cilantro
- 2 tablespoons lime juice
- 2 tablespoons chopped roasted salted peanuts

1. In a 5- to 6-quart pan, bring about 3 quarts water to a boil over high heat; stir in pasta and cook, uncovered, until just tender to bite (2 to 3 minutes for fresh pasta, 7 to 9 minutes for dried pasta). Or cook pasta according to package directions.

2. While water for pasta comes to a boil, pour broth into a 2- to 3-quart pan and stir in vinegar, soy sauce, ginger, garlic, and red pepper flakes. Cover and bring to a boil over medium-high heat, stirring occasionally; then reduce heat and simmer, stirring occasionally, until pasta is ready.

3. Drain pasta well and return to cooking pan. Add broth mixture, turkey, cilantro, and lime juice; toss to mix. Pour into a serving bowl or onto 4 individual plates; sprinkle with peanuts.

MAKES 4 SERVINGS

Per serving: 393 calories (16% calories from fat), 7 g total fat, 1 g saturated fat, 106 mg cholesterol, 788 mg sodium, 53 g carbohydrates, 2 g fiber, 9 g protein, 40 mg calcium, 4 mg iron

Turkey Tamale Pie

Here's a good example of a classic Western recipe reinvented for heart-healthier dining. In this version, lean ground turkey replaces the traditional beef, and we use just a modest amount of reduced-fat jack cheese instead of a generous helping of the full-fat kind.

PREPARATION TIME: *About 15 minutes*
COOKING TIME: *45 to 50 minutes*

1 teaspoon vegetable oil

12 ounces lean ground turkey

1 cup thinly sliced green onions

2 tablespoons chili powder

1 teaspoon ground cumin

1 jar (about 14 oz.) fat-free spaghetti sauce

1 can (about 15 oz.) black beans or red kidney beans, rinsed and drained

1 large egg

¼ cup low-fat (1%) milk

1 can (about 4 oz.) diced green chiles

1 package (about 8½ oz.) cornbread mix

½ cup shredded reduced-fat jack cheese

¾ cup fat-free sour cream

1. Heat oil in a wide nonstick frying pan over medium-high heat. Crumble turkey into pan; then add onions. Cook, stirring often, until onions are soft (about 3 minutes); if pan appears dry, add water, 1 tablespoon at a time.

2. Add chili powder and cumin to pan; cook, stirring, for 2 to 3 minutes. Add ¾ cup water, spaghetti sauce, and beans. Bring to a boil. Then reduce heat and simmer, uncovered, for 10 to 12 minutes to blend flavors; stir occasionally.

3. Meanwhile, in a large bowl, lightly beat together egg and milk. Stir in chiles and cornbread mix.

4. Pour turkey mixture into a shallow 2½- to 3-quart baking dish; sprinkle with cheese, then top evenly with cornbread batter. Bake in a 375° oven until cornbread is golden brown (25 to 30 minutes).

5. To serve, scoop out portions of pie with a spoon. Offer sour cream to add to taste.

MAKES 6 SERVINGS

Per serving: 430 calories (27% calories from fat), 13 g total fat, 4 g saturated fat, 87 mg cholesterol, 941 mg sodium, 54 g carbohydrates, 6 g fiber, 24 g protein, 271 mg calcium, 4 mg iron

Turkey Chiles Rellenos Casserole

A fluffy egg batter cloaks chiles stuffed with spicy turkey sausage in this hearty dish. It's a great choice for brunch, lunch, or supper.

PREPARATION TIME: *About 25 minutes*
COOKING TIME: *About 40 minutes*

12 ounces hot turkey Italian sausage, casings removed

1 cup low-fat (2%) cottage cheese

1 can (about 15 oz.) cream-style corn

½ teaspoon ground cumin

2 large cans (about 7 oz. *each*) whole green chiles

2 large eggs

6 large egg whites (about ¾ cup)

⅔ cup fat-free milk

1 cup all-purpose flour

1 teaspoon baking powder

½ cup shredded reduced-fat Cheddar cheese

1 jar (about 1 lb.) mild red salsa

2 teaspoons chili powder

1 cup fat-free sour cream

1. Crumble sausage into a wide nonstick frying pan. Cook over medium-high heat, stirring often, until meat is tinged with brown (5 to 7 minutes). Drain and discard any drippings. Stir cottage cheese, corn, and cumin into sausage. Cut a slit down one side of each chile; fill chiles equally with sausage mixture (filling will be mounded above chiles). Arrange chiles side by side in a lightly oiled 8-inch-square baking pan. Set aside.

2. In a large bowl, beat eggs and egg whites with an electric mixer on high speed until thick and foamy. Add milk, flour, and baking powder; beat until smooth. Fold in ¼ cup of the Cheddar cheese. Pour egg mixture over chiles; sprinkle with remaining ¼ cup Cheddar cheese.

3. Bake in a 375° oven until top is tinged with brown (about 35 minutes). Meanwhile, in a food processor or blender, whirl salsa and chili powder until puréed. Set aside.

4. To serve, spoon casserole onto 8 individual plates and top with some of the salsa. Offer remaining salsa and sour cream to add to taste.

MAKES 8 SERVINGS

Per serving: 348 calories (30% calories from fat), 12 g total fat, 4 g saturated fat, 88 mg cholesterol, 1,657 mg sodium, 38 g carbohydrates, 2 g fiber, 22 g protein, 206 mg calcium, 2 mg iron

Turkey & Cranberry Burgers

Thanksgiving flavors star in these lean burgers. Don't limit them to holiday meals, though; they make an appealing quick supper at any time of the year. You might serve spoonfuls of crunchy Classic Coleslaw (page 57) alongside.

PREPARATION TIME: *About 5 minutes*
COOKING TIME: *8 to 10 minutes*

12 ounces lean ground turkey

¾ cup minced onion

1 teaspoon dried sage

¼ teaspoon white pepper

4 hamburger buns, split and toasted

4 teaspoons Dijon mustard

¾ cup whole-berry cranberry sauce

4 large butter lettuce leaves, rinsed and crisped

1. In a large bowl, thoroughly mix turkey, onion, sage, and pepper. Shape into 4 patties, each about 4 inches wide.

2. Set a wide nonstick frying pan over medium-high heat. When pan is hot, add patties and cook, turning once, until browned on outside and no longer pink in center; cut to test (8 to 10 minutes).

3. Spread cut sides of buns with mustard. Then spoon about 2 tablespoons of the cranberry sauce over bottom half of each bun; top with a lettuce leaf and a turkey patty. Spoon remaining cranberry sauce atop patties; set top halves of buns in place.

MAKES 4 SERVINGS

Per serving: 345 calories (23% calories from fat), 9 g total fat, 2 g saturated fat, 62 mg cholesterol, 469 mg sodium, 46 g carbohydrates, 2 g fiber, 19 g protein, 80 mg calcium, 3 mg iron

Spaghetti with Spiced Turkey Sauce

Here's a leaner twist on spaghetti and meatballs. Meatballs made from lightly seasoned ground turkey are browned under the broiler, then simmered briefly in fat-free marinara sauce (choose your favorite brand) and spooned over hot pasta. For the most efficient preparation, put the water for the spaghetti on to boil as soon as the meatballs come out of the oven; that way, sauce and pasta should be ready at about the same time.

PREPARATION TIME: *About 10 minutes*
COOKING TIME: *About 20 minutes*

- 12 ounces lean ground turkey
- ½ cup chopped onion
- ¼ cup grated Parmesan cheese
- ¼ cup chopped parsley
- ½ teaspoon dried oregano
- 12 ounces dried spaghetti
- 1 large jar (about 26 oz.) fat-free or low-fat marinara sauce with mushrooms
- Parsley sprigs

1. In a large bowl, thoroughly mix turkey, onion, cheese, 3 tablespoons of the chopped parsley, and oregano. Shape into 20 equal balls and place on an oiled rack in a broiler pan. Broil 3 inches below heat, turning as needed, until well browned all over (10 to 12 minutes).

2. Bring about 3 quarts water to a boil in a 5- to 6-quart pan over high heat; stir in pasta and cook, uncovered, until just tender to bite (about 10 minutes). Or cook pasta according to package directions.

3. Meanwhile, pour marinara sauce into a 2- to 3-quart pan. Stir over medium-high heat until simmering (about 5 minutes). Reduce heat. Add browned meatballs and simmer, uncovered, for 5 minutes to blend flavors, stirring occasionally.

4. Drain pasta and pour onto a platter. Spoon meatballs and sauce over pasta, sprinkle with remaining 1 tablespoon chopped parsley, and garnish with parsley sprigs.

MAKES 4 TO 6 SERVINGS

Per serving: 422 calories (16% calories from fat), 7 g total fat, 2 g saturated fat, 53 mg cholesterol, 605 mg sodium, 62 g carbohydrates, 3 g fiber, 25 g protein, 130 mg calcium, 5 mg iron

Fusilli with Turkey Italian Sausage

Mild or hot, it's your choice—either way, spicy turkey sausage is delicious in this robust tomato-basil-fennel sauce for corkscrew-shaped fusilli.

PREPARATION TIME: *About 20 minutes*
COOKING TIME: *About 15 minutes*

- 12 ounces dried fusilli
- 8 ounces mild or hot turkey Italian sausage, casings removed
- 2 cans (about 14½ oz. *each*) Italian-style stewed tomatoes
- 2 teaspoons fennel seeds, crushed
- 1 cup lightly packed chopped fresh basil
- ¼ cup grated Asiago or Parmesan cheese
- Salt and pepper
- Basil sprigs

1. In a 5- to 6-quart pan, bring about 3 quarts water to a boil over high heat; stir in pasta and cook, uncovered, until just tender to bite (about 10 minutes). Or cook pasta according to package directions.

2. Meanwhile, crumble sausage into a wide nonstick frying pan. Cook over medium-high heat, stirring often, until browned (7 to 10 minutes). Stir in tomatoes and fennel seeds. Bring to a boil; then reduce heat and simmer, uncovered, for 5 minutes. Stir in chopped basil.

3. Drain pasta and return to cooking pan. Add tomato-sausage sauce and cheese; toss to coat pasta well. Season to taste with salt and pepper; garnish with basil sprigs.

MAKES 4 TO 6 SERVINGS

Per serving: 398 calories (17% calories from fat), 8 g total fat, 3 g saturated fat, 28 mg cholesterol, 1,087 mg sodium, 63 g carbohydrates, 5 g fiber, 20 g protein, 132 mg calcium, 5 mg iron

CORNISH HENS WITH APRICOT PILAF

POULTRY

Cornish Hens with Apricot Pilaf

Serve these plump, apricot-glazed little birds with a packaged rice pilaf mix enhanced with herbs, dried apricots, and currants; a cup of unsweetened applesauce adds extra moisture. We suggest using the pilaf as stuffing and serving any leftovers on the side, but you can also roast the hens unstuffed and arrange them atop a bed of pilaf. Present the birds whole, if you like; then cut each in half with poultry shears before serving.

PREPARATION TIME: *About 30 minutes*
COOKING TIME: *About 1½ hours*

1¾ cups fat-free reduced-sodium chicken broth

2 packages (about 6 oz. *each*) rice pilaf mix

1 cup (about 6 oz.) thinly sliced dried apricots

2 teaspoons dried oregano

1 cup unsweetened applesauce

1⅔ cups currants

⅓ cup snipped chives or thinly sliced green onions

1 tablespoon toasted pine nuts

4 Rock Cornish game hens (about 1½ lbs. *each*)

1½ cups apricot jam

1 tablespoon lemon juice

Lemon slices and whole chives (optional)

1. In a wide nonstick frying pan, bring broth and 1¾ cups water to a boil over medium-high heat. Add rice pilaf mixes, ½ cup of the apricots, and oregano. Then cook according to pilaf package directions. Let pilaf cool; stir in applesauce, currants, snipped chives, and pine nuts.

2. Reserve game hen necks and giblets for other uses; pull off and discard any lumps of fat. Rinse hens inside and out and pat dry. Fill each hen with pilaf, packing firmly (reserve any remaining pilaf to serve alongside hens; reheat just before serving). Use poultry skewers to close cavities securely.

3. Place hens, breast up, on a rack in a 10- by 15-inch baking pan. Cover with foil and roast in a 400° oven for 30 minutes. Meanwhile, in a 1- to 2-quart pan, combine jam, 1 tablespoon water, lemon juice, and remaining ½ cup apricots. Stir over medium heat until jam is melted and mixture is hot. Remove from heat; keep warm.

4. Uncover hens and roast for 15 more minutes; then baste with half the apricot glaze. Roast for 10 more minutes; baste with remaining glaze. Continue to roast until hens are golden brown and meat near thighbone is no longer pink; cut to test (about 10 more minutes). If pan appears dry at any point during roasting, add water, ¼ cup at a time, stirring to loosen browned bits from pan; do not let drippings scorch.

5. Let hens rest for at least 5 minutes. Meanwhile, pour pan drippings into a bowl; skim and discard fat. Garnish hens with lemon slices and whole chives, if desired; serve with skimmed drippings and reheated reserved pilaf.

MAKES 8 SERVINGS

Per serving: 824 calories (30% calories from fat), 29 g total fat, 7 g saturated fat, 187 mg cholesterol, 915 mg sodium, 109 g carbohydrates, 5 g fiber, 39 g protein, 87 mg calcium, 5 mg iron

Seafood

Sea Bass with Chiles & Tomatoes

A hot, spicy tomato sauce complements baked white-fleshed fish such as delicate Chilean sea bass. Depending on what looks best at the market, you can use other kinds of fish, too; try halibut or rockfish, for example.

PREPARATION TIME: *About 10 minutes*
COOKING TIME: *10 to 15 minutes*

1½ to 2 pounds firm white-fleshed fish fillets, such as Chilean sea bass, halibut, or rockfish (*each about 1 inch thick*)
1 tablespoon olive oil
1 medium-size onion, chopped
2 cloves garlic, minced or pressed
2 to 4 tablespoons minced fresh jalapeño chiles
1 can (about 14½ oz.) diced tomatoes
1 tablespoon lemon juice
1½ tablespoons cornstarch
   Salt and pepper
2 tablespoons chopped cilantro
   Cilantro sprigs (optional)

1. Rinse fish, pat dry, and cut into 6 serving-size pieces; then rub all over with 2 teaspoons of the oil. Arrange fish pieces slightly apart in a 10- by 15-inch baking pan. Bake in a 425° oven until just opaque but still moist in thickest part; cut to test (10 to 15 minutes).

2. Meanwhile, heat remaining 1 teaspoon oil in a wide frying pan over medium-high heat. Add onion, garlic, and chiles. Cook, stirring often, until onion is lightly browned (about 5 minutes).

3. Drain tomatoes, reserving juice. In a small bowl, stir together reserved tomato juice, lemon juice, and cornstarch to blend smoothly. Add tomatoes and tomato juice mixture to pan with onion; cook, stirring, until sauce boils and thickens. Season to taste with salt and pepper. If sauce is done before fish, remove from heat and keep warm.

4. With a slotted spatula, transfer fish to 6 individual plates. Spoon sauce over fish; sprinkle with chopped cilantro. Garnish with cilantro sprigs, if desired.

MAKES 6 SERVINGS

Per serving: 180 calories (26% calories from fat), 5 g total fat, 1 g saturated fat, 54 mg cholesterol, 204 mg sodium, 7 g carbohydrates, 1 g fiber, 26 g protein, 40 mg calcium, 1 mg iron

Spicy Swordfish

Swordfish has been described as one of the meatiest of all fish, in both texture and flavor. As such, it stands up nicely to the invigorating flavors of this vivid sauce—a simple combination of purchased salsa and diced fresh tomato sparked with green onion, lime, and as much hot pepper seasoning as you like.

PREPARATION TIME: *About 10 minutes*
COOKING TIME: *10 to 12 minutes*

4 swordfish steaks (*each ¾ to 1 inch thick; about 1½ lbs. total*)
1 medium-size tomato (about 6 oz.)
1 green onion
1 cup chunky red salsa
1 tablespoon lime juice
   Liquid hot pepper seasoning (optional)

1. Rinse fish, pat dry, and arrange on an oiled rack in a broiler pan. Broil 4 to 6 inches below heat, turning once, until fish is just opaque but still moist in thickest part; cut to test (10 to 12 minutes).

2. Meanwhile, dice tomato and thinly slice onion. In a small bowl, mix tomato, onion, salsa, and lime juice. Season to taste with hot pepper seasoning, if desired.

3. To serve, arrange fish on a platter or 4 individual plates; top with salsa mixture.

MAKES 4 SERVINGS

Per serving: 214 calories (28% calories from fat), 6 g total fat, 2 g saturated fat, 59 mg cholesterol, 782 mg sodium, 6 g carbohydrates, 1 g fiber, 30 g protein, 11 mg calcium, 1 mg iron

Salmon with Rice Triangles, Pineapple Salsa & Sweet-Sour Sauce

A beautiful choice for a company meal, this entrée teams silky salmon with a simple pineapple salsa and a bright sauce of fresh carrot, pineapple, and lime juices. Serve with whimsical rice triangles, easily made by pressing warm cooked rice into a square pan, then turning it out and cutting it into shapes.

PREPARATION TIME: *About 25 minutes*
COOKING TIME: *About 30 minutes*

Pressed Rice Triangles (recipe follows)

¼ teaspoon cumin seeds

2 cups fresh carrot juice

1 cup unsweetened pineapple juice

2½ tablespoons lime juice

2 teaspoons chopped cilantro

1 teaspoon minced fresh jalapeño chile

½ cup diced fresh pineapple; or ½ cup canned juice-packed pineapple tidbits, drained

1 to 1⅓ pounds salmon fillet, cut into 4 serving-size pieces

1 teaspoon vegetable oil

Salt and pepper

Cilantro sprigs

1. Begin cooking rice for Pressed Rice Triangles.

2. While rice is cooking, place cumin seeds in a 3- to 4-quart pan over medium-high heat; heat, shaking pan often, until seeds begin to smoke (about 2 minutes). Remove from heat. Pour seeds from pan and crush them with a mortar and pestle or a rolling pin; set aside.

3. Pour carrot and pineapple juices into pan. Bring to a boil over high heat; boil, stirring occasionally, until reduced to ½ cup (15 to 20 minutes). Stir in cumin seeds and 2 tablespoons of the lime juice. Remove from heat and keep warm.

4. While juice is boiling, in a small bowl, mix remaining 1½ teaspoons lime juice, chopped cilantro, chile, and pineapple; set aside.

5. Complete Pressed Rice Triangles.

6. Rinse fish, pat dry, and rub all over with oil; sprinkle with salt and pepper. Place fish in a wide nonstick frying pan over medium-high heat. Cook, turning once, until just opaque but still moist in thickest part; cut to test (5 to 7 minutes).

7. Spoon sauce over bottom of a rimmed platter. Arrange fish on sauce; spoon pineapple salsa in a band across fish. Garnish with cilantro sprigs. Serve with Pressed Rice Triangles.

MAKES 4 SERVINGS

Pressed Rice Triangles. In a 2- to 3-quart pan, combine 1 cup **long-grain white rice**, 1¾ cups **water**, and ½ teaspoon **salt** (optional). Bring to a boil over high heat. Then reduce heat, cover, and simmer until liquid has been absorbed and rice is tender to bite (about 20 minutes).

With the back of a wet spoon, firmly press rice into an 8-inch-square pan to form an even layer. Let cool for 5 minutes. Run a knife around edges of pan; turn rice out onto a board. Cut rice into 12 triangles. Makes 4 servings.

Per serving of fish: 517 calories (28% calories from fat), 16 g total fat, 3 g saturated fat, 78 mg cholesterol, 118 mg sodium, 60 g carbohydrates, 1 g fiber, 31 g protein, 69 mg calcium, 3 mg iron

Per serving of rice: 169 calories (2% calories from fat), .40 g total fat, 0 g saturated fat, 0 mg cholesterol, 2 mg sodium, 37 g carbohydrates, 0 g fiber, 3 g protein, 13 mg calcium, 2 mg iron

Teriyaki Sea Bass

Start with purchased teriyaki sauce, then refresh it with lime juice, cilantro, and minced ginger to season tender sea bass for the barbecue. You might serve fish and sauce on a bed of long-grain white and wild rice accented with a sprinkling of toasted pine nuts.

PREPARATION TIME: *About 5 minutes, plus at least 15 minutes to marinate*
COOKING TIME: *15 to 18 minutes*

1½ **cups teriyaki sauce**
 ¼ **cup lime juice**
 1 **cup lightly packed chopped cilantro**
 3 **tablespoons minced fresh ginger**
 1 **pound Chilean sea bass fillets (*each* about 1 inch thick)**
   Lime wedges

1. In a 9- by 13-inch dish, stir together teriyaki sauce, lime juice, cilantro, and ginger. Rinse fish, pat dry, and cut into 4 serving-size pieces. Place fish in marinade; turn to coat. Cover and refrigerate for at least 15 minutes or up to 4 hours, turning occasionally.

2. Lift fish from marinade and drain briefly (reserve marinade). Place fish on an oiled grill 4 to 6 inches above a solid bed of hot coals or over high heat on a gas grill (you can hold your hand at grill level for 2 to 3 seconds). Close lid on gas grill. Cook for 5 minutes, basting occasionally with marinade. Then turn fish over and continue to cook, basting occasionally, until just opaque but still moist in thickest part; cut to test (10 to 13 more minutes). Offer lime wedges to squeeze over fish to taste.

MAKES 4 SERVINGS

Per serving: 160 calories (13% calories from fat), 2 g total fat, 1 g saturated fat, 47 mg cholesterol, 2,148 mg sodium, 10 g carbohydrates, 0 g fiber, 24 g protein, 28 mg calcium, 1 mg iron

SALMON WITH RICE TRIANGLES, PINEAPPLE SALSA & SWEET-SOUR SAUCE

Snapper with Fruit Salsa

Whole wheat couscous makes a good accompaniment for this lean fish. Sauté the fillets in a nonstick pan barely glazed with oil, then top them with a tropical-tasting fresh salsa of pineapple, papaya, ginger, and lime.

PREPARATION TIME: *About 15 minutes*
COOKING TIME: *About 6 minutes*

- ¼ cup chopped red onion
- ¾ cup chopped fresh pineapple; or ¾ cup canned juice-packed pineapple tidbits, drained
- ¾ cup chopped ripe papaya
- ¼ cup lime juice
- 1 tablespoon minced fresh ginger
- ¼ teaspoon crushed red pepper flakes
- 4 rockfish fillets (*each* about ½ inch thick; about 1 lb. *total*), such as snapper
- Salt and pepper
- 1 teaspoon vegetable oil
- Lime wedges

1. Place onion in a small bowl and cover with ice water. In another small bowl, combine pineapple, papaya, lime juice, ginger, and red pepper flakes. Set onion and fruit mixture aside.

2. Rinse fish, pat dry, and sprinkle with salt and pepper. Heat oil in a wide nonstick frying pan over medium-high heat. Add fish and cook, turning as needed, until browned on outside and just opaque but still moist in thickest part; cut to test (about 6 minutes). Transfer to 4 individual plates; keep warm.

3. Drain onion and stir into fruit mixture. Spoon fruit salsa over fish. Offer lime, salt, and pepper to season fish to taste.

MAKES 4 SERVINGS

Per serving: 150 calories (19% calories from fat), 3 g total fat, 1 g saturated fat, 40 mg cholesterol, 73 mg sodium, 8 g carbohydrates, 1 g fiber, 22 g protein, 24 mg calcium, 1 mg iron

Halibut with Horseradish Mashed Potatoes & Chard

This dish is so sophisticated that few will suspect it began with instant mashed potatoes! The red Swiss chard sandwiched between the moist halibut fillets and horseradish-nipped potatoes is a fall and winter favorite.

PREPARATION TIME: *About 10 minutes*
COOKING TIME: *15 to 20 minutes*

- Instant mashed potatoes for 8 servings (enough to make 4 cups)
- 1 to 2 tablespoons prepared horseradish
- 1 pound halibut fillets (*each* 1 to 1½ inches thick)
- 1½ teaspoons olive oil
- Salt and freshly ground pepper
- 1 pound red Swiss chard
- About ¼ cup balsamic vinegar

1. Prepare potatoes according to package directions, but omit butter. Stir in horseradish; keep warm.

2. Rinse fish, pat dry, and cut into 4 serving-size pieces. Rub fish all over with oil; sprinkle with salt and pepper. Place fish in a wide nonstick frying pan and cook over medium-high heat, turning occasionally, until just opaque but still moist in thickest part; cut to test (10 to 12 minutes).

3. Meanwhile, remove and discard tough stems from chard; then chop chard coarsely. In a 5- to 6-quart pan, bring ¼ cup water to a boil over high heat. Add chard, cover, and cook until wilted (about 3 minutes). Drain and discard any cooking liquid.

4. Spoon potatoes equally onto 4 individual plates, flattening top of each mound of potatoes. Top potatoes with chard, then with fish. Offer vinegar, salt, and pepper to season each serving to taste.

MAKES 4 SERVINGS

Per serving: 296 calories (16% calories from fat), 5 g total fat, 1 g saturated fat, 39 mg cholesterol, 353 mg sodium, 32 g carbohydrates, 2 g fiber, 30 g protein, 193 mg calcium, 3 mg iron

Poached Seafood with Potatoes & Fennel

Yukon Gold potatoes and fresh fennel absorb the subtly rich flavors of mussels, sea bass, and shrimp poached in a wine broth smoothed with a little heavy cream. Serve the stew in shallow bowls, with a green salad and crusty French bread baguettes alongside.

PREPARATION TIME: *About 15 minutes*
COOKING TIME: *About 35 minutes*

- 4 cups fat-free reduced-sodium chicken broth
- 1 cup Sauvignon Blanc or other dry white wine
- ½ cup whipping cream
- 1 teaspoon fennel seeds
- 2 to 3 teaspoons minced fresh thyme or ¾ teaspoon dried thyme
- 1½ pounds Yukon Gold or other thin-skinned potatoes, peeled and thinly sliced
- 2 large heads fennel (*each* 3½ to 4 inches in diameter; about 1½ lbs. *total*)
- 8 ounces mussels in shells
- 8 to 12 ounces very large raw shrimp (16 to 20 per lb.)
- 1 pound Chilean sea bass fillets

1. In a 6- to 8-quart pan, combine broth, wine, cream, fennel seeds, thyme, and potatoes. Place over high heat.

2. Rinse fennel. Trim base, stems, and any bruised portions from each head; reserve feathery leaves. Thinly slice fennel crosswise and add to pan. Bring mixture to a boil; then reduce heat, cover, and simmer until potatoes are very tender when pierced (about 20 minutes).

3. Meanwhile, chop reserved fennel leaves. Scrub mussels and pull off beards; shell and devein shrimp (leave tails on, if desired). Rinse fish, pat dry, and cut into 1-inch chunks.

4. When potatoes are tender, add mussels. Cover and simmer for 3 minutes. Add shrimp and fish; continue to simmer until mussels pop open (5 to 7 more minutes). Fish and shrimp should be just opaque but still moist in thickest part; cut to test.

5. To serve, ladle into 6 individual bowls; sprinkle with chopped fennel leaves.

MAKES 6 SERVINGS

Per serving: 294 calories (28% calories from fat), 4 g total fat, 9 g saturated fat, 115 mg cholesterol, 630 mg sodium, 23 g carbohydrates, 3 g fiber, 29 g protein, 101 mg calcium, 3 mg iron

Shrimp with Chanterelle Sauce

If you're looking for an elegant entrée, you've found it! Sautéed shrimp sauced with a rich-tasting, tarragon-seasoned sauce of dried chanterelle mushrooms in wine make a lovely special-occasion meal. You'll find the chanterelles in specialty food stores and some well-stocked supermarkets; be sure to allow at least half an hour to soak them.

PREPARATION TIME: *About 20 minutes, plus at least 30 minutes to soak chanterelles*
COOKING TIME: *About 1 hour*

- ½ ounce (about 1 cup) dried chanterelles
- 1½ cups long-grain white rice
- 2 teaspoons butter or margarine
- 1 pound large raw shrimp (31 to 35 per lb.), shelled and deveined
- ¾ cup bottled clam juice or fat-free reduced-sodium chicken broth
- ¼ cup chardonnay
- 2 teaspoons chopped fresh tarragon or 1 teaspoon dried tarragon
- 2 tablespoons whipping cream or half-and-half
  Pepper
  Tarragon sprigs
  Lemon wedges

1. Place chanterelles in a 1½- to 2-quart pan and add 1½ cups water. Bring to a boil over high heat; then reduce heat, cover, and simmer gently until mushrooms are very tender when pierced (about 30 minutes). Remove from heat and let stand for 30 minutes. Then lift chanterelles from pan and squeeze liquid from them back into cooking water; reserve cooking water. Set chanterelles aside.

2. In a 4- to 5-quart pan, bring 3 cups water to a boil over high heat; stir in rice. Reduce heat, cover, and simmer until liquid has been absorbed and rice is tender to bite (about 20 minutes).

3. Meanwhile, melt butter in a wide nonstick frying pan over medium-high heat. Add shrimp and cook, stirring often, until just opaque but still moist in center; cut to test (3 to 4 minutes). Remove shrimp from pan with a slotted spoon and keep warm.

4. Add chanterelles to pan. Cook, stirring, until tinged a darker brown (about 3 minutes); if pan appears dry, add water, 1 tablespoon at a time. Carefully pour reserved mushroom cooking water into pan, taking care not to add any grit that has settled at bottom of pan. Add clam juice, wine, and chopped tarragon. Bring to a boil; then boil, stirring, until liquid is reduced to ⅓ cup. Add cream; return to a boil, stirring. Remove from heat and stir in shrimp. Season to taste with pepper.

5. Spoon rice onto a rimmed platter or 4 individual plates. Spoon shrimp mixture over rice. Garnish with tarragon sprigs; offer lemon wedges to season individual servings.

MAKES 4 SERVINGS

Per serving: 409 calories (15% calories from fat), 7 g total fat, 3 g saturated fat, 155 mg cholesterol, 260 mg sodium, 59 g carbohydrates, 2 g fiber, 25 g protein, 84 mg calcium, 6 mg iron

SHRIMP WITH CHANTERELLE SAUCE

PIZZAS WITH PESTO & SHRIMP

SEAFOOD

Pizzas with Pesto & Shrimp

An individual pizza is always an engaging main course. These use big, round crusty rolls as a base; you spread the bread with a blend of purchased pesto and puréed garbanzos; then add tangy artichoke hearts, tomatoes, and shredded Parmesan. Bake the pizzas just until hot, then top with tiny shrimp and serve.

PREPARATION TIME: *About 20 minutes*
BAKING TIME: *12 to 15 minutes*

- 4 large crusty Italian rolls (*each* 4 to 5 inches in diameter); or 8 small Italian bread shells (*each* 4 oz. and 5½ inches in diameter)
- 1 jar (about 6½ oz.) marinated artichoke hearts
- 1 can (about 15 oz.) garbanzo beans, rinsed and drained
- 1 carton (about 4 oz.) reduced-fat pesto
- 2 tablespoons drained capers
- 2 large tomatoes (about 1 lb. *total*), chopped and drained
- ¾ cup shredded Parmesan cheese
- 8 ounces small cooked shrimp
- ½ cup thinly sliced green onions

1. If using rolls, carefully cut each in half horizontally. Set roll halves, cut side up, on a large baking sheet. Set aside.

2. Drain marinade from artichokes into a blender or food processor. Thinly slice artichokes and set aside. Add garbanzos, pesto, and capers to blender; whirl until smoothly puréed. Spread sauce over rolls, nearly to edges; scatter equally with artichokes and tomatoes, then sprinkle with cheese.

3. Bake in a 350° oven until cheese is melted and beginning to brown (12 to 15 minutes). Place each pizza on an individual plate; top pizzas equally with shrimp and onions.

MAKES 8 SERVINGS

Per serving: 339 calories (30% calories from fat), 11 g total fat, 3 g saturated fat, 65 mg cholesterol, 930 mg sodium, 41 g carbohydrates, 5 g fiber, 18 g protein, 226 mg calcium, 4 mg iron

Grilled Fish Tacos

Simple and simply delicious are these soft corn tortillas filled with grilled sea bass and spoonfuls of salsa and sour cream. Use your favorite salsa, either purchased or homemade; opt for a reduced-sodium recipe if you can.

PREPARATION TIME: *10 to 15 minutes*
COOKING TIME: *10 to 12 minutes*

- 12 corn tortillas (*each* about 6 inches in diameter)
- 1½ pounds Chilean sea bass fillets (*each* about 1 inch thick)
- Salt and pepper
- About 2 cups hot or mild salsa
- About ¾ cup fat-free sour cream
- Lime wedges

1. Stack tortillas, wrap in foil, and heat in a 350° oven until hot (about 10 minutes).

2. Meanwhile, rinse fish and pat dry. Cut into 2 or 3 pieces, then place on an oiled grill 4 to 6 inches above a solid bed of hot coals or over high heat on a gas grill (you can hold your hand at grill level for 2 to 3 seconds). Close lid on gas grill. Cook, turning once, until fish is just opaque but still moist in thickest part; cut to test (10 to 12 minutes). Transfer fish to a platter; break into chunks, then sprinkle with salt and pepper.

3. To assemble each taco, stack 2 tortillas; fill with chunks of fish, salsa, and sour cream. Squeeze lime wedges over filling, fold tortillas to enclose filling, and eat out of hand.

MAKES 6 SERVINGS

Per serving: 303 calories (11% calories from fat), 4 g total fat, 1 g saturated fat, 50 mg cholesterol, 543 mg sodium, 40 g carbohydrates, 4 g fiber, 27 g protein, 166 mg calcium, 1 mg iron

Shrimp with Lemon Shells

This colorful medley of pasta, plump shrimp, and vegetables is good hot or cool—so you can enjoy any leftovers the next day as a chilled salad.

PREPARATION TIME: *About 25 minutes*
COOKING TIME: *About 15 minutes*

 2 teaspoons grated lemon peel
¼ cup lemon juice
¼ cup fat-free reduced-sodium chicken broth
 2 cloves garlic, minced or pressed
 1 tablespoon minced fresh dill or 1 teaspoon dried dill weed
 2 tablespoons minced fresh ginger
 1 package (about 9 oz.) frozen broccoli flowerets, thawed
 1 small zucchini (about 4 oz.), thinly sliced
 8 ounces dried medium-size pasta shells
12 ounces frozen medium-size cooked shelled, deveined shrimp (36 to 50 per lb.)

1. In a small bowl, stir together lemon peel, lemon juice, broth, garlic, dill, and ginger. Set aside. Also place broccoli in a colander to drain; place zucchini on top of broccoli in colander.

2. In a 4- to 5-quart pan, bring about 8 cups water to a boil over high heat; stir in pasta and cook, uncovered, for 10 minutes. Add shrimp and return to boil. Pasta should be just tender to bite; if necessary, continue to boil until it reaches this stage.

3. Pour pasta and shrimp over vegetables in colander.

4. Pour lemon mixture into pan used to cook pasta. Bring to a boil over high heat, stirring; then boil, stirring, for 1 minute. Reduce heat to low; add shrimp, pasta, broccoli, and zucchini. Toss to coat with sauce, then serve.

MAKES 4 SERVINGS

Per serving: 326 calories (6% calories from fat), 2 g total fat, 0 g saturated fat, 166 mg cholesterol, 259 mg sodium, 48 g carbohydrates, 3 g fiber, 28 g protein, 82 mg calcium, 5 mg iron

Coriander-Curry Shrimp

Serve this mildly spicy stir-fry over vermicelli or other pasta strands, perhaps with a selection of tropical fruits on the side.

PREPARATION TIME: *About 20 minutes*
COOKING TIME: *About 10 minutes*

12 ounces to 1 pound dried vermicelli
⅔ cup pineapple-coconut juice
 2 teaspoons cornstarch
 1 teaspoon vegetable oil
 1 large onion, thinly sliced
 1 clove garlic, minced or pressed
 1 tablespoon curry powder
 1 tablespoon ground coriander
¼ teaspoon ground red pepper (cayenne)
1½ pounds large raw shrimp (31 to 35 per lb.), shelled and deveined
 2 tablespoons minced cilantro
 Lime wedges

1. In a 6- to 8-quart pan, bring about 4 quarts water to a boil over high heat; stir in pasta and cook, uncovered, until just tender to bite (7 to 9 minutes). Or cook pasta according to package directions.

2. Meanwhile, in a small bowl, stir together pineapple-coconut juice and cornstarch until smoothly blended. Set aside.

3. Heat oil in a wide frying pan over high heat. Add onion, garlic, and 2 tablespoons water. Cook, stirring often, until water has evaporated and onion is soft and beginning to brown slightly (about 5 minutes). Stir in curry powder, coriander, and red pepper.

4. Add shrimp to onion mixture and stir for 2 minutes. Stir pineapple juice mixture; pour into pan, stirring. Then cook, stirring, until sauce comes to a boil and shrimp are just opaque but still moist in center; cut to test (3 to 4 minutes). Stir in cilantro.

5. Drain pasta well; pour onto a platter. Spoon shrimp and sauce over pasta. Offer lime wedges to season individual servings.

MAKES 6 SERVINGS

Per serving: 354 calories (12% calories from fat), 4 g total fat, 1 g saturated fat, 140 mg cholesterol, 148 mg sodium, 50 g carbohydrates, 3 g fiber, 26 g protein, 77 mg calcium, 5 mg iron

Prawns with Pasta & Parsley Pesto

The pesto for this pretty entrée is made from parsley and roasted almonds rather than the usual basil and pine nuts; rice vinegar gives it a little tang. Serve the dish with warm No-knead French Rolls (page 210) and a salad of mixed lettuces.

PREPARATION TIME: *About 10 minutes*
COOKING TIME: *15 to 20 minutes*

- ¼ cup roasted salted almonds
- 3 cups lightly packed parsley sprigs
- ¼ cup plus 1 teaspoon olive oil
- 6 tablespoons seasoned rice vinegar
- 1 clove garlic, peeled
- 1 tablespoon drained capers
- ¼ teaspoon crushed red pepper flakes
- 1 pound dried medium-size pasta shells or other pasta shapes
- 1 pound large raw shrimp (31 to 35 per lb.), shelled and deveined
- 1 large tomato (about 8 oz.), chopped and drained
  Parsley sprigs

1. In a food processor or blender, combine almonds, the 3 cups parsley, ¼ cup of the oil, ¼ cup of the vinegar, garlic, capers, and red pepper flakes. Whirl until smooth. Set aside.

2. In a 6- to 8-quart pan, bring about 4 quarts water to a boil over high heat; stir in pasta and cook, uncovered, until just tender to bite (10 to 12 minutes). Or cook pasta according to package directions.

3. Meanwhile, heat remaining 1 teaspoon oil in a wide nonstick frying pan over medium-high heat. Add shrimp and cook, stirring often, until just opaque but still moist in center; cut to test (3 to 4 minutes). Remove from heat and stir in tomato. Keep warm.

4. Drain pasta, rinse with hot water, and drain well again. Quickly return drained pasta to cooking pan; add remaining 2 tablespoons vinegar and lift with 2 forks to mix.

5. To serve, stir pesto well, then spread evenly on 6 individual plates. Top with pasta, then with shrimp mixture. Garnish with parsley sprigs and serve at once.

MAKES 6 SERVINGS

Per serving: 504 calories (29% calories from fat), 16 g total fat, 2 g saturated fat, 93 mg cholesterol, 522 mg sodium, 65 g carbohydrates, 4 g fiber, 24 g protein, 103 mg calcium, 7 mg iron

OVEN-FRIED CRAB CAKES WITH GREEN AÏOLI

Oven-fried Crab Cakes with Green Aïoli

Crunchy on the outside, sweet and creamy on the inside, these baked crab cakes offer a variation on the usual recipe; they're held together with polenta (cooked in milk and clam juice) rather than bread or cracker crumbs. The garlicky aïoli you spoon on top is likewise unorthodox: it's made with cream-style corn, parsley, roasted almonds, and piquant capers.

PREPARATION TIME: *About 15 minutes, plus 15 minutes for crab mixture to stand*
COOKING TIME: *About 45 minutes*

- 2 cups low-fat (1%) milk
- ½ cup bottled clam juice or fat-free reduced-sodium chicken broth
- 1 cup polenta or yellow cornmeal
- 1½ teaspoons chopped fresh thyme or ½ teaspoon dried thyme
- 1 large egg, lightly beaten
- 8 ounces cooked crabmeat
- ½ cup diced red bell pepper
- 2 tablespoons sliced green onion
- 2 teaspoons Worcestershire
- Salt and white pepper
- Green Aïoli (recipe follows)
- Whole green onions or thyme sprigs (optional)

1. In a 4- to 5-quart pan, combine milk and clam juice. Bring just to a boil over medium-high heat. Stir in polenta and chopped thyme. Reduce heat and simmer, uncovered, stirring often and scraping pan bottom with a long-handled spoon (mixture will spatter), until polenta is thick and tastes creamy (about 15 minutes).

2. Remove pan from heat and quickly stir in egg. Gently stir in crab, bell pepper, sliced onion, and Worcestershire. Season to taste with salt and white pepper. Let mixture cool for at least 15 minutes, stirring occasionally.

3. Meanwhile, prepare Green Aïoli.

4. Moisten your hands with water to keep polenta-crab mixture from sticking to them; then shape mixture into 12 patties, each about 3 inches wide. Arrange patties in a single layer in 1 or 2 lightly greased nonstick 10- by 15-inch baking pans.

5. Bake in a 450° oven until golden brown; turn cakes over as needed and rotate pans halfway through baking, if necessary. If any cakes begin to overbrown before remaining cakes are done, remove them from pan and keep warm.

6. Arrange 3 crab cakes on each of 4 individual plates; top with Green Aïoli. Garnish with whole green onions, if desired.

MAKES 4 SERVINGS

Green Aïoli. In a blender or food processor, combine 2 cups lightly packed **parsley sprigs**; 1 small can (about 8¾ oz.) **cream-style corn**; ¼ cup **roasted salted almonds**; 3 tablespoons **white wine vinegar**; 2 tablespoons drained **capers**; 1 clove **garlic** (peeled); and ¼ teaspoon **crushed red pepper flakes**. Whirl until smoothly puréed. Cover and refrigerate until ready to use.

Per serving, including aïoli: 517 calories (19% calories from fat), 11 g total fat, 2 g saturated fat, 115 mg cholesterol, 774 mg sodium, 78 g carbohydrates, 11 g fiber, 27 g protein, 318 mg calcium, 6 mg iron

Scallop Sauté

This pretty green-and-white dish goes together fast. If you can't find sugar snap peas, use fresh Chinese pea pods; the flavor will be just as good. You might serve the dish with hot linguine or capellini, sesame-seeded whole wheat rolls, and a salad of mixed baby greens.

PREPARATION TIME: *About 15 minutes*
COOKING TIME: *About 10 minutes*

1	pound sea scallops
2	tablespoons butter or margarine
1	pound sugar snap peas
2½	cups diagonally sliced celery
¼	cup Chablis or other dry white wine
3	tablespoons lemon juice
½	teaspoon dried dill weed
½	teaspoon freshly ground pepper
3	tablespoons chopped parsley

1. Rinse scallops and pat dry; set aside.

2. Melt butter in a wide nonstick frying pan over medium-high heat. Add peas and celery; cook, stirring, until vegetables are tender-crisp to bite (3 to 4 minutes). Remove vegetables from pan with a slotted spoon; set aside.

3. Add scallops, wine, lemon juice, dill, and pepper to pan; bring to a boil. Reduce heat, cover, and simmer until scallops are just opaque but still moist in center; cut to test (about 5 minutes). Return vegetables to pan and cook just until heated through.

4. Using a slotted spoon, divide scallop mixture among 4 individual plates. Sprinkle with parsley.

MAKES 4 SERVINGS

Per serving: 223 calories (29% calories from fat), 7 g total fat, 4 g saturated fat, 53 mg cholesterol, 311 mg sodium, 15 g carbohydrates, 4 g fiber, 22 g protein, 121 mg calcium, 3 mg iron

Clams & Fennel in Tomato Broth

Breadsticks and steamed broccoli are good alongside big bowls of clams and sliced fresh fennel simmered in a flavorsome tomato-wine broth. Serve the dish with forks and oversize spoons.

PREPARATION TIME: *About 15 minutes*
COOKING TIME: *About 25 minutes*

- 2 medium-size heads fennel (about 1 lb. *total*)
- 4 cloves garlic, minced or pressed
- 2 bottles (about 8 oz. *each*) clam juice
- 2 cups fat-free reduced-sodium chicken broth
- 1 cup dry white wine
- 1 can (about 14½ oz.) no-salt-added sliced tomatoes
- 4 pounds small hard-shell clams in shells, suitable for steaming, scrubbed
  Freshly ground pepper

1. Rinse fennel. Trim base, stems, and any bruised portions from each head; reserve feathery leaves. Thinly slice fennel crosswise and place in a 5- to 6-quart pan. Add garlic, clam juice, broth, and wine. Bring to a boil over high heat; then reduce heat, cover, and simmer until fennel is tender when pierced (about 10 minutes). Meanwhile, mince enough of the reserved fennel leaves to make 2 teaspoons; set aside along with remaining feathery leaves.

2. Stir in tomatoes and their liquid; then add clams. Increase heat to high, cover, and return to a simmer; then reduce heat and simmer, stirring occasionally, until clams pop open (3 to 4 minutes).

3. To serve, ladle clams and sauce into 4 individual bowls. Top with the 2 teaspoons minced fennel leaves; top each serving with a few fennel leaves. Season to taste with pepper.

MAKES 4 SERVINGS

Per serving: 155 calories (9% calories from fat), 1 g total fat, 0 g saturated fat, 29 mg cholesterol, 695 mg sodium, 11 g carbohydrates, 2 g fiber, 15 g protein, 139 mg calcium, 14 mg iron

Spaghetti with Clams & Tuna

If you have a well-stocked pantry, you probably have most of the ingredients for this zesty pasta at hand. For a springtime menu, add a sliced tomato and cucumber salad, sourdough bread, and fresh strawberries.

PREPARATION TIME: *About 12 minutes*
COOKING TIME: *About 15 minutes*

- 1 pound dried spaghetti
- 5 ounces bacon, chopped
- 5 cloves garlic, minced or pressed
- ½ cup fat-free reduced-sodium chicken broth
- 1 can (about 6½ oz.) chopped clams
- 1 can (about 2¼ oz.) sliced ripe olives, drained
- 1 can (about 6 oz.) water-packed albacore tuna, drained and flaked
  Minced parsley
  Lemon wedges

1. In a 6- to 8-quart pan, bring about 4 quarts water to a boil over high heat; stir in pasta and cook, uncovered, until just tender to bite (about 10 minutes). Or cook pasta according to package directions.

2. Meanwhile, cook bacon in a wide nonstick frying pan over medium-high heat, stirring often, for 5 minutes. Add garlic; continue to cook, stirring often, until bacon is browned and crisp (about 3 more minutes). Pour off and discard all but 2 tablespoons of the drippings from pan.

3. Add broth, clams and their liquid, and olives to pan with bacon. Bring mixture to a boil over high heat; reduce heat, cover, and keep warm.

4. Drain pasta well; return to cooking pan. Pour bacon mixture over pasta, then top with tuna; toss to mix well. Pour onto a platter, sprinkle with parsley; offer lemon wedges to season individual servings.

MAKES 6 SERVINGS

Per serving: 429 calories (22% calories from fat), 10 g total fat, 3 g saturated fat, 31 mg cholesterol, 399 mg sodium, 59 g carbohydrates, 2 g fiber, 23 g protein, 45 mg calcium, 8 mg iron

Pasta, Grains & Legumes

PASTA, PEARS & GORGONZOLA

172

Pasta, Pears & Gorgonzola

Spaghetti tossed with mild, juicy ripe pears and tangy Gorgonzola makes a simple entrée with out-of-the-ordinary appeal. Top the dish with a sprinkling of crisp toasted pecans.

PREPARATION TIME: *About 10 minutes*
COOKING TIME: *About 15 minutes*

12 ounces dried spaghetti

2 large soft-ripe Bartlett, red Bartlett, or d'Anjou pears (about 1 lb. *total*)

1 tablespoon lemon juice

1 cup (about 5 oz.) crumbled Gorgonzola or other blue-veined cheese

½ cup chopped Italian parsley

½ cup fat-free reduced-sodium chicken broth

½ teaspoon cornstarch

Salt and pepper

¼ cup toasted pecan halves

1. In a 5- to 6-quart pan, bring about 3 quarts water to a boil over high heat; stir in pasta and cook, uncovered, until just tender to bite (about 10 minutes). Or cook pasta according to package directions. Drain well; return to pan.

2. While pasta is cooking, cut each pear lengthwise into eighths; cut cores from pear wedges, then cut wedges crosswise into ¼-inch-thick slices. In a medium-size bowl, gently mix pears, lemon juice, cheese, and parsley; set aside.

3. In a 1- to 2-quart pan, stir together broth and cornstarch. Bring to a boil over high heat, stirring. Gently mix broth mixture and pear mixture into drained pasta. Season to taste with salt and pepper. Pour into a serving dish and sprinkle with pecans.

MAKES 4 SERVINGS

Per serving: 554 calories (28% calories from fat), 18 g total fat, 8 g saturated fat, 31 mg cholesterol, 567 mg sodium, 82 g carbohydrates, 5 g fiber, 20 g protein, 227 mg calcium, 4 mg iron

Smoked Salmon & Capellini

A creamy smoked salmon sauce tinged with lemon, orange, and fresh dill complements delicate capellini (sometimes called angel hair pasta). To make the sauce, you whisk fat-free sour cream into hot, seasoned broth, then keep the mixture warm over lowest heat (if the temperature is too high, the sauce may curdle or separate).

PREPARATION TIME: *About 10 minutes*
COOKING TIME: *8 to 10 minutes*

12 ounces fresh or dried capellini

1 cup fat-free reduced-sodium chicken broth

1 tablespoon grated lemon peel

1 tablespoon grated orange peel

1 cup fat-free sour cream

2 tablespoons minced fresh dill

5 to 8 ounces smoked salmon, cut into bite-size pieces

Dill sprigs and lemon wedges

1. In a 5- to 6-quart pan, bring about 3 quarts water to a boil over high heat; stir in pasta and cook, uncovered, until just tender to bite (1 to 2 minutes for fresh pasta, about 3 minutes for dried). Or cook pasta according to package directions.

2. While pasta water is heating, combine broth, lemon peel, and orange peel in a 2- to 3-quart pan. Cover and bring to a boil over high heat. Remove from heat and whisk in sour cream until smooth; then keep warm over very low heat.

3. Drain pasta well, rinse with hot water, and drain again. Return to cooking pan and add sour cream mixture, minced dill, and salmon. Toss to mix. Transfer to a serving bowl or 4 individual plates; garnish with dill sprigs and lemon wedges.

MAKES 4 SERVINGS

Per serving: 378 calories (10% calories from fat), 4 g total fat, 1 g saturated fat, 79 mg cholesterol, 1,166 mg sodium, 59 g carbohydrates, 2 g fiber, 23 g protein, 103 mg calcium, 3 mg iron

Capellini with Prosciutto & Capers

Convenient prewashed spinach speeds the preparation for this colorful side dish. The slivered leaves combine with red pepper strips and smoky prosciutto to dress up thin pasta strands.

PREPARATION TIME: *About 15 minutes*
COOKING TIME: *About 15 minutes*

- 1 package (about 10 oz.) prewashed fresh spinach
- 3 green onions
- 1 large red or yellow bell pepper (about 8 oz.), seeded and cut into thin strips
- 2 tablespoons drained capers
- 8 ounces dried capellini, broken in half
- 3 ounces prosciutto or bacon, coarsely chopped
- ⅓ cup balsamic vinegar
- ½ teaspoon fennel seeds

1. Remove and discard tough stems and any yellow or wilted leaves from spinach. Rinse and drain spinach; cut leaves lengthwise into slivers. Trim and discard root ends of onions; cut onions into 3-inch lengths, then sliver each piece lengthwise. Place spinach, onions, bell pepper, and capers in a large serving bowl and set aside.

2. In a 4- to 5-quart pan, bring about 8 cups water to a boil over high heat; stir in pasta and cook, uncovered, until just tender to bite (about 3 minutes). Or cook pasta according to package directions. Drain well, rinse with hot water, and drain again; keep warm.

3. In a wide nonstick frying pan, combine prosciutto and 2 tablespoons water. Cook over medium-high heat, stirring often, until prosciutto is tinged with brown (about 4 minutes). Add vinegar and fennel seeds to pan, stirring to loosen any browned bits. Bring to a boil; then boil, stirring, for 30 seconds.

4. Add pasta to vegetables, then pour prosciutto mixture over pasta and vegetables; toss until spinach is slightly wilted. Serve at once.

MAKES 4 TO 6 SERVINGS

Per serving: 232 calories (13% calories from fat), 3 g total fat, 1 g saturated fat, 14 mg cholesterol, 500 mg sodium, 39 g carbohydrates, 3 g fiber, 12 g protein, 54 mg calcium, 3 mg iron

Pasta with Fresh Puttanesca Sauce

Here's a quick, light version of a pasta classic. The simple sauce is based on fresh Roma tomatoes, diced and heated briefly with the traditional seasonings of garlic, olives, and anchovies.

PREPARATION TIME: *10 to 15 minutes*
COOKING TIME: *About 15 minutes*

- 8 ounces dried vermicelli
- 1 tablespoon olive oil
- 3 cloves garlic, minced or pressed
- 1 can (about 2 oz.) anchovies, drained, patted dry, and minced
- 1½ pounds pear-shaped (Roma-type) tomatoes, cut into ½-inch cubes
- 1 can (about 2¼ oz.) sliced ripe olives, drained
- 3 tablespoons drained capers
- ¾ to 1 teaspoon crushed red pepper flakes (optional)
- Grated Parmesan cheese

1. In a 4- to 5-quart pan, bring about 8 cups water to a boil over high heat; stir in pasta and cook, uncovered, until just tender to bite (7 to 9 minutes). Or cook pasta according to package directions.

2. Meanwhile, heat oil in a wide frying pan over medium-high heat. Add garlic and cook, stirring, just until soft but not browned (about 1 minute). Stir in anchovies, increase heat to high, and add tomatoes, olives, capers, and (if desired) red pepper flakes. Stir until tomatoes are heated through (about 3 minutes).

3. Drain pasta well and pour into a serving bowl; pour sauce over pasta and toss to mix. Offer cheese to add to taste.

MAKES 4 SERVINGS

Per serving: 322 calories (21% calories from fat), 8 g total fat, 1 g saturated fat, 6 mg cholesterol, 855 mg sodium, 52 g carbohydrates, 4 g fiber, 12 g protein, 62 mg calcium, 4 mg iron

CAPELLINI WITH PROSCIUTTO & CAPERS

Asparagus Pasta Risotto

A lookalike for rice, orzo provides quick satisfaction when you have a hankering for pasta. Stir in asparagus midway through the cooking time; top your "risotto" with a handful of fresh sage, heated in olive oil to release its flavor.

PREPARATION TIME: *About 20 minutes*
COOKING TIME: *About 20 minutes*

- 2 cups dried orzo or other tiny rice-shaped pasta
- 6 cups fat-free reduced-sodium chicken broth
- 4 cups sliced asparagus (1- to 2-inch pieces)
- ½ cup grated Parmesan cheese
- 2 tablespoons extra-virgin olive oil
- ½ cup fresh sage leaves
- Pepper
- Fresh sage leaves

1. In a 4- to 5-quart pan, stir together pasta and broth. Cover and bring to a boil over high heat. Reduce heat to medium-high; uncover and cook for 5 minutes, stirring occasionally. Add asparagus and continue to cook, uncovered, stirring occasionally, until pasta is barely tender to bite (8 to 10 minutes). Stir in cheese and remove from heat.

2. While pasta is cooking, heat oil in a small frying pan over medium heat. Add the ½ cup sage leaves and heat, stirring often, until edges just begin to curl (2 to 3 minutes). Remove pan from heat. With a slotted spoon, transfer sage leaves to paper towels to drain. Pour oil from pan over pasta mixture (use a spatula to scrape all oil from pan).

3. Crumble sage leaves; add to pasta and mix. Season to taste with pepper and garnish with additional sage leaves.

MAKES 4 SERVINGS

Per serving: 476 calories (22% calories from fat), 12 g total fat, 3 g saturated fat, 8 mg cholesterol, 1,037 mg sodium, 69 g carbohydrates, 3 g fiber, 24 g protein, 199 mg calcium, 5 mg iron

Penne with Sausage, Roasted Peppers & Greens

For a quick, trattoria-style supper, serve hearty penne in a bold red pepper–tomato sauce accented with spicy sausage and vitamin-rich mustard greens. Complete the menu with Italian rolls and a salad of mixed baby lettuces.

PREPARATION TIME: *About 10 minutes*
COOKING TIME: *About 15 minutes*

- 12 ounces dried penne
- 8 ounces turkey Italian sausage, casings removed
- 3 cloves garlic, minced or pressed
- 1 medium-size onion, chopped
- 1 large can (about 15 oz.) no-salt-added tomato sauce
- ½ cup dry red wine
- 1 jar (about 7¼ oz.) roasted red peppers (not oil-packed), drained and cut into thin strips
- 3 cups thinly sliced mustard greens
- ¼ cup shredded Parmesan cheese

1. In a 5- to 6-quart pan, bring about 3 quarts water to a boil over high heat; stir in pasta and cook, uncovered, until just tender to bite (8 to 10 minutes). Or cook pasta according to package directions. Drain well and return to cooking pan.

2. While pasta is cooking, crumble sausage into a 3- to 4-quart pan. Add garlic and onion. Cook over medium-high heat, stirring often, until sausage is browned (about 10 minutes). Add tomato sauce, wine, and red peppers. Bring to a boil over high heat, stirring often; then reduce heat to low and stir in mustard greens and 3 tablespoons of the cheese.

3. Pour tomato-sausage sauce over pasta and mix well; then pour into a serving bowl or onto 4 individual plates. Sprinkle with remaining 1 tablespoon cheese.

MAKES 4 SERVINGS

Per serving: 527 calories (17% calories from fat), 9 g total fat, 3 g saturated fat, 34 mg cholesterol, 569 mg sodium, 82 g carbohydrates, 5 g fiber, 25 g protein, 133 mg calcium, 6 mg iron

Orzo with Mint & Tomatoes

Cool, minted orzo with juicy fresh tomatoes is a refreshing accompaniment for broiled lamb or chicken on a warm evening. To preserve the mint's color, wait until just before serving to chop it and add it to the pasta.

PREPARATION TIME: *About 20 minutes*
COOKING TIME: *About 15 minutes*

- 2 **tablespoons olive oil**
- 2 **large onions, chopped**
- 3 **cups dried orzo or other tiny rice-shaped pasta**
- ½ **cup fat-free reduced-sodium chicken broth**
- ⅓ **cup lemon juice**
- ¼ **cup minced parsley**
- 2 **large tomatoes (about 1 lb. *total*), seeded and chopped**
- ½ **cup minced fresh mint**

1. Heat oil in a wide nonstick frying pan over medium-high heat. Add onions and cook, stirring often, until browned and sweet tasting (about 15 minutes). Remove from heat.

2. While onions are cooking, bring about 3 quarts water to a boil in a 5- to 6-quart pan over high heat; stir in pasta and cook, uncovered, until just tender to bite (about 10 minutes). Or cook pasta according to package directions. Drain, rinse with cold water and drain again.

3. Pour pasta into a large bowl and mix in onions, broth, lemon juice, and parsley. (At this point, you may cover and refrigerate for up to 3 hours.) Just before serving, gently stir in tomatoes and mint.

MAKES 10 SERVINGS

Per serving: 244 calories (14% calories from fat), 4 g total fat, 1 g saturated fat, 0 mg cholesterol, 40 mg sodium, 45 g carbohydrates, 3 g fiber, 8 g protein, 32 mg calcium, 3 mg iron

Asparagus Pesto Pasta

Preserve all the nutrition of asparagus by puréeing the cooked stems with garlic and basil to make a glorious sauce for fresh fettuccine. Keep the tips whole, then toss them with the finished pasta.

PREPARATION TIME: *About 20 minutes*
COOKING TIME: *About 10 minutes*

- 3 **tablespoons lemon juice**
- 2 **tablespoons extra-virgin olive oil**
- 3 **or 4 cloves garlic, peeled**
- ¼ **cup coarsely chopped fresh basil**
- 2 **pounds asparagus**
- 1 **pound fresh fettuccine or linguine**
  Salt and pepper
- ¼ **cup grated Parmesan cheese**

1. Place lemon juice, oil, garlic, and basil in a blender or food processor; set aside.

2. In a 5- to 6-quart pan, bring about 3 quarts water to a boil over high heat. Snap off and discard tough ends of asparagus. Add asparagus to boiling water. Cook, uncovered, until barely tender to bite (4 to 5 minutes). Lift asparagus from water with tongs; drain, then let cool slightly. Return water in pan to a boil; stir in pasta and cook, uncovered, until just tender to bite (about 3 minutes). Or cook pasta according to package directions.

3. Meanwhile, diagonally trim off top 3 to 4 inches of asparagus spears and place in a colander. Coarsely chop remaining part of asparagus spears and add to blender along with 6 tablespoons hot water from pasta pan. Whirl until mixture is smoothly puréed.

4. Drain pasta into colander containing asparagus tips. Transfer asparagus and pasta to a serving bowl; top with asparagus purée and toss to mix. Season to taste with salt and pepper; sprinkle with cheese.

MAKES 6 SERVINGS

Per serving: 308 calories (22% calories from fat), 8 g total fat, 2 g saturated fat, 58 mg cholesterol, 86 mg sodium, 48 g carbohydrates, 3 g fiber, 14 g protein, 93 mg calcium, 4 mg iron

Bow Tie Pasta Primavera

This springtime favorite is bright with a garden's worth of fresh vegetables —steamed until just tender, then tossed with fanciful farfalle and a light, creamy sauce. The recipe serves eight as a first course, four as a main dish.

PREPARATION TIME: *About 30 minutes*
COOKING TIME: *About 30 minutes*

- 8 ounces asparagus
- 1½ cups fresh broccoli flowerets
- 1 large carrot, peeled and sliced diagonally
- 1 cup sliced yellow zucchini or crookneck squash
- 2 teaspoons olive oil
- 1 cup sliced mushrooms
- ½ cup chopped onion
- ½ cup chopped red bell pepper
- 1 clove garlic, minced or pressed
- 8 ounces dried pasta bow ties (farfalle)
- 1 tablespoon butter or margarine
- 1 tablespoon all-purpose flour
- ¾ cup fat-free milk
- ¼ cup fat-free reduced-sodium chicken broth
- Salt and black pepper
- ⅓ cup grated Parmesan cheese
- 1 tablespoon chopped parsley
- 1 tablespoon chopped fresh basil

1. Snap off and discard tough ends of asparagus. Cut spears diagonally into 1-inch pieces. Arrange asparagus, broccoli, and carrot on a rack in a pan over boiling water. Cover and steam for 5 minutes. Add squash; cover and steam until all vegetables are tender-crisp to bite (about 5 more minutes). Set aside.

2. While vegetables are steaming, heat oil in a wide nonstick frying pan over medium heat. Add mushrooms, onion, bell pepper, and garlic; cook, stirring often, until onion is tender to bite (about 5 minutes). Set aside.

3. In a 4- to 5-quart pan, bring about 8 cups water to a boil over high heat; stir in pasta and cook, uncovered, until just tender to bite (8 to 10 minutes). Or cook pasta according to package directions. Drain well; keep warm.

4. Melt butter in a small pan over low heat. Stir in flour until smooth; then stir for 1 minute. Gradually add milk and broth, stirring constantly. Increase heat to medium and stir until sauce is thickened and bubbly. Season to taste with salt and black pepper. Reduce heat; keep warm.

5. Combine steamed vegetables, mushroom mixture, and pasta in a large serving bowl. Add sauce, ¼ cup of the cheese, parsley, and basil; toss to mix. Sprinkle with remaining cheese and serve.

MAKES 8 SERVINGS

Per serving: 187 calories (21% calories from fat), 4 g total fat, 2 g saturated fat, 7 mg cholesterol, 205 mg sodium, 29 g carbohydrates, 3 g fiber, 8 g protein, 115 mg calcium, 2 mg iron

Capellini with White Beans & Bell Peppers

Delicate angel hair pasta in a simple sauce of mild cannellini, bright bell peppers, and fresh oregano makes an easy light supper dish. Serve with a green salad and a crusty loaf such as Dried Tomato Basil Bread (page 211).

PREPARATION TIME: *About 20 minutes*
COOKING TIME: *About 10 minutes*

- 6 green onions
- 8 ounces dried capellini
- 1 tablespoon olive oil
- 2 large red bell peppers (about 1 lb. *total*), seeded and cut lengthwise into strips
- 2 cans (about 15 oz. *each*) cannellini (white kidney beans)
- 2 tablespoons chopped fresh oregano or 2 teaspoons dried oregano
- ¼ cup balsamic vinegar
- 2 tablespoons chopped fresh basil or 2 teaspoons dried basil

. Trim and discard root ends of onions. Cut onions into 2-inch lengths; then sliver each piece lengthwise. Set aside.

2. In a 4- to 5-quart pan, bring about 8 cups water to a boil over high heat; stir in pasta and cook, uncovered, until just tender to bite (about 3 minutes). Or cook pasta according to package directions. Drain, rinse with hot water, and drain again; return to pan and keep warm.

3. While pasta is cooking, heat oil in a 3- to 4-quart pan over medium-high heat. Add peppers and cook, stirring often, until tender-crisp to bite (3 to 4 minutes). Add beans and their liquid; stir in oregano. Bring to a boil; then reduce heat and simmer, stirring often, for 3 minutes.

4. Add bean mixture, onions, vinegar, and basil to pasta; lift with 2 forks to mix. Transfer pasta to a wide, shallow serving bowl.

MAKES 4 SERVINGS

Per serving: 440 calories (11% calories from fat), 5 g total fat, 1 g saturated fat, 0 mg cholesterol, 452 mg sodium, 80 g carbohydrates, 12 g fiber, 17 g protein, 112 mg calcium, 6 mg iron

Curry-spiced Couscous

Enriched with apricots, raisins, diced carrots, and an array of aromatic spices, this couscous accompanies roasted or broiled poultry with style. Try it with smoky barbecued pork tenderloin, too.

PREPARATION TIME: *About 15 minutes*
COOKING TIME: *About 15 minutes*

- 1 teaspoon vegetable oil
- 1 large onion, chopped
- 1 cup chopped carrots
- 1 teaspoon ground coriander
- ½ teaspoon ground cumin
- ½ teaspoon ground ginger
- ¼ teaspoon ground cinnamon
- 3⅓ cups fat-free reduced-sodium chicken broth
- 2 cups couscous
- ½ cup chopped dried apricots
- ½ cup golden raisins
-   Salt and pepper
- ⅓ cup chopped cilantro

1. Heat oil in a 5- to 6-quart pan over medium-high heat. Add onion and carrots; cook, stirring often, until onion is soft (about 8 minutes). If pan appears dry, add water, 1 tablespoon at a time. Stir in coriander, cumin, ginger, and cinnamon.

2. Add broth and bring to a boil over high heat. Stir in couscous, apricots, and raisins. Cover, remove from heat, and let stand until liquid has been absorbed (about 5 minutes). Fluff couscous with a fork; season to taste with salt and pepper. Stir in cilantro.

MAKES 8 SERVINGS

Per serving: 249 calories (4% calories from fat), 1 g total fat, 0 g saturated fat, 0 mg cholesterol, 246 mg sodium, 52 g carbohydrates, 4 g fiber, 8 g protein, 32 mg calcium, 1 mg iron

Couscous with Dill

Cool, dill-seasoned couscous is a perfect partner for chilled salmon or sliced cold chicken breast on a warm evening.

PREPARATION TIME: *About 15 minutes, plus at least 45 minutes to cool and chill*
COOKING TIME: *About 10 minutes*

1½ cups couscous
1 small cucumber (about 6 oz.), peeled, seeded, and diced
½ cup minced fresh dill
2 tablespoons olive oil
⅓ cup lemon juice
½ teaspoon ground cumin
Salt and pepper
Large butter lettuce leaves, rinsed and crisped
2 large tomatoes (about 1 lb. *total*), thinly sliced
Dill sprigs
1 cup fat-free sour cream

1. In a 3- to 4-quart pan, bring 2¼ cups water to a boil over high heat. Stir in couscous; cover, remove from heat, and let stand until liquid has been absorbed (about 5 minutes). Transfer couscous to a large, shallow bowl and let cool for about 15 minutes, fluffing occasionally with a fork.

2. Add cucumber, minced dill, oil, lemon juice, and cumin to couscous. Mix well; season to taste with salt and pepper. Cover and refrigerate until cool (at least 30 minutes) or for up to 4 hours; fluff occasionally with a fork.

3. Line a platter with lettuce leaves. Mound couscous in center; arrange tomatoes around couscous. Garnish with dill sprigs. Offer sour cream to add to taste.

MAKES 6 TO 8 SERVINGS

Per serving: 244 calories (16% calories from fat), 4 g total fat, 1 g saturated fat, 3 mg cholesterol, 42 mg sodium, 42 g carbohydrates, 2 g fiber, 8 g protein, 63 mg calcium, 1 mg iron

Mango Basmati Rice

The fragrance of basmati rice makes it a natural match for fruits, as in this refreshing side dish. Flavored with a nutmeg-scented mixture of orange and lime juices, it's a nice partner for grilled chicken or tuna. Garnish with rose petals, nasturtiums, or other edible flowers, if you like.

PREPARATION TIME: *About 20 minutes, plus 15 minutes for rice to cool*
COOKING TIME: *About 20 minutes*

2 cups white basmati rice
1 cup orange juice
½ cup lime juice
4 teaspoons sugar
About ¼ teaspoon freshly grated or ground nutmeg
2 medium-size firm-ripe mangoes (about 1 lb. *each*)
Salt

1. Place rice in a large bowl and add enough cool water to cover. Stir; then drain. Repeat this process several times, or until water is no longer cloudy. Drain rice well.

2. Transfer rice to a 2- to 3-quart pan and add 3 cups water. Bring to a boil over high heat; then reduce heat to very low, cover, and simmer until rice is tender to bite (about 15 minutes). Do not stir during cooking.

3. Pour hot rice into a colander to drain; let stand until warm (about 15 minutes).

4. In a wide bowl, combine orange juice, lime juice, sugar, and ¼ teaspoon of the nutmeg. Peel mangoes, then cut fruit from pits in small pieces and add to juice mixture in bowl. Mix in rice and season to taste with salt. Sprinkle with more nutmeg.

MAKES 8 SERVINGS

Per serving: 232 calories (4% calories from fat), 1 g total fat, 0 g saturated fat, 0 mg cholesterol, 25 mg sodium, 56 g carbohydrates, 1 g fiber, 6 g protein, 13 mg calcium, 0 mg iron

Cilantro Rice

Zesty green rice is good with a variety of main courses, from mild beef or turkey loaf to zippier choices such as Cornmeal-crusted Chicken (page 142) or Sea Bass with Chiles & Tomatoes (page 157). The green color comes from a purée of fresh cilantro, garlic, and jalapeño chile.

PREPARATION TIME: *About 10 minutes*
COOKING TIME: *About 20 minutes*

 1 cup lightly packed cilantro leaves
 2 cloves garlic, peeled
 1 fresh jalapeño chile, stemmed
2½ cups vegetable broth
 2 teaspoons olive oil
1½ cups long-grain white rice
 ½ teaspoon ground cumin
 ⅓ cup grated carrot
 ¼ cup sliced green onions
    Salt (optional)
    Cilantro sprigs

1. In a blender, whirl cilantro leaves, garlic, chile, and 1 cup of the broth until smoothly puréed. Set aside.

2. Heat oil in a 3- to 4-quart pan over medium heat. Add rice and cumin; cook, stirring often, until rice is pale golden (5 to 8 minutes). Stir in cilantro purée, remaining 1½ cups broth, carrot, and onions. Bring to a boil over high heat; then reduce heat, cover, and simmer until liquid has been absorbed and rice is tender to bite (about 18 minutes). Season to taste with salt, if desired.

3. To serve, spoon into a serving dish; garnish with cilantro sprigs.

MAKES 4 SERVINGS

Per serving: 297 calories (9% calories from fat), 3 g total fat, 0 g saturated fat, 0 mg cholesterol, 165 mg sodium, 60 g carbohydrates, 1 g fiber, 7 g protein, 33 mg calcium, 3 mg iron

Pine Nut Pilaf

A generous measure of sweet sherry and a lavish sprinkling of rich pine nuts give this simple rice-and-pasta pilaf a luxurious air.

PREPARATION TIME: *About 20 minutes*
COOKING TIME: *30 to 35 minutes*

 ½ cup 1-inch lengths of dried vermicelli
 2 tablespoons butter or margarine
 1 cup long-grain white rice
1⅓ cups fat-free reduced-sodium chicken broth
 ¾ cup cream sherry
 1 tablespoon chopped fresh thyme or 1 teaspoon dried thyme
 ⅓ cup sliced green onions
 ⅓ cup toasted pine nuts
    Thyme sprigs

1. Toast pasta in a wide frying pan over medium-high heat, stirring, until golden brown (about 2 minutes). Remove from pan and set aside.

2. Melt butter in pan; then add rice and cook, stirring, until grains begin to turn opaque (2 to 3 minutes).

3. Add vermicelli, broth, sherry, and chopped thyme. Bring to a boil over high heat; then reduce heat, cover, and simmer until liquid has been absorbed and rice is tender to bite (20 to 25 minutes).

4. Remove from heat and stir in onions. Pour pilaf into a serving bowl, sprinkle with pine nuts, and garnish with thyme sprigs.

MAKES 6 SERVINGS

Per serving: 242 calories (30% calories from fat), 8 g total fat, 3 g saturated fat, 10 mg cholesterol, 170 mg sodium, 37 g carbohydrates, 2 g fiber, 6 g protein, 21 mg calcium, 3 mg iron

PINE NUT PILAF

Rice with Coconut

A Caribbean favorite, this golden-hued rice gets its deceptively rich, creamy texture and flavor from reduced-fat coconut milk.

PREPARATION TIME: *About 20 minutes*
COOKING TIME: *35 to 40 minutes*

- 1 tablespoon olive oil
- 1 large onion, chopped
- 1 clove garlic, minced or pressed
- 1 large red bell pepper (about 8 oz.), seeded and chopped
- 2 cups long-grain white rice
- ½ teaspoon ground turmeric
- 1 can (about 14 oz.) light coconut milk
- 1½ cups vegetable broth or fat-free reduced-sodium chicken broth
- 2 tablespoons unsweetened shredded coconut

1. Heat oil in a 3- to 4-quart nonstick pan over medium-high heat. Add onion and cook, stirring often, until soft (about 5 minutes). Add garlic and bell pepper; cook, stirring often, until pepper is soft (about 3 minutes).

2. Add rice to pan; stir until grains begin to turn opaque (2 to 3 minutes). Add turmeric; stir for about 30 seconds. Add coconut milk and broth. Bring to a boil; then reduce heat, cover, and simmer until liquid has been absorbed and rice is tender to bite (20 to 25 minutes).

3. Spoon rice into a serving dish and sprinkle with coconut.

MAKES 6 TO 8 SERVINGS

Per serving: 274 calories (19% calories from fat), 6 g total fat, 3 g saturated fat, 0 mg cholesterol, 73 mg sodium, 50 g carbohydrates, 2 g fiber, 6 g protein, 25 mg calcium, 3 mg iron

Quinoa-stuffed Squash

Tiny, beadlike quinoa, a staple of the ancient Incas, contains more protein than any other grain—making it a good choice for vegetarian main dishes.

PREPARATION TIME: *About 30 minutes*
COOKING TIME: *About 1¼ hours*

- 10 to 12 Sweet Dumpling, Carnival, or Delicata squash (about 12 oz. each)
- ½ cup chopped pecans
- 1 tablespoon olive oil
- 2 large onions, chopped
- 2 cups chopped celery
- 5¼ cups vegetable broth
- 1½ cups wild rice, rinsed and drained
- 2 tablespoons chopped fresh sage or 2 teaspoons dried sage
- 1½ cups quinoa, rinsed and drained
- ⅔ cup chopped dried apricots
- ⅓ cup chopped dried cherries
- ⅓ cup chopped dried cranberries

1. Rinse squash and pierce each one with a fork several times. Set squash in two 9- by 13-inch baking pans. Add ¾ cup water to each pan and cover pans tightly with foil. Bake in a 350° oven until squash are tender when pierced (45 minutes to 1 hour), switching positions of baking pans halfway through baking. Keep cooked squash warm.

2. While squash are baking, pour pecans into a 4- to 5-quart pan and stir over medium heat until golden (about 5 minutes). Remove from pan and set aside.

3. Add oil, onions, and celery to pan; cook over medium-high heat, stirring often, until onions are soft (about 6 minutes). Add broth, rice, and sage. Bring to a boil over high heat; then reduce heat, cover, and simmer for 40 minutes. Stir in quinoa, cover, and continue to simmer until rice and quinoa are tender to bite (15 to 20 more minutes). Stir in pecans, apricots, cherries, and cranberries. Keep warm.

4. Hold each hot cooked squash with a thick towel to protect your hands. Then cut a ½- to ¾-inch-thick "lid" from top of each squash (or from side, if using Delicata). Scoop out and discard seeds. If needed, trim squash bases slightly so squash will sit steady and level.

5. Mound rice-quinoa stuffing into squash. Set lids atop, then serve.

MAKES 10 TO 12 SERVINGS

Per serving: 366 calories (16% calories from fat), 7 g total fat, 1 g saturated fat, 0 mg cholesterol, 166 mg sodium, 71 g carbohydrates, 11 g fiber, 12 g protein, 118 mg calcium, 5 mg iron

Pumpkin Risotto

Golden with canned pumpkin, this smooth risotto is a wholesome meatless main dish. Accompany it with a loaf of crusty Italian-style ciabatta and Red & Green Salad (page 95).

PREPARATION TIME: *About 5 minutes*
COOKING TIME: *About 10 minutes*

- 2 teaspoons butter or margarine
- 1 large onion, chopped
- 1/8 to 1/4 teaspoon ground nutmeg
- 2 tablespoons cornstarch
- 3 1/2 cups fat-free reduced-sodium chicken broth
- 1/2 cup dry white wine
- 1 cup canned solid-pack pumpkin
- 3 cups precooked dried white rice
- 1 cup (about 4 oz.) grated Parmesan cheese
- Salt and freshly ground pepper

1. Melt butter in a 4- to 5-quart pan over high heat. Add onion and nutmeg. Cook, stirring often, until onion is soft (3 to 4 minutes).

2. In a small bowl, stir together cornstarch and a little of the broth to blend smoothly; stir into onion mixture. Then add remaining broth, wine, pumpkin, and rice. Stir over high heat until mixture comes to a boil (3 to 4 minutes). Cover, remove from heat, and let stand until rice is tender to bite (about 5 minutes).

3. Stir 3/4 cup of the cheese into rice mixture; season to taste with salt and pepper. Spoon risotto onto 4 individual plates and sprinkle with remaining 1/4 cup cheese.

MAKES 4 SERVINGS

Per serving: 470 calories (17% calories from fat), 8 g total fat, 5 g saturated fat, 21 mg cholesterol, 893 mg sodium, 74 g carbohydrates, 3 g fiber, 18 g protein, 319 mg calcium, 4 mg iron

Creamy Corn Polenta

Craving comfort food? Polenta cooked with creamed corn soothes frayed nerves after a hectic day. Serve it with crusty bread and an antipasto assortment of cherry tomatoes, artichoke hearts, and tangy olives.

PREPARATION TIME: *About 5 minutes*
COOKING TIME: *About 25 minutes*

- 4 cups vegetable broth or fat-free reduced-sodium chicken broth
- 1 cup polenta or yellow cornmeal
- 2 cans (about 15 oz. *each*) cream-style corn
- 6 ounces teleme or Münster cheese, thinly sliced (cut teleme into small chunks if it is too soft to slice)
- 1/2 cup thinly sliced green onions
- 1/2 cup bottled roasted red peppers (not oil-packed), drained and cut into strips
- Freshly ground black pepper

1. In a 3- to 4-quart pan, smoothly mix broth and polenta. Bring to a boil over medium-high heat. Reduce heat and simmer, uncovered, stirring often and scraping pan bottom with a long-handled spoon (mixture will spatter), until polenta is thick and tastes creamy (about 15 minutes). Stir in corn; cook, stirring often, until mixture is hot (about 5 minutes).

2. Spoon polenta into 4 individual bowls. Lay a fourth of the cheese atop each bowl of polenta; sprinkle with onions. Arrange red peppers decoratively over polenta. Sprinkle with black pepper.

MAKES 4 SERVINGS

Per serving: 553 calories (19% calories from fat), 12 g total fat, 5 g saturated fat, 15 mg cholesterol, 1,101 mg sodium, 98 g carbohydrates, 10 g fiber, 19 g protein, 325 mg calcium, 3 mg iron

Spicy Bean Enchiladas

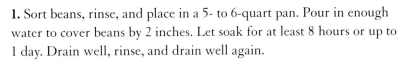

Family and guests alike will appreciate these hearty enchiladas. If you like, you can use canned beans in the filling; just simmer two or three 15-ounce cans of pinto beans with a little minced garlic for flavor, drain and mash them, and mix them with homemade tomato sauce and spices as the recipe directs.

PREPARATION TIME: *About 20 minutes, plus at least 8 hours to soak beans*
COOKING TIME: *About 2 hours*

- 12 **ounces dried pinto beans**
- 2 **cloves garlic, minced or pressed**
- 1 **dried bay leaf**
- ⅛ **teaspoon salt**
  Tomato-Chile Sauce (recipe follows)
- 12 **corn tortillas (*each* about 6 inches in diameter)**
- 2 **teaspoons chili powder**
- ¼ **teaspoon pepper**
- 1 **cup (about 4 oz.) shredded reduced-fat Cheddar cheese**
- ¾ **cup fat-free sour cream**
- ¼ **cup chopped green onions**

1. Sort beans, rinse, and place in a 5- to 6-quart pan. Pour in enough water to cover beans by 2 inches. Let soak for at least 8 hours or up to 1 day. Drain well, rinse, and drain well again.

2. Return beans to pan and add 8 cups water, garlic, bay leaf, and salt. Bring to a boil; then reduce heat, cover, and simmer until beans are soft when mashed (about 1½ hours).

3. Meanwhile, prepare Tomato-Chile Sauce.

4. Stack tortillas, wrap in foil, and heat in a 350° oven until warm (about 10 minutes). Meanwhile, drain beans; remove and discard bay leaf. Place beans in a large bowl and mash with a potato masher or fork. Stir in ½ cup of the Tomato-Chile Sauce, ½ cup water, chili powder, and pepper.

5. Spread ⅓ cup of the bean mixture down center of each tortilla. Loosely roll tortillas around filling and place, seam side down, in a lightly oiled 9- by 13-inch baking dish. Spoon remaining Tomato-Chile Sauce over tortillas.

6. Cover and bake in a 350° oven until enchiladas are hot in center (about 20 minutes). Uncover, sprinkle with cheese, and continue to bake until cheese is melted (about 5 more minutes). Offer sour cream and onions to add to taste.

MAKES 6 SERVINGS.

Tomato-Chile Sauce. In a 1½- to 2-quart pan, combine 2 cans (about 8 oz. *each*) **no-salt-added tomato sauce;** 1 can (about 4 oz.) **diced green chiles;** ¾ cup chopped **green onions;** 2 teaspoons **chili powder;** 1 teaspoon **ground cumin;** ¼ teaspoon **dried oregano;** and 1 clove **garlic,** minced or pressed. Cook over medium heat until hot, stirring occasionally (about 5 minutes). Then remove from heat, cover, and refrigerate until ready to use.

Per serving: 439 calories (12% calories from fat), 6 g total fat, 3 g saturated fat, 16 mg cholesterol, 459 mg sodium, 75 g carbohydrates, 12 g fiber, 24 g protein, 389 mg calcium, 6 mg iron

Polenta with Tomato-Mushroom Sauce

This satisfying vegetarian treat features creamy polenta topped with meaty portabella mushrooms in an herbed tomato-wine sauce.

PREPARATION TIME: *About 15 minutes*
COOKING TIME: *About 30 minutes*

- 8 ounces portabella mushrooms, coarsely chopped
- 1 large onion, chopped
- 1 tablespoon olive oil
- 1 cup dry white or red wine
- 1 can (about 6 oz.) tomato paste
- 1 teaspoon dried oregano
- ¾ teaspoon dried thyme
- 1½ cups polenta or yellow cornmeal
- 1 cup low-fat (1%) milk
- ½ cup grated Parmesan cheese

1. In a wide nonstick frying pan, combine mushrooms and ¼ cup water. Cook over high heat, stirring often, until mushrooms are soft (5 to 7 minutes); if pan appears dry, add water, 2 tablespoons at a time. Add onion and oil; cook, stirring often, until onion is lightly browned (about 5 minutes).

2. Add wine, 1 cup water, tomato paste, oregano, and thyme. Bring to a boil; then reduce heat and simmer, uncovered, stirring occasionally, until sauce is reduced to 3 cups (about 10 minutes).

3. While sauce is simmering, smoothly mix polenta, 4½ cups water, and milk in a 3- to 4-quart pan. Bring to a boil over medium-high heat, stirring. Reduce heat and simmer, uncovered, stirring often and scraping pan bottom with a long-handled spoon (mixture will spatter), until polenta is thick and tastes creamy (about 15 minutes). To serve, spoon polenta into 6 individual shallow bowls; top with sauce. Offer cheese to add to taste.

MAKES 6 SERVINGS

Per serving: 393 calories (14% calories from fat), 7 g total fat, 2 g saturated fat, 7 mg cholesterol, 373 mg sodium, 67 g carbohydrates, 9 g fiber, 12 g protein, 182 mg calcium, 4 mg iron

Black Bean Chili

The unusual topping for this mildly seasoned chili is a colorful mix of chopped orange and radish, piquant with fresh lime juice. For dessert, offer ripe Comice pear wedges to dip into warmed chocolate sauce.

PREPARATION TIME: *About 15 minutes*
COOKING TIME: *About 20 minutes*

- 3 medium-size oranges (about 8 oz. *each*)
- 2 tablespoons vegetable oil
- 1 large onion, chopped
- 4 cans (about 15 oz. *each*) black beans
- 3 tablespoons chili powder
- 1½ teaspoons cumin seeds
- ½ teaspoon ground red pepper (cayenne)
- ½ cup coarsely chopped radishes
- 3 tablespoons lime juice
- ½ cup fat-free sour cream

1. Squeeze juice from one of the oranges to make ½ cup. Set juice and remaining 2 oranges aside.

2. Heat oil in a 3- to 4-quart pan over high heat. Add onion and cook, stirring often, until soft (about 4 minutes). Reduce heat to low. Drain beans, reserving liquid; then rinse beans and add to pan along with chili powder, cumin seeds, red pepper, and the ½ cup orange juice. Stir to combine. Cover and simmer, stirring occasionally, for 15 minutes; if chili becomes too thick or begins to stick to pan, stir in some of the reserved bean liquid.

3. Meanwhile, cut peel and all white membrane from remaining 2 oranges; then cut oranges into ½-inch chunks and place in a small bowl. Stir in radishes and lime juice.

4. Spoon chili equally into 4 individual bowls. Top with orange-radish mixture. Offer sour cream to add to taste.

MAKES 4 SERVINGS

Per serving: 431 calories (21% calories from fat), 10 g total fat, 1 g saturated fat, 3 mg cholesterol, 777 mg sodium, 68 g carbohydrates, 17 g fiber, 20 g protein, 202 mg calcium, 6 mg iron

Lentil & Vegetable Ragout

This hearty medley of lentils and braised vegetables is a great partner for roast turkey breast or chicken. Or serve it as a satisfying main dish, perhaps accompanied by Sunflower Soda Bread (page 213) and a fresh fruit plate.

PREPARATION TIME: *About 20 minutes*
COOKING TIME: *30 to 35 minutes*

- 2 cups vegetable broth or fat-free reduced-sodium chicken broth
- 1 cup lentils, sorted and rinsed
- ¼ cup golden raisins
- 1 teaspoon dried oregano
- 1 medium-size onion, slivered
- 1 medium-size red bell pepper (about 6 oz.), seeded and cut into thin strips
- 1 small eggplant (about 1 lb.), peeled and cut into ½-inch cubes
- 1 tablespoon chopped fresh basil or ½ teaspoon dried basil
- 1 tablespoon chopped fresh thyme or 1 teaspoon dried thyme
- 1 small zucchini (about 6 oz.), cut crosswise into ¼-inch-thick slices
- 1 large tomato (about 8 oz.), chopped and drained

1. In a 1½- to 2-quart pan, bring broth to a boil over high heat. Add lentils, raisins, and oregano; then reduce heat, cover, and simmer just until lentils are tender to bite (25 to 30 minutes).

2. Meanwhile, combine onion, bell pepper, eggplant, chopped basil, thyme, and ½ cup water in a wide nonstick frying pan. Cover and cook over medium-high heat until vegetables are almost tender when pierced (about 5 minutes). Uncover pan and add zucchini; continue to cook, uncovered, stirring gently, until almost all liquid has evaporated and zucchini is just tender to bite (about 3 more minutes). If vegetables are cooked before lentils are done, remove them from heat and keep warm.

3. Drain any remaining cooking liquid from lentils; then add lentils and tomato to eggplant mixture. Stir gently over medium heat just until well combined and heated through.

MAKES 4 TO 6 SERVINGS

Per serving: 215 calories (3% calories from fat), 1 g total fat, 0 g saturated fat, 0 mg cholesterol, 114 mg sodium, 42 g carbohydrates, 8 g fiber, 14 g protein, 74 mg calcium, 5 mg iron

Tuscan Beans

Dotted with vegetables and fresh rosemary, these fragrant beans are a quick accompaniment to roasted or grilled pork tenderloin or leg of lamb.

PREPARATION TIME: *About 15 minutes*
COOKING TIME: *25 to 35 minutes*

- 1 teaspoon olive oil
- 1 medium-size carrot, finely chopped
- 1 stalk celery, finely chopped
- 1 small onion, finely chopped
- 1 clove garlic, minced or pressed
- 2 ounces sliced prosciutto, finely chopped
- 2 cans (about 15 oz. *each*) cannellini (white kidney beans), rinsed and drained
- 2 teaspoons minced fresh rosemary
- ¼ cup fat-free reduced-sodium chicken broth
- 1 pear-shaped (Roma-type) tomato, seeded and chopped
- Salt and freshly ground pepper

1. Heat oil in a 2½- to 3-quart pan over medium-high heat. Add carrot, celery, and onion; cook, stirring often, until onion is soft (3 to 5 minutes). Mix in garlic and prosciutto; stir just until mixture is lightly browned (about 1 more minute).

2. Stir in beans, rosemary, broth, and tomato. Bring to a boil; then reduce heat, cover, and simmer until vegetables are very tender to bite (20 to 25 minutes). Season to taste with salt and pepper.

MAKES 6 TO 8 SERVINGS

Per serving: 126 calories (18% calories from fat), 3 g total fat, 0 g saturated fat, 7 mg cholesterol, 332 mg sodium, 17 g carbohydrates, 6 g fiber, 9 g protein, 38 mg calcium, 2 mg iron

White Bean Gratin

Here's a hearty casserole to serve with broiled reduced-fat sausages—or on its own, as a filling supper dish. Either way, accompany it with a crisp green salad and a loaf of warm rye bread.

PREPARATION TIME: *About 20 minutes*
COOKING TIME: *About 1 hour*

3 slices sourdough sandwich bread (about 3 oz. *total*), torn into pieces

1 slice bacon, chopped

2 medium-size red onions (about 1 lb. *total*), finely chopped

2 cans (about 15 oz. *each*) cannellini (white kidney beans), rinsed and drained

1 tablespoon chopped fresh basil or 1 teaspoon dried basil

1 teaspoon cider vinegar
   Salt and pepper

½ cup beef broth (skimmed of fat) or water

2 to 3 tablespoons brandy, beef broth (skimmed of fat), or water

¾ cup shredded Parmesan cheese

1. In a food processor, whirl bread to form coarse crumbs. Sprinkle half the crumbs over bottom of a lightly greased shallow 2½- to 3-quart baking dish.

2. Combine bacon and onions in a wide nonstick frying pan over medium-high heat; cook, stirring often, until onions are tinged with brown (5 to 7 minutes). If pan appears dry, add water, 1 tablespoon at a time. Remove from heat. Stir in beans, remaining bread crumbs, basil, and vinegar; season to taste with salt and pepper. Spoon bean mixture over crumbs in baking dish.

3. In a cup, stir together broth and brandy; pour over bean mixture. Cover and bake in a 400° oven until bean mixture is bubbly and heated through (about 30 minutes). Uncover, sprinkle with cheese, and continue to bake until cheese is melted and tinged with brown (about 15 more minutes).

MAKES 6 SERVINGS

Per serving: 264 calories (26% calories from fat), 8 g total fat, 4 g saturated fat, 14 mg cholesterol, 624 mg sodium, 32 g carbohydrates, 8 g fiber, 17 g protein, 263 mg calcium, 2 mg iron

Beer-baked Beans

For picnics, potlucks, and casual parties, baked beans are an all-time favorite. This quick-to-make version starts with canned beans and gets a little extra flavor from a half-cup of beer (either regular or nonalcoholic, as you prefer).

PREPARATION TIME: *About 5 minutes*
COOKING TIME: *About 30 minutes*

6 slices bacon, coarsely chopped

2 medium-size red onions (about 1 lb. *total*), chopped

2 cans (about 15 oz. *each*) pinto beans

1 can (about 8 oz.) tomato sauce

½ cup regular or nonalcoholic beer

3 tablespoons molasses

1 to 2 tablespoons Dijon mustard

¼ teaspoon pepper
   Salt

1. In a 3- to 4-quart pan, cook bacon and half the onions over medium heat, stirring often, until browned bits form on pan bottom and onions are soft (8 to 10 minutes). Remove from heat; pour off and discard any drippings from pan.

2. Drain beans, reserving ¼ cup of the liquid; transfer to a 2- to 2½-quart baking dish. Stir in tomato sauce, ¼ cup of the beer, molasses, mustard, pepper, and onion mixture. If mixture looks dry, add enough of the reserved bean liquid for desired consistency. Cover and bake in a 350° oven until bubbly and heated through (about 20 minutes).

3. To serve, stir in remaining ¼ cup beer and season to taste with salt. Offer remaining onions to sprinkle over individual servings.

MAKES 6 SERVINGS

Per serving: 235 calories (28% calories from fat), 7 g total fat, 2 g saturated fat, 8 mg cholesterol, 861 mg sodium, 33 g carbohydrates, 6 g fiber, 9 g protein, 85 mg calcium, 3 mg iron

Split Pea Tagine

Green split peas simmered in a sweetly spiced broth with plenty of golden raisins make a hearty vegetarian entrée that's very low in fat. Serve with fluffy rice and a sliced cucumber salad.

PREPARATION TIME: *About 25 minutes*
COOKING TIME: *About 35 minutes*

2 cups vegetable broth

1 cup green split peas, sorted and rinsed

1 cup golden raisins

½ teaspoon dried thyme

¼ cup orange marmalade

¼ teaspoon ground ginger

¼ teaspoon ground cinnamon

⅛ teaspoon ground saffron or a large pinch of saffron threads

2 large tomatoes (about 1 lb. *total*), diced

⅓ cup cilantro leaves

⅓ cup thinly sliced green onions
   About 4 cups hot cooked rice

4 to 8 whole green onions, ends trimmed

1. In a 1½- to 2-quart pan, bring broth to a boil over high heat. Add peas, raisins, and thyme. Reduce heat, cover, and simmer until peas are almost tender to bite (about 20 minutes). Drain and discard any remaining cooking liquid.

2. Add marmalade, ginger, cinnamon, and saffron to pea mixture. Stir over medium-high heat until marmalade is melted and mixture is hot. Stir in tomatoes and reduce heat so mixture boils very gently; then cook, stirring gently, just until heated through (about 3 minutes). Remove from heat and stir in cilantro and sliced onions.

3. To serve, spoon rice onto a platter or 4 individual plates; top with pea mixture. Garnish with whole green onions.

MAKES 4 SERVINGS

Per serving: 577 calories (2% calories from fat), 2 g total fat, 0 g saturated fat, 0 mg cholesterol, 165 mg sodium, 126 g carbohydrates, 8 g fiber, 20 g protein, 104 mg calcium, 6 mg iron

Vegetables

Maple-Mustard Green Beans

Tender-crisp whole green beans in a sweet-tart mustard sauce are just right with holiday dinners of turkey breast, chicken, or pork tenderloin.

PREPARATION TIME: *About 10 minutes*
COOKING TIME: *About 10 minutes*

2 **pounds green beans, ends trimmed**

2 **tablespoons coarse-grained Dijon mustard**

3 **tablespoons balsamic vinegar**

1½ **tablespoons maple syrup**

2 **teaspoons extra-virgin olive oil**

Salt and freshly ground pepper

2 **tablespoons thinly sliced green onion**

1. In a 4- to 5-quart pan, bring about 8 cups water to a boil over high heat. Add beans and cook, uncovered, until tender-crisp to bite (5 to 8 minutes).

2. Meanwhile, in a small bowl, mix mustard, vinegar, syrup, and oil.

3. Drain beans and pour into a serving bowl. Pour mustard mixture over hot beans and mix to coat. Season to taste with salt and pepper and sprinkle with onion.

MAKES 8 SERVINGS

Per serving: 56 calories (20% calories from fat), 1 g total fat, 0 g saturated fat, 0 mg cholesterol, 97 mg sodium, 10 g carbohydrates, 2 g fiber, 2 g protein, 41 mg calcium, 1 mg iron

Green Beans with Garlic Crumbs

If you feel that fresh green beans need a little adornment, try this recipe. Slender beans are boiled just until tender-crisp, then topped with a pan-toasted combination of sourdough crumbs and garlic.

PREPARATION TIME: *5 to 10 minutes*
COOKING TIME: *About 15 minutes*

3 **slices sourdough sandwich bread (about 3 oz.** *total***), torn into pieces**

2 **teaspoons olive oil**

2 **cloves garlic, minced or pressed**

2 **pounds slender green beans, ends trimmed**

About ⅛ teaspoon salt

Freshly ground pepper

1. In a food processor or blender, whirl bread to form fine crumbs. Pour crumbs into a wide nonstick frying pan; add oil and garlic. Cook over medium-high heat, stirring often, until crumbs are lightly browned (5 to 7 minutes). Remove crumbs from pan and set aside. Wipe pan clean (be careful; pan is hot).

2. To pan, add beans, ⅓ cup water, and salt. Cover and cook over medium-high heat until beans are just tender-crisp to bite (5 to 6 minutes). Then uncover and continue to cook, stirring, until all liquid has evaporated.

3. Arrange beans on a platter and sprinkle with crumb mixture. Season to taste with pepper.

MAKES 8 SERVINGS

Per serving: 71 calories (18% calories from fat), 2 g total fat, 0 g saturated fat, 0 mg cholesterol, 107 mg sodium, 13 g carbohydrates, 2 g fiber, 3 g protein, 46 mg calcium, 1 mg iron

Asparagus with Rosemary & Prosciutto

Thick, sweet springtime asparagus doesn't need much dressing up, and it doesn't get much here—the tender spears are seasoned with nothing more than prosciutto, garlic, and fresh rosemary.

PREPARATION TIME: *About 10 minutes*
COOKING TIME: *About 20 minutes*

18 thick asparagus spears (about 1½ lbs. *total*)
½ to 1 ounce sliced prosciutto or bacon, chopped
2 cloves garlic, minced or pressed
1½ teaspoons chopped fresh rosemary or ½ teaspoon dried rosemary
   Lemon wedges and rosemary sprigs

1. Snap off and discard tough ends of asparagus. Then trim ends of spears so that spears are all the same length (reserve trimmings for soups or salads). For the sweetest flavor and most tender texture, peel spears with a vegetable peeler.

2. In a wide nonstick frying pan, bring about 1 inch water to a boil over medium-high heat. Add as much asparagus as will fit without crowding (6 to 9 spears) and cook, uncovered, until just tender when pierced (about 4 minutes). Lift from pan with a slotted spoon and place in a bowl of ice water to cool. Repeat to cook remaining asparagus. Drain cooled asparagus well; arrange on a large platter and set aside.

3. Wipe pan dry. Add prosciutto to pan and cook over medium-high heat, stirring often, just until crisp (about 1 minute). Remove from pan with a slotted spoon and set aside. Add garlic, chopped rosemary, and 2 tablespoons water to pan; stir just until garlic is fragrant (about 30 seconds; do not scorch). Pour garlic mixture over asparagus; sprinkle with prosciutto and garnish with lemon wedges and rosemary sprigs.

MAKES 4 SERVINGS.

Per serving: 45 calories (17% calories from fat), 1 g total fat, 0 g saturated fat, 4 mg cholesterol, 101 mg sodium, 6 g carbohydrates, 1 g fiber, 6 g protein, 33 mg calcium, 1 mg iron

Yam Puff

Lemon peel and nutmeg accent this delicate puff of steamed yams. It's light, seemingly creamy, and perfect with roast or grilled chicken or turkey—and it has just 1 gram of fat per serving.

PREPARATION TIME: *About 15 minutes*
COOKING TIME: *About 40 minutes*

3¼ to 3½ pounds yams or sweet potatoes
¾ cup fat-free or light sour cream
   About 2 tablespoons grated lemon peel
¼ teaspoon ground nutmeg
   Salt

1. Peel yams and cut into ½-inch chunks. Arrange on a rack in a pan over boiling water; cover and steam until tender when pierced (about 15 minutes).

2. Place cooked yams in a large bowl. Add sour cream, 2 tablespoons of the lemon peel, and nutmeg; beat with an electric mixer on medium speed until very smooth (about 3 minutes). Season to taste with salt. Spoon into a buttered 1½- to 2-quart casserole.

3. Cover and bake in a 375° oven until yam mixture is hot in center (about 20 minutes). Garnish with a sprinkling of lemon peel.

MAKES 6 SERVINGS

Per serving: 302 calories (3% calories from fat), 1 g total fat, 0 g saturated fat, 5 mg cholesterol, 52 mg sodium, 68 g carbohydrates, 9 g fiber, 5 g protein, 81 mg calcium, 1 mg iron

ASPARAGUS WITH ROSEMARY & PROSCIUTTO

Brandied Potatoes

Festive accompaniments can elevate simply cooked poultry or meat to heights of holiday splendor. One good example of such a dish is this golden gratin of sliced russet potatoes and yams, baked in a brandy-spiked broth and crowned with a light crust of Parmesan cheese.

PREPARATION TIME: *About 15 minutes*
BAKING TIME: *About 1½ hours*

2 **pounds russet potatoes**
2 **pounds yams or sweet potatoes**
   Freshly ground pepper
¾ **cup fat-free reduced-sodium chicken broth (or beef broth, skimmed of fat)**
⅓ **cup brandy (or additional broth)**
8 **ounces teleme or jack cheese, thinly sliced (cut teleme into small chunks if it is too soft to slice)**
⅓ **cup grated Parmesan cheese**

1. Peel potatoes and yams; then cut them crosswise into slices about ⅛ inch thick.

2. Cover bottom of a lightly greased shallow 2½- to 3-quart baking dish with a layer of alternating potato and yam slices, overlapping slices to fit. Sprinkle lightly with pepper. Repeat layers to use remaining potatoes and yams.

3. In a small pan, bring broth to a simmer over high heat. Remove from heat, stir in brandy, and pour over potatoes. Cover and bake in a 375° oven until potatoes and yams are tender when pierced (about 1¼ hours).

4. Uncover dish and top potato mixture evenly with teleme and Parmesan cheeses. Continue to bake until cheese is melted and browned (about 15 more minutes).

MAKES 8 SERVINGS

Per serving: 298 calories (26% calories from fat), 9 g total fat, 4 g saturated fat, 14 mg cholesterol, 276 mg sodium, 46 g carbohydrates, 6 g fiber, 10 g protein, 262 mg calcium, 1 mg iron

Potato & Gruyère Gratin

The traditional potato gratin is made with a buttery crumb topping and plenty of cheese and cream. This lighter alternative retains a deceptively rich flavor, and it's very easy to make. The potato slices bake in fat-free broth and are gilded with just a thin layer of shredded Gruyère cheese.

PREPARATION TIME: *About 15 minutes*
BAKING TIME: *1 to 1¼ hours*

3¼ **to 3½ pounds thin-skinned potatoes**
3 **cups fat-free reduced-sodium chicken broth or vegetable broth**
½ **teaspoon ground nutmeg**
½ **teaspoon pepper**
½ **cup shredded Gruyère, Cheddar, or fontina cheese**

1. Peel potatoes, cut into ⅛- to ¼-inch-thick slices, and place in a shallow 3-quart baking dish. Shake dish to settle potatoes.

2. In a small bowl, stir together broth, nutmeg, and pepper. Pour broth mixture over potatoes and bake in a 425° oven until potatoes are very tender when pierced (1 to 1¼ hours). As potatoes get dry on top, tilt casserole and spoon up some of the broth to baste them.

3. Sprinkle potatoes evenly with cheese. Continue to bake until cheese is melted (about 3 more minutes).

4. Let potatoes stand for 5 to 10 minutes to allow most of the remaining liquid to soak into them; then serve.

MAKES 6 SERVINGS

Per serving: 230 calories (13% calories from fat), 3 g total fat, 2 g saturated fat, 10 mg cholesterol, 326 mg sodium, 42 g carbohydrates, 4 g fiber, 9 g protein, 113 mg calcium, 2 mg iron

Garlic Mashed Potatoes

Cooked with whole cloves of garlic in chicken broth, these potatoes are mashed, seasoned with yogurt and fresh herbs, and baked with a light topping of reduced-fat cheese.

PREPARATION TIME: *About 15 minutes*
COOKING TIME: *About 1 hour*

- 4 pounds russet potatoes, peeled and quartered
- 2 to 4 cloves garlic, peeled
- 8 cups fat-free reduced-sodium chicken broth
- 1 cup fat-free milk
- ½ cup plain nonfat yogurt
- 2 tablespoons snipped chives
- 1 tablespoon minced fresh dill
- 1 teaspoon salt
  White pepper
- ¾ cup shredded reduced-fat jack cheese

1. In a 6- to 8-quart pan, combine potatoes, garlic, and broth. Bring to a boil over high heat; then reduce heat, cover, and simmer until potatoes are tender when pierced (about 20 minutes).

2. Drain potatoes and garlic, discarding any remaining cooking liquid; return to pan. Add milk and mash with a potato masher until smooth. Stir in yogurt, chives, dill, and salt; season to taste with pepper. Spoon potatoes into a shallow 2- to 3-quart baking dish; sprinkle with cheese. (At this point, you may cover and refrigerate for up to 1 day.)

3. Bake in a 375° oven until potatoes are hot in center and cheese is lightly browned (about 30 minutes; about 1 hour if refrigerated).

MAKES 8 SERVINGS

Per serving: 223 calories (9% calories from fat), 2 g total fat, 1 g saturated fat, 8 mg cholesterol, 697 mg sodium, 40 g carbohydrates, 3 g fiber, 11 g protein, 163 mg calcium, 1 mg iron

Spinach Pesto Potato Casserole

A lattice of spinach-parsley pesto and a sprinkling of crisp, garlicky crumbs top mashed potatoes enriched with cream cheese. (You can make the potatoes fresh, or use leftover or instant mashed potatoes.)

PREPARATION TIME: *About 20 minutes*
COOKING TIME: *40 to 45 minutes*

- 3 slices sourdough sandwich bread (about 3 oz. *total*), torn into pieces
- 4 cloves garlic, peeled and chopped
- 2 cups firmly packed fresh spinach leaves
- 1½ cups firmly packed parsley sprigs
- 2 tablespoons olive oil or vegetable oil
- 1 teaspoon grated lemon peel
- 1 large package (about 8 oz.) fat-free cream cheese, at room temperature
- 1 large egg
- 2 large egg whites (about ¼ cup)
  About 8 cups unseasoned mashed potatoes
- 1½ cups fat-free sour cream

1. In a food processor or blender, whirl bread and 2 cloves of the garlic until bread is in coarse crumbs. Sprinkle two-thirds of the crumb mixture over bottom of a shallow 3- to 3½-quart baking dish; set aside. Reserve remaining crumb mixture.

2. To food processor, add spinach, parsley, remaining 2 cloves garlic, oil, 2 tablespoons water, and lemon peel. Whirl until smoothly puréed. Set aside.

3. In a large bowl, beat cream cheese with an electric mixer on high speed until fluffy. Beat in egg, then egg whites. Add potatoes and stir to mix well. Spread potato mixture over crumbs in baking dish. With tip of a knife, make shallow stripes or a lattice pattern atop potatoes; spoon spinach pesto into these depressions.

4. Cover tightly and bake in a 375° oven until potatoes are hot in center (about 35 minutes). Uncover, sprinkle with remaining crumb mixture, and bake until crumbs are tinged with brown (5 to 10 more minutes). Offer sour cream to add to taste.

MAKES 10 TO 12 SERVINGS

Per serving: 284 calories (30% calories from fat), 10 g total fat, 2 g saturated fat, 28 mg cholesterol, 665 mg sodium, 40 g carbohydrates, 4 g fiber, 11 g protein, 203 mg calcium, 3 mg iron

ROASTED BEETS WITH BALSAMIC GLAZE

Roasted Beets with Balsamic Glaze

Like Roasted Roots (page 205), these beets gain extra sweetness from baking in a very hot oven. Once the beets and the red onion that bakes with them are done, stir in a few spoonfuls of fruity balsamic vinegar; its tartness nicely complements the vegetables' sweet flavor.

PREPARATION TIME: *About 20 minutes*
BAKING TIME: *35 to 45 minutes*

- 2 **bunches beets (about 2¾ lbs. total)**
- 1 **medium-size red onion (about 8 oz.), cut into ¾-inch chunks**
- 2 **teaspoons olive oil**
- 2 **tablespoons (or to taste) balsamic vinegar**
  Salt and pepper
- 1 **tablespoon chopped fresh oregano or parsley**
  Oregano sprigs

1. Trim and discard roots from beets. Remove stems and leafy greens (reserve greens for other uses). Peel beets, rinse well, and cut into ¾-inch chunks. In a 9- by 13-inch baking pan, stir together beets, onion, and 2 tablespoons water; drizzle with oil.

2. Bake in a 475° oven until vegetables are richly browned and tender when pierced (35 to 45 minutes), stirring occasionally. During last 15 minutes or so, watch carefully to prevent scorching; if pan appears dry, add water, 1 tablespoon at a time. If any pieces start to over-brown, remove them and keep warm until all vegetables are done.

3. Remove pan from oven and quickly drizzle vegetables with vinegar. Stir to combine; season to taste with salt and pepper. Transfer vegetables and any pan liquid to a serving dish, sprinkle with oregano, and garnish with oregano sprigs.

MAKES 4 TO 6 SERVINGS

Per serving: 80 calories (21% calories from fat), 2 g total fat, 0 g saturated fat, 0 mg cholesterol, 77 mg sodium, 15 g carbohydrates, 2 g fiber, 2 g protein, 33 mg calcium, 1 mg iron

Curried Cauliflower

Creamy white cauliflower sauced with a sweet-tart, yogurt-based curry sauce is a good partner for main dishes such as oven-fried fish or chicken. Be careful not to boil the yogurt sauce once you've added it to the cauliflower; if you do, it may curdle.

PREPARATION TIME: *About 15 minutes*
COOKING TIME: *7 to 10 minutes*

- 1 **cup plain nonfat yogurt**
- 2 **tablespoons cornstarch**
- 1 **tablespoon olive oil**
- 2 **teaspoons curry powder**
- 1 **clove garlic, minced or pressed**
- 1 **large cauliflower (about 2 lbs.), cut into bite-size flowerets**
- ½ **cup apricot jam**
  Salt and pepper
- ½ **cup thinly sliced green onions**

1. In a small bowl, stir together yogurt and cornstarch until smoothly blended; set aside.

2. Heat oil in a wide nonstick frying pan over medium-high heat. Add curry powder and garlic; stir just until fragrant (about 30 seconds; do not scorch). Add cauliflower and ⅓ cup water. Cover and cook just until cauliflower is tender when pierced (about 4 minutes). Uncover and continue to cook, stirring, until liquid has evaporated. Add jam; stir just until jam is melted.

3. Stir yogurt mixture well; then pour into pan. Reduce heat to medium-low and simmer gently, stirring constantly, until sauce is slightly thickened (do not boil). Season to taste with salt and pepper. Remove from heat and stir in onions.

MAKES 4 SERVINGS

Per serving: 203 calories (16% calories from fat), 4 g total fat, 1 g saturated fat, 1 mg cholesterol, 75 mg sodium, 40 g carbohydrates, 3 g fiber, 6 g protein, 162 mg calcium, 1 mg iron

Corn Frittata

Fresh corn, fresh basil, ripe tomatoes—this dish says summertime. It's a good choice for a brunch or supper entrée; try it with whole-grain rolls and Gingered Triple Melon Medley (page 47).

PREPARATION TIME: *About 25 minutes*
COOKING TIME: *20 to 25 minutes*

- 3 medium-size ears corn (*each* about 8 inches long; about 1½ lbs. *total*), husks and silk removed
- ¼ cup thinly sliced green onions
- 3 large eggs
- 2 large egg whites (about ¼ cup)
- 2 tablespoons fat-free milk
- 1 tablespoon cornstarch
- 2 teaspoons chopped fresh basil or ½ teaspoon dried basil
- ⅛ teaspoon salt
- ⅛ teaspoon pepper
- 1 tablespoon butter or margarine
- 1 pound russet potatoes, peeled and finely chopped
- 2 large tomatoes (about 1 lb. *total*), *each* cut into 6 wedges
- 1 cup (about 4 oz.) shredded reduced-fat Cheddar cheese
  Basil sprigs

1. In a large, shallow bowl, hold one ear of corn upright and, with a sharp knife, cut kernels from cob. Then, using blunt edge of knife, scrape juice from cob into bowl. Repeat with remaining ears of corn. Discard cobs. Sprinkle corn in bowl with onions and set aside.

2. In a medium-size bowl, beat eggs, egg whites, milk, cornstarch, chopped basil, salt, and pepper until well blended. Set aside.

3. Melt butter in a wide ovenproof frying pan over medium heat. Add potatoes and ½ cup water. Cover and cook, stirring occasionally, until potatoes are tender to bite (12 to 15 minutes); if pan appears dry, add water, 1 tablespoon at a time. Uncover and cook until any liquid has evaporated.

4. Whisk egg mixture and pour over corn; quickly stir to blend well. At once, pour corn mixture over potatoes; increase heat to medium-high and cook, lifting edges with a spatula to let uncooked eggs flow underneath, until frittata is set around edges (2 to 3 minutes). Broil about 4 inches below heat until puffed and golden (about 2 minutes).

5. Decoratively arrange tomato wedges over top of frittata and sprinkle with cheese. Broil until cheese is melted (about 3 minutes). Garnish with basil sprigs.

MAKES 6 SERVINGS

Per serving: 256 calories (29% calories from fat), 9 g total fat, 5 g saturated fat, 125 mg cholesterol, 394 mg sodium, 33 g carbohydrates, 4 g fiber, 14 g protein, 196 mg calcium, 2 mg iron

Golden Squash & Feta Casserole

Made with frozen mashed squash, this savory casserole goes together quickly. Tangy feta and a tart, garlicky yogurt sauce you add at the table offer a nice counterpoint to the nutty sweetness of the squash.

PREPARATION TIME: *About 15 minutes, plus at least 15 minutes to chill sauce*
BAKING TIME: *About 20 minutes*

- 2 packages (about 10 oz. *each*) frozen cooked squash, thawed
- ¾ cup fat-free sour cream
- 1 teaspoon dried thyme
  Salt
- 1 cup (about 4 oz.) crumbled feta cheese
- 1½ cups plain nonfat yogurt
- 2 tablespoons minced cilantro
- 1 clove garlic, minced or pressed
- 1 teaspoon cumin seeds
- ⅓ cup thinly sliced green onions

1. In a large bowl, combine squash, sour cream, and thyme; beat with an electric mixer on medium speed until very smooth (about 3 minutes). Season to taste with salt. Spoon half the squash mixture into a lightly oiled 1- to 1½-quart casserole; sprinkle evenly with cheese, then top with remaining squash mixture.

2. Cover and bake in a 375° oven until squash is heated through (about 20 minutes).

3. Meanwhile, in a small bowl, stir together yogurt, cilantro, garlic, and cumin seeds. Cover and refrigerate for at least 15 minutes.

4. Garnish casserole with onions; offer yogurt sauce to add to taste.

MAKES 8 SERVINGS

Per serving: 138 calories (24% calories from fat), 4 g total fat, 3 g saturated fat, 18 mg cholesterol, 242 mg sodium, 19 g carbohydrates, 3 g fiber, 8 g protein, 228 mg calcium, 1 mg iron

Stuffed Zucchini

Small, tender zucchini stuffed with brown rice and Swiss cheese make an attractive side dish. Try them with beef or turkey burgers or herb-sprinkled baked chicken.

PREPARATION TIME: *About 15 minutes*
COOKING TIME: *About 30 minutes*

- 4 small zucchini (*each* about 5 inches long; about 1¼ lbs. *total*)
- 1 tablespoon butter or margarine
- 6 green onions, finely chopped
- 1 cup cooked brown rice
- ½ cup shredded reduced-fat Swiss cheese
- 1 large egg, lightly beaten
- ¼ cup seasoned fine dry bread crumbs

1. Cut each zucchini in half lengthwise. With a small knife or sharp-edged spoon, scoop out zucchini centers, leaving ¼-inch-thick shells. Finely chop zucchini centers; set shells aside.

2. In a small nonstick frying pan, combine chopped zucchini, 2 teaspoons of the butter, and onions. Cook over medium-high heat, stirring often, until zucchini is lightly browned (about 10 minutes). If pan appears dry, add water, 2 tablespoons at a time.

3. Transfer zucchini mixture to a medium-size bowl; stir in rice, cheese, and egg. Arrange zucchini shells in a 9- by 13-inch baking pan; mound filling equally in shells. Cover tightly and bake in a 400° oven until zucchini shells are tender when pierced (about 20 minutes).

4. Rinse and dry frying pan. Melt remaining 1 teaspoon butter in pan over medium-high heat; mix in bread crumbs. Uncover zucchini, sprinkle evenly with crumb mixture, and broil 4 to 6 inches below heat until crumbs are browned (1 to 2 minutes).

MAKES 8 SERVINGS

Per serving: 112 calories (29% calories from fat), 4 g total fat, 2 g saturated fat, 34 mg cholesterol, 239 mg sodium, 14 g carbohydrates, 1 g fiber, 6 g protein, 109 mg calcium, 1 mg iron

Petite Peas with Browned Butter

Lime, thyme, and green onions quickly dress up packaged frozen peas.

PREPARATION TIME: *About 10 minutes*
COOKING TIME: *About 5 minutes*

- ½ cup thinly sliced green onions
- ½ teaspoon grated lime peel
- 1 tablespoon lime juice
- 1 tablespoon chopped fresh thyme or 1 teaspoon dried thyme
- 1 tablespoon butter or margarine
- 2 packages (about 10 oz. *each*) frozen tiny peas, thawed
- Thyme sprigs

1. In a large bowl, combine onions, lime peel, lime juice, 1 tablespoon water, and chopped thyme; set aside.

2. Melt butter in a wide nonstick frying pan over medium heat. Heat until butter just begins to brown; do not scorch (about 3 minutes). Add peas and cook, stirring, just until heated through.

3. Working quickly, pour pea mixture over onion mixture and mix gently but thoroughly. Garnish with thyme sprigs and serve at once.

MAKES 6 SERVINGS

Per serving: 82 calories (24% calories from fat), 2 g total fat, 1 g saturated fat, 5 mg cholesterol, 139 mg sodium, 12 g carbohydrates, 5 g fiber, 5 g protein, 25 mg calcium, 1 mg iron

Southwestern Stuffed Portabellas

Big portabella mushrooms are perfect for stuffing—they're wide enough to hold a generous amount. Here, they're filled with a nippy combination of corn, beans, chiles, and crushed tortilla chips; creamy jalapeño jack cheese melts on top for a little more zip. Another time, you might choose a crabmeat stuffing (see page 66).

PREPARATION TIME: *About 15 minutes*
BAKING TIME: *About 30 minutes*

- 4 large portabella mushrooms (*each* about 4 inches in diameter; about 12 oz. *total*)
- 2½ cups baked tortilla chips, finely crushed
- 1 small can (about 8¾ oz.) cream-style corn
- 1 small can (about 8¾ oz.) red kidney beans, rinsed and drained
- 1 can (about 4 oz.) diced green chiles
- ¼ teaspoon ground cumin
- Salt
- 3 ounces jalapeño or regular jack cheese, thinly sliced
- ½ cup fat-free sour cream
- Cilantro sprigs
- Pepper

1. Rinse mushrooms and pat dry. Remove and chop stems. In a large bowl, mix chopped mushroom stems with crushed tortilla chips, corn, beans, chiles, and cumin. Season to taste with salt.

2. Place mushrooms, cup side up, in a lightly greased 9- by 13-inch baking pan. Spoon stuffing equally atop mushrooms; press lightly to compact stuffing so it fits within caps.

3. Bake in a 350° oven for 15 minutes. Top with cheese and continue to bake until cheese is melted and lightly browned (about 15 more minutes). Let stand for 5 minutes before serving.

4. To serve, top mushrooms with sour cream and cilantro sprigs. Season to taste with pepper.

MAKES 4 SERVINGS

Per serving: 339 calories (22% calories from fat), 9 g total fat, 4 g saturated fat, 25 mg cholesterol, 768 mg sodium, 53 g carbohydrates, 7 g fiber, 16 g protein, 252 mg calcium, 3 mg iron

Baked Eggplant Stew

Baking eggplant with just a drizzling of olive oil is a good way to cook it without adding much fat. Here, the versatile vegetable joins tomatoes, garbanzos, and a generous measure of onions to make a dish that's good hot or cool. It can double as a pasta sauce; spoon it over hot fettuccine for a vegetarian entrée.

PREPARATION TIME: *About 15 minutes*
BAKING TIME: *About 1 hour and 5 minutes*

- 2 pounds eggplant
- 3 medium-size onions, chopped
- 1 tablespoon olive oil
- 2 cans (about 14½ oz. *each*) diced tomatoes
- 1 can (about 15 oz.) garbanzo beans, rinsed and drained
  Salt and pepper

1. Cut unpeeled eggplant into 2-inch cubes; place in a 9- by 13-inch baking pan and mix in onions and oil.

2. Bake in a 450° oven, stirring occasionally, until eggplant is very soft when pressed (about 45 minutes).

3. Drain tomatoes, reserving juice. Measure juice and add enough water to make 1⅓ cups. Add tomatoes, tomato juice mixture, and garbanzos to eggplant. Continue to bake, stirring occasionally, until vegetable mixture is bubbly and heated through (about 20 more minutes). Season to taste with salt and pepper.

MAKES 6 TO 8 SERVINGS

Per serving: 140 calories (20% calories from fat), 3 g total fat, 0 g saturated fat, 0 mg cholesterol, 261 mg sodium, 25 g carbohydrates, 6 g fiber, 5 g protein, 103 mg calcium, 2 mg iron

Moroccan Vegetable Stew

Vegetable lovers will appreciate this satisfying dish. A spicy, quick-to-cook sauce of stewed tomatoes, garbanzo beans, and a medley of frozen vegetables tops fluffy couscous cooked in broth.

PREPARATION TIME: *About 10 minutes*
COOKING TIME: *About 20 minutes*

- 1 teaspoon olive oil
- 1 large onion, coarsely chopped
- 1 teaspoon ground ginger
- 1 teaspoon ground cumin
- ½ teaspoon ground red pepper (cayenne)
- ¼ teaspoon ground turmeric
- 2 cans (about 14½ oz. *each*) stewed tomatoes
- 1 can (about 15 oz.) garbanzo beans, rinsed and drained
- 2¼ cups vegetable broth or fat-free reduced-sodium chicken broth
- 1½ cups couscous
- 1 package (about 1 lb.) frozen mixed vegetables (carrots, broccoli and cauliflower flowerets, green beans), thawed
- 2 tablespoons chopped fresh mint or parsley

1. Heat oil in a 3- to 4-quart pan over high heat. Add onion and cook, stirring often, until soft (about 5 minutes). Stir in ginger, cumin, red pepper, and turmeric. Add tomatoes; bring to a boil. Stir in garbanzos, reduce heat to medium, and simmer until beans are heated through (about 5 more minutes).

2. Meanwhile, in a 2- to 3-quart pan, bring broth to a boil over high heat. Stir in couscous. Cover, remove from heat, and let stand until liquid has been absorbed (about 5 minutes).

3. Stir thawed vegetables into tomato-garbanzo sauce. Cover and continue to simmer over medium heat until vegetables are heated through (about 5 minutes).

4. To serve, spoon couscous into 4 individual bowls or a large serving dish. Top with vegetable sauce and sprinkle with mint.

MAKES 4 SERVINGS

Per serving: 500 calories (6% calories from fat), 3 g total fat, 0 g saturated fat, 0 mg cholesterol, 836 mg sodium, 101 g carbohydrates, 8 g fiber, 20 g protein, 185 mg calcium, 5 mg iron

Roasted Roots

Rich color and sweet flavor are the rewards of roasting beets, carrots, onions, potatoes, and yams at a very high temperature—500°. You might serve the medley alongside broiled fish, roast lean beef, or barbecued chicken breasts.

PREPARATION TIME: *About 10 minutes*
BAKING TIME: *About 35 minutes*

2 tablespoons olive oil

1 pound Yukon Gold or other thin-skinned potatoes, scrubbed and cut into ¾-inch cubes

¾ cup fresh baby-cut carrots

1 large red onion (about 12 oz.), coarsely chopped

1 yam or sweet potato (about 8 oz.)

1 beet (about 8 oz.)

Salt and pepper

Parsley sprigs or thinly sliced green onion (optional)

1. Pour oil into a 10- by 15-inch baking pan and heat in a 500° oven just until hot (about 1½ minutes). Add potatoes, carrots, and red onion. Bake for 15 minutes, stirring after 10 minutes.

2. Meanwhile, peel yam and beet; cut each into about ½-inch cubes.

3. Add yam and beet to baking pan; bake until all vegetables are golden brown (about 20 more minutes), stirring every 10 minutes. Season to taste with salt and pepper.

4. To serve, spoon onto a platter; garnish with parsley, if desired.

MAKES 4 SERVINGS

Per serving: 273 calories (23% calories from fat), 7 g total fat, 1 g saturated fat, 0 mg cholesterol, 61 mg sodium, 49 g carbohydrates, 7 g fiber, 5 g protein, 49 mg calcium, 2 mg iron

FENNEL WITH MUSHROOMS & PROSCIUTTO

Fennel with Mushrooms & Prosciutto

Known to Italians as finocchio, fennel has been a Mediterranean favorite since ancient Roman times. Poached in wine and filled with sautéed mushrooms and crisp prosciutto pieces, the mildly licorice-flavored vegetable makes an impressive partner for grilled or broiled steaks or chops.

PREPARATION TIME: *About 30 minutes*
COOKING TIME: *1 to 1¼ hours*

> 8   large heads fennel (*each* 3½ to 4 inches in diameter; 6 to 6½ lbs. *total*)
>
> 1¼   cups fat-free reduced-sodium chicken broth
>
> ¾   cup slightly sweet, fruity white wine, such as Johannisberg Riesling
>
> 1   pound mushrooms, sliced
>
> 2   ounces thinly sliced prosciutto, minced

1. Rinse fennel. Trim base, stems, and any bruised portions from each head; reserve feathery leaves. Mince enough leaves to make ¼ cup; then set minced leaves and remaining feathery sprigs aside.

2. Arrange fennel in a single layer in a 5- to 6-quart pan. Add broth and wine; cover and bring to a boil over high heat. Then reduce heat, cover, and simmer until fennel is very tender when pierced (35 to 45 minutes). Lift from pan and set aside until cool enough to handle; reserve cooking liquid.

3. While fennel is cooking, combine mushrooms, prosciutto, and 2 tablespoons of the minced fennel leaves in a wide nonstick frying pan. Cover and cook over medium-high heat until mushrooms release their liquid (about 7 minutes). Uncover and cook, stirring often, until liquid has evaporated and mushrooms are browned (about 15 minutes). Remove from heat and set aside.

4. With a small knife and a sharp-edged spoon, carefully scoop out inner part of each fennel head to make a ¼-inch-thick shell. (Reserve scooped-out fennel for soups or other uses, if desired.) Fill fennel heads with mushroom mixture. Arrange fennel in a baking dish large enough to hold it in a single layer; spoon reserved cooking liquid over fennel. (At this point, you may cover and refrigerate for up to 1 day.)

5. Cover dish and bake in a 375° oven for 15 minutes; uncover and continue to bake until stuffing and fennel are heated through (about 10 more minutes; about 25 more minutes if refrigerated). Transfer fennel to a platter and sprinkle with remaining 2 tablespoons minced fennel leaves; garnish with fennel sprigs.

MAKES 8 SERVINGS

Per serving: 83 calories (16% calories from fat), 2 g total fat, 0 g saturated fat, 6 mg cholesterol, 518 mg sodium, 11 g carbohydrates, 4 g fiber, 7 g protein, 150 mg calcium, 4 mg iron

Breads

Asiago Bagels

Making your own bagels is an adventure—unlike other yeast breads, they're boiled before baking to produce the characteristic dense, chewy texture. These husky bagels get their crusty topping from chunks of piquant Asiago cheese. Eaten plain or spread lightly with your favorite topping, they make a satisfying breakfast along with a glass of fresh fruit juice.

PREPARATION TIME: *About 35 minutes*
RISING TIME: *About 50 minutes*
COOKING TIME: *50 to 60 minutes*

2 packages active dry yeast
2 cups warm water (about 110°F)
3 tablespoons sugar
1½ teaspoons salt
 About 6 cups all-purpose flour
4 ounces Asiago or Parmesan cheese
1 large egg yolk

1. In a large bowl, sprinkle yeast over warm water and let stand until dissolved (about 5 minutes). Add sugar, salt, and 5½ cups of the flour; stir until flour is evenly moistened.

2. Spread ½ cup more flour on a board. Scrape dough out onto board and knead until very smooth and elastic (10 to 15 minutes), adding more flour as required to prevent sticking. Place dough in a lightly oiled bowl and turn over to oil top. Cover with oiled plastic wrap and let rise in a warm place until almost doubled (about 40 minutes).

3. Bring 3 quarts water to a boil in a covered 4- to 5-quart pan over high heat.

4. Meanwhile, turn dough out onto lightly floured board and knead briefly to expel air. Divide dough into 12 equal pieces. To shape each bagel, knead one piece of dough into a smooth ball; then hold ball with both hands and poke your thumbs through center to form a hole, working around edges to make a smooth, evenly thick ring. Set shaped bagels on lightly floured baking sheets. Cover lightly and let rise in a warm place just until slightly puffy (about 10 minutes).

5. With your hand, lift 4 bagels, one by one, from baking sheets and gently slip them into boiling water (refrigerate remaining bagels). Adjust heat to maintain a gentle boil and turn bagels often until they feel firm but are still slightly spongy (3 to 5 minutes). With a slotted spoon, lift bagels from water and transfer to a towel to drain briefly; then arrange slightly apart on lightly oiled baking sheets.

6. Repeat step 5 with remaining 8 bagels, boiling them in 2 batches.

7. Coarsely chop cheese. In a small bowl, beat egg yolk with 1 tablespoon water to blend; brush mixture over bagels. Then pat cheese onto bagels, pressing it gently to make it stick.

8. Bake bagels in a 375° oven until browned (30 to 35 minutes), switching positions of baking sheets halfway through baking. Let cool on racks. Serve warm or cool.

MAKES 1 DOZEN BAGELS

Per bagel: 297 calories (13% calories from fat), 4 g total fat, 2 g saturated fat, 24 mg cholesterol, 401 mg sodium, 52 g carbohydrates, 2 g fiber, 10 g protein, 94 mg calcium, 3 mg iron

No-knead French Rolls

If you like homemade bread and shortcuts too, try these classic dinner rolls. There's no kneading; you just mix the dough well and let it rise, then shape and bake.

PREPARATION TIME: *About 20 minutes*
RISING TIME: *55 to 80 minutes*
BAKING TIME: *15 to 18 minutes*

1 package active dry yeast
1½ cups warm water (about 110°F)
1 tablespoon sugar
2 tablespoons butter or margarine, melted
1 teaspoon salt
4 cups all-purpose flour
Vegetable oil cooking spray

1. In a large bowl, combine yeast, warm water, sugar, butter, and salt; let stand until yeast is dissolved (about 5 minutes). Add flour; beat with a heavy spoon until dough is well blended and stretchy. Cover with oiled plastic wrap and let rise in a warm place until almost doubled (45 to 60 minutes).

2. Coat 2 baking sheets with cooking spray; set aside. Turn dough out onto a floured board and knead briefly to release air. Cut dough into 16 equal portions. Roll each piece into a smooth ball; place balls 2 to 3 inches apart on baking sheets. Cover lightly and let stand in a warm place until almost doubled (10 to 20 minutes).

3. Bake in a 400° oven until golden brown (15 to 18 minutes), switching positions of baking sheets halfway through baking. Transfer to racks to cool; serve warm or cool.

MAKES 16 ROLLS

Per roll: 135 calories (14% calories from fat), 2 g total fat, 1 g saturated fat, 4 mg cholesterol, 161 mg sodium, 25 g carbohydrates, 1 g fiber, 3 g protein, 6 mg calcium, 2 mg iron

Onion-Herb Batter Bread

Serve this old favorite warm (the better to tempt appetites with the savory fragrance!), as a partner for just about any main course.

PREPARATION TIME: *About 20 minutes*
RISING TIME: *1 to 1¼ hours*
BAKING TIME: *About 45 minutes*

1 package active dry yeast
1½ tablespoons sugar
½ cup warm water (about 110°F)
½ cup fat-free milk
1 tablespoon butter or margarine
2 tablespoons dried minced onion
½ teaspoon dried rosemary or 1 teaspoon chopped fresh rosemary
½ teaspoon dried dill weed or 1 teaspoon chopped fresh dill
2¼ cups all-purpose flour

1. In a large bowl, sprinkle yeast and sugar over warm water; let stand until yeast is dissolved (about 5 minutes).

2. In a 1- to 1½-quart pan, heat milk and butter just until mixture reaches 110°F. Stir milk mixture into yeast mixture; then stir in onion, rosemary, dill, and flour. With a heavy-duty mixer or a heavy spoon, beat to form a stretchy batter (it will be very sticky). Cover with oiled plastic wrap and let rise in a warm place until tripled (45 to 60 minutes).

3. With a floured spoon, stir batter down; then scrape into an oiled 4½- by 8½-inch loaf pan and spread to level. Cover lightly and let rise in a warm place until puffy (about 15 minutes).

4. Bake in a 350° oven until richly browned (about 45 minutes). Let cool in pan on a rack for 10 minutes; then invert onto rack. Serve warm or cool.

MAKES 1 LOAF (ABOUT 8 SERVINGS)

Per serving: 170 calories (15% calories from fat), 3 g total fat, 1 g saturated fat, 6 mg cholesterol, 24 mg sodium, 31 g carbohydrates, 1 g fiber, 5 g protein, 28 mg calcium, 2 mg iron

Dried Tomato Basil Bread

The transformation of flour, water, yeast, and salt into a fragrant loaf is nothing short of magical. These herb- and tomato-flecked loaves are especially rewarding, both to bake and to eat.

PREPARATION TIME: *About 30 minutes*
RISING TIME: *1¼ to 1½ hours*
BAKING TIME: *About 18 minutes*

- 1 **package active dry yeast**
- 1¼ **cups warm water (about 110°F)**
- 1 **tablespoon dried basil**
- 2 **tablespoons olive oil**
- 1½ **teaspoons salt**
- 1 **cup whole wheat flour (regular or bread flour)**
- 2½ **to 2¾ cups all-purpose flour or white bread flour**
- ⅓ **cup chopped dried tomatoes (not oil-packed)**

1. In a large bowl, sprinkle yeast over warm water and let stand until dissolved (about 5 minutes). Stir in basil, oil, salt, and whole wheat flour; then gradually mix in 1½ cups of the all-purpose flour. Beat with a heavy spoon until stretchy (about 5 minutes). Add ¾ cup more all-purpose flour and stir until dough pulls away from sides of bowl.

2. Turn dough out onto a lightly floured board and knead until smooth, elastic, and no longer sticky (about 10 minutes), adding more flour as required to prevent sticking. When dough has been sufficiently kneaded, you'll see tiny stretch marks beneath surface. Knead in tomatoes until evenly distributed.

3. Place dough in a lightly oiled bowl and turn over to oil top. Cover with oiled plastic wrap and let rise in a warm place until doubled (1 to 1¼ hours). Then turn out onto floured board and knead briefly to expel air.

4. Divide dough in half. Shape each half into a smooth ball; place each ball on an unfloured board and roll with your hands to make a very smooth 2-inch wide log. If necessary, smooth the surface by gently stretching dough from underside of log to its top all along its length, pinching to make a long seam. Place loaves, seam side down and 4 inches apart, on an oiled 12- by 15-inch baking sheet.

5. Cover loaves lightly and let rise in a warm place until puffy (15 to 20 minutes); dough should hold a faint impression when lightly pressed.

6. Holding a razor blade or very sharp knife at a 45° angle, cut a ¾-inch-deep slash lengthwise down center of each loaf, extending to within 2 inches of each end.

7. Bake in a 425° oven until deep golden (about 18 minutes). Let cool on racks. Serve warm or cool.

MAKES 2 LOAVES (ABOUT 8 SERVINGS EACH)

Per serving: 127 calories (18% calories from fat), 3 g total fat, 0 g saturated fat, 0 mg cholesterol, 221 mg sodium, 22 g carbohydrates, 2 g fiber, 4 g protein, 12 mg calcium, 1 mg iron

Sunflower Soda Bread

A generous helping of cornmeal and plenty of sunflower seeds give this big loaf a nice crunch and a wonderful nutty flavor. Serve it alongside a pot of Lentil & Kale Soup (page 112) for a perfect cold-weather dinner.

PREPARATION TIME: *5 to 10 minutes*
BAKING TIME: *25 to 30 minutes*

2½ cups all-purpose flour
1 cup whole wheat flour
1 cup yellow cornmeal
½ cup dry-roasted unsalted sunflower seeds
⅓ cup sugar
2 teaspoons baking powder
1 teaspoon baking soda
½ teaspoon salt
2 cups reduced-fat (1½%) buttermilk
1 large egg
Vegetable oil cooking spray

1. In a large bowl, stir together all-purpose flour, whole wheat flour, cornmeal, sunflower seeds, sugar, baking powder, baking soda, and salt. In a small bowl, beat together buttermilk and egg; add to flour mixture and beat with a heavy spoon until dough is thoroughly moistened and stretchy (about 2 minutes).

2. Coat two 10- by 15-inch baking pans with cooking spray. Divide dough in half; spoon one half in center of each pan. With floured hands, pat each portion of dough into an 8-inch round. With a floured sharp knife, cut a large, ½-inch-deep cross on top of each round.

3. Bake in a 375° oven until bread is golden brown (25 to 30 minutes), switching positions of baking pans halfway through baking. Let cool on racks. Serve warm or cool.

MAKES 2 LOAVES (10 TO 12 SERVINGS EACH)

Per serving: 139 calories (15% calories from fat), 2 g total fat, 0 g saturated fat, 11 mg cholesterol, 169 mg sodium, 25 g carbohydrates, 2 g fiber, 4 g protein, 59 mg calcium, 1 mg iron

Irish Brown Bread

Simple enough for children to make, this crusty free-form loaf is delicious warm or cool; you can slice it or simply break it into chunks.

PREPARATION TIME: *About 10 minutes*
BAKING TIME: *About 40 minutes*

1 cup all-purpose flour
2 tablespoons sugar
1 teaspoon baking powder
1 teaspoon baking soda
½ teaspoon salt
1½ tablespoons butter or margarine, cut into chunks
2 cups whole wheat flour
¼ cup regular or quick-cooking rolled oats
1½ cups plain nonfat yogurt
Fat-free milk
Vegetable oil cooking spray

1. In a large bowl, stir together all-purpose flour, sugar, baking powder, baking soda, and salt. Using a pastry blender or 2 knives, cut in butter until mixture resembles fine crumbs. Stir in whole wheat flour and oats.

2. Add yogurt to flour mixture and stir gently. If dough is too dry to hold together, stir in milk, 1 teaspoon at a time, just until dough holds together; it should not be sticky. Turn dough out onto a lightly floured board and knead gently just long enough to form a ball (about 5 turns).

3. Coat a baking sheet with cooking spray. Place dough in center of baking sheet. With floured hands, pat dough into a 7-inch round. With a floured sharp knife, cut a large, ½-inch-deep cross on top of round.

4. Bake in a 375° oven until well browned (about 40 minutes). Let cool on a rack. Serve warm or cool.

MAKES 1 LOAF (ABOUT 14 SERVINGS)

Per serving: 133 calories (14% calories from fat), 2 g total fat, 1 g saturated fat, 4 mg cholesterol, 240 mg sodium, 24 g carbohydrates, 3 g fiber, 5 g protein, 76 mg calcium, 3 mg iron

Yogurt Cornbread

Nonfat yogurt replaces the fat in this hearty cornbread. It has a slightly springy texture, making it ideal for dunking into thick soups and bean stews such as Black Bean Chili (page 188).

PREPARATION TIME: *About 5 minutes*
BAKING TIME: *20 to 25 minutes*

- 1 cup all-purpose flour
- 1 cup yellow cornmeal
- ¼ cup sugar
- 1 teaspoon baking soda
- ¾ teaspoon salt
- 1 cup plain nonfat yogurt
- 2 large eggs
  Vegetable oil cooking spray

1. In a large bowl, stir together flour, cornmeal, sugar, baking soda, and salt. In a small bowl, beat together yogurt and eggs; add to flour mixture and stir just until blended.

2. Coat an 8- or 9-inch baking pan with cooking spray; pour batter into pan. Bake in a 400° oven until center of bread springs back when gently pressed (20 to 25 minutes). Serve warm; to serve, cut into squares or wedges.

MAKES 9 SERVINGS

Per serving: 163 calories (11% calories from fat), 2 g total fat, 1 g saturated fat, 49 mg cholesterol, 372 mg sodium, 30 g carbohydrates, 1 g fiber, 6 g protein, 59 mg calcium, 1 mg iron

Berry Breakfast Braid

Your favorite fruit preserves fill a lemon-glazed braid made from a simple, biscuitlike cream cheese dough. To shape the braid a bit more quickly, you can make the strips you fold over the filling wider, spacing the cuts about 3 inches apart.

PREPARATION TIME: *About 15 minutes*
BAKING TIME: *About 20 minutes*

- 1 small package (about 3 oz.) cream cheese, cut into chunks
- ¼ cup butter or margarine, cut into chunks
- 2 cups all-purpose flour
- 1 tablespoon baking powder
- ⅔ cup low-fat (1%) milk
  Vegetable oil cooking spray
- ¾ cup raspberry, blueberry, or other fruit preserves or jam
- ⅔ cup powdered sugar
- 2 teaspoons lemon juice
- 2 teaspoons water

1. In a food processor or a medium-size bowl, combine cream cheese, butter, flour, and baking powder. Whirl or cut with a pastry blender or 2 knives until mixture resembles fine crumbs. If using a food processor, transfer mixture to a medium-size bowl. Slowly add milk, stirring until dough forms a soft ball.

2. Coat a 10- by 15-inch baking pan with cooking spray; set aside. Place dough between 2 sheets of lightly oiled wax paper and roll out to make a 10- by 15-inch rectangle. Remove top sheet of paper and invert dough into baking pan; remove second sheet of paper. If needed, push dough with fingers to fit pan.

3. Spread preserves lengthwise down center of dough in a 3-inch-wide band, leaving a ½-inch border without preserves at each end. With a sharp knife, make 3-inch-long slits from long edge of dough toward preserves on either side, spacing cuts 1 to 1½ inches apart. Alternating between sides, gently fold dough strips over preserves, overlapping ends in center to resemble a braid. Pinch to secure strips.

4. Bake in a 400° oven until bread is lightly browned (about 20 minutes). Let cool slightly. Meanwhile, in a small bowl, smoothly mix powdered sugar, lemon juice, and water. Drizzle bread with icing. Serve warm.

MAKES 8 SERVINGS

Per serving: 321 calories (29% calories from fat), 11 g total fat, 6 g saturated fat, 28 mg cholesterol, 296 mg sodium, 53 g carbohydrates, 1 g fiber, 5 g protein, 148 mg calcium, 2 mg iron

BERRY BREAKFAST BRAID

ORANGE YOGURT SCONES

Orange Yogurt Scones

Orange-flavored yogurt, orange peel, and orange juice give these moist, sugar-sprinkled scones their emphatically citrusy flavor.

PREPARATION TIME: *About 10 minutes*
BAKING TIME: *About 25 minutes*

  2 cups all-purpose flour
 ⅓ cup plus 2 teaspoons sugar
  2 tablespoons baking powder
 ¼ teaspoon baking soda
 ¼ teaspoon salt
  3 tablespoons butter or margarine, cut into chunks
 ¾ cup orange- or lemon-flavored low-fat yogurt
  2 teaspoons grated orange peel
 ¼ cup orange juice
    Vegetable oil cooking spray

1. In a large bowl or a food processor, combine flour, ⅓ cup of the sugar, baking powder, baking soda, and salt. Stir or whirl until blended. Add butter; cut in with a pastry blender or 2 knives or whirl until mixture resembles fine crumbs.

2. In a small bowl, stir together yogurt, orange peel, and orange juice. Add to flour mixture and stir or whirl just until evenly moistened.

3. Coat a baking sheet with cooking spray. Mound dough on baking sheet. With well-floured hands, pat mound into a 9-inch round. With a floured sharp knife, cut through dough to make 8 wedges, but do not separate wedges. Sprinkle with remaining 2 teaspoons sugar.

4. Bake in a 375° oven until golden brown (about 25 minutes). Serve hot or warm. To serve, cut apart into wedges.

MAKES 8 SCONES

Per scone: 221 calories (22% calories from fat), 5 g total fat, 3 g saturated fat, 12 mg cholesterol, 533 mg sodium, 39 g carbohydrates, 1 g fiber, 4 g protein, 243 mg calcium, 2 mg iron

Lemon-Date Tea Bread

Studded with walnuts and dates, this tangy bread is deliciously moist: you soak it in a sweet lemon syrup when it's hot from the oven.

PREPARATION TIME: *About 15 minutes, plus 2 hours for loaf to stand and at least 8 hours to chill*
BAKING TIME: *About 1 hour*

  1 large lemon (about 5 oz.), coarsely chopped, including rind (discard seeds)
  1 cup chopped pitted dates
 1¼ cups sugar
  2 tablespoons butter or margarine, at room temperature
  1 large egg
 1¾ cups all-purpose flour
  1 teaspoon baking soda
  1 teaspoon salt
 ¾ cup chopped walnuts
 ½ cup lemon juice

1. In a food processor, whirl lemon and dates until evenly chopped. Add ¾ cup of the sugar, butter, and egg; whirl until ingredients are well blended and lemon and dates are finely chopped.

2. In a small bowl, stir together flour, baking soda, and salt. Add to date mixture; whirl until blended. Stir in walnuts. Spread batter in a buttered, floured 4½- by 8½-inch glass loaf pan. Bake in a 325° oven until a wooden pick inserted in center of loaf comes out clean (about 1 hour). Remove from oven.

3. Combine lemon juice and remaining ½ cup sugar in a 1- to 1½-quart pan. Stir over medium heat until sugar is dissolved (about 2 minutes). Use a long, thin skewer to poke holes about ½ inch apart all over surface of hot bread, piercing about halfway through loaf each time. Pour hot syrup evenly over bread in pan. Let stand at room temperature until bread has absorbed all syrup (about 2 hours). Turn out of pan onto a plate; cover airtight and refrigerate for at least 8 hours or up to 3 days. To serve, cut into thin slices. Refrigerate any leftover bread airtight.

MAKES 1 LOAF (18 TO 24 SERVINGS)

Per serving: 154 calories (24% calories from fat), 4 g total fat, 1 g saturated fat, 14 mg cholesterol, 189 mg sodium, 28 g carbohydrates, 1 g fiber, 2 g protein, 15 mg calcium, 1 mg iron

Banana-Walnut Muffins

These fruit-nut muffins are tender, moist, and delicious—and each one has just 2 grams of fat. To make them, you will need about five medium-size (6-oz.) bananas—four to mash, one to dice.

PREPARATION TIME: *About 35 minutes*
BAKING TIME: *About 25 minutes*

4   cups all-purpose flour
1   tablespoon baking powder
2   teaspoons baking soda
1   teaspoon salt
2   cups sugar
½   cup prune purée
½   cup plain nonfat yogurt
2   tablespoons vegetable oil
1   tablespoon vanilla
2   cups mashed ripe bananas
½   cup diced banana
5   large egg whites (about ⅔ cup)
⅛   teaspoon cream of tartar
⅓   cup finely chopped walnuts

1. In a large bowl, stir together flour, baking powder, baking soda, and salt. Set aside.

2. In another large bowl, combine 1¾ cups of the sugar, prune purée, yogurt, oil, and vanilla. Beat with an electric mixer on medium speed until blended. Fold in mashed and diced bananas; set aside.

3. In a clean large bowl, using clean beaters, beat egg whites and cream of tartar on high speed until foamy. Gradually add remaining ¼ cup sugar, about 1 tablespoon at a time, beating until soft peaks form. Gently fold whites into banana mixture; then fold in flour mixture just until blended. (Avoid overmixing; it will toughen muffins.)

4. Divide batter evenly among 24 paper-lined 2½-inch muffin cups; sprinkle evenly with walnuts.

5. Bake in a 350° oven until muffins are just firm to the touch and edges are golden (about 25 minutes). Let cool on racks. Serve warm or at room temperature.

MAKES 2 DOZEN MUFFINS

Per muffin: 201 calories (11% calories from fat), 2 g total fat, 0 g saturated fat, 0 mg cholesterol, 281 mg sodium, 42 g carbohydrates, 1 g fiber, 4 g protein, 50 mg calcium, 1 mg iron

Raisin Bran Muffins

Moist muffins based on bran cereal have been popular for years—for speedy breakfasts, as partners for fruit salads, and just for snacking. These are sweetened with brown sugar and applesauce and dotted with raisins.

PREPARATION TIME: *About 15 minutes*
BAKING TIME: *About 20 minutes*

1½   cups shredded wheat bran cereal
¾   cup unsweetened applesauce
½   cup fat-free buttermilk
½   cup firmly packed brown sugar
2   large eggs, beaten
2   tablespoons water
2   tablespoons vegetable oil
1¼   cups all-purpose flour
2   teaspoons baking powder
¼   teaspoon salt
½   teaspoon ground cinnamon
¾   cup raisins
    Vegetable oil cooking spray

1. In a large bowl, combine cereal, applesauce, and buttermilk; let stand for 5 minutes. Add ¼ cup of the brown sugar, eggs, water, and oil; stir to blend well.

2. In another large bowl, mix flour, baking powder, salt, and cinnamon. Make a well in center of dry ingredients and add cereal mixture; stir just until dry ingredients are evenly moistened. Fold in raisins.

3. Coat twelve 2½-inch muffin cups with cooking spray. Spoon batter into cups, filling them three-fourths full. Sprinkle batter evenly with remaining ¼ cup brown sugar. Bake in a 400° oven until muffins are lightly browned and a wooden pick inserted in centers comes out clean (about 20 minutes).

MAKES 1 DOZEN MUFFINS

Per muffin: 177 calories (19% calories from fat), 4 g total fat, 1 g saturated fat, 36 mg cholesterol, 227 mg sodium, 34 g carbohydrates, 4 g fiber, 4 g protein, 102 mg calcium, 2 mg iron

Herbed Popovers

Unlike traditional popovers, these are made with egg whites alone, beaten until foamy to give you the classic "pop" without the added fat. Dried herbs and chili powder add a zesty flavor that makes the popovers just right with soups or bean dishes such as Tuscan Beans (page 189).

PREPARATION TIME: *About 10 minutes*
BAKING TIME: *About 50 minutes*

⅓ cup yellow or white cornmeal

1 cup bread flour or all-purpose flour

¼ teaspoon dried thyme

¼ teaspoon dried oregano

¼ teaspoon chili powder

¼ teaspoon salt

6 large egg whites (about ¾ cup)

1 cup fat-free milk

2 tablespoons butter or margarine, melted

1. Sprinkle cornmeal equally over bottoms and sides of 12 lightly oiled 2½-inch muffin cups. Set aside.

2. In a small bowl, stir together flour, thyme, oregano, chili powder, and salt. In a large bowl, beat egg whites with an electric mixer on high speed until foamy. Add milk and butter; beat on medium speed until well blended. Then add flour mixture, beating until batter is smooth.

3. Pour batter into muffin cups, filling them three-fourths full. Bake in a 375° oven until popovers are golden brown (about 45 minutes); then cut a small slit in top of each popover, return to oven, and continue to bake for 5 more minutes to dry interiors of popovers slightly. Serve at once.

MAKES 1 DOZEN POPOVERS

Per popover: 93 calories (27% calories from fat), 3 g total fat, 1 g saturated fat, 6 mg cholesterol, 106 mg sodium, 12 g carbohydrates, 0 g fiber, 4 g protein, 30 mg calcium, 1 mg iron

Parsley-Lemon Quick Bread

Chopped parsley and grated lemon peel, classic garnishes for Italian main dishes, are used in this quick loaf bread. Serve it for lunch with a leafy salad, offering light cream cheese to spread on each slice. You can bake the loaf up to a day in advance; after it cools, wrap it airtight and hold at room temperature.

PREPARATION TIME: *About 15 minutes*
BAKING TIME: *About 1 hour*

2⅓ cups all-purpose flour

½ cup sugar

2 teaspoons baking powder

¼ teaspoon salt

1 large egg

2 large egg whites (about ¼ cup)

1 cup low-fat (1%) milk

3 tablespoons vegetable oil

1½ tablespoons grated lemon peel

⅓ cup chopped parsley

Vegetable oil cooking spray

1. In a large bowl, stir together flour, sugar, baking powder, and salt; set aside. In a medium-size bowl, combine egg and egg whites; beat just until yolk and whites are blended. Then stir in milk, oil, lemon peel, and parsley. Add egg mixture to flour mixture; stir just until dry ingredients are moistened.

2. Coat a 4½- by 8½-inch loaf pan with cooking spray. Spread batter in loaf pan. Bake in a 325° oven until loaf begins to pull away from sides of pan and a wooden pick inserted in center comes out clean (about 1 hour).

3. Let loaf cool in pan on a rack for 10 minutes; then turn out onto rack. Let cool almost to room temperature before slicing.

MAKES 1 LOAF (ABOUT 16 SERVINGS).

Per serving: 128 calories (23% calories from fat), 3 g total fat, 1 g saturated fat, 14 mg cholesterol, 116 mg sodium, 21 g carbohydrates, 1 g fiber, 3 g protein, 60 mg calcium, 1 mg iron

Desserts

FRESH APPLE COFFEE CAKE

Fresh Apple Coffee Cake

Filled and topped with cinnamon-spiced apples, this big cake is a satisfying close to a simple meal. Fat-free mayonnaise is the secret to the moist texture.

PREPARATION TIME: *About 20 minutes, plus about hour to cool*
BAKING TIME: *1 to 1¼ hours*

- 4 large Golden Delicious apples (about 2 lbs. *total*)
- ⅓ cup orange juice
- 1½ teaspoons ground cinnamon
- 3 cups all-purpose flour
- 2 teaspoons baking powder
- ½ teaspoon salt
- 2 cups granulated sugar
- 1 cup fat-free mayonnaise
- ½ cup fat-free milk
- 2½ teaspoons vanilla
- 3 large eggs
  Vegetable oil cooking spray
- ⅔ cup firmly packed brown sugar

1. Peel, core, and coarsely chop apples; place in a medium-size bowl and mix in orange juice and cinnamon. Set aside.

2. In another medium-size bowl, stir together flour, baking powder, and salt; set aside. In a large bowl, beat granulated sugar, mayonnaise, milk, and vanilla until well blended. Beat in eggs.

3. Coat a 9- or 10-inch tube pan with cooking spray. Add flour mixture to egg mixture; stir to blend thoroughly. Pour half the batter into pan and top with half the apples. Pour remaining batter evenly over apples; top with remaining apples. Sprinkle with brown sugar.

4. Bake in a 350° oven until center of cake springs back when lightly pressed (1 to 1¼ hours). Let cool in pan on a rack for about 1 hour. Run a long, thin knife around sides of pan and tube. Carefully invert cake onto rack; lift off pan. Then carefully reinvert cake onto a serving plate.

MAKES 16 SERVINGS

Per serving: 274 calories (6% calories from fat), 2 g total fat, 0 g saturated fat, 40 mg cholesterol, 259 mg sodium, 61 g carbohydrates, 1 g fiber, 4 g protein, 64 mg calcium, 2 mg iron

Banana Ginger Cake

This flavorful cake is versatile: you can make it with ordinary bananas or with a more unusual type (such as red, manzano, or nino), and bake it in a square pan or a loaf pan. It's delicious topped with sliced strawberries, diced pineapple, or other fresh fruit.

PREPARATION TIME: *About 25 minutes*
BAKING TIME: *45 to 50 minutes*

- 2¼ cups all-purpose flour
- 1 teaspoon baking powder
- ¾ teaspoon baking soda
- ½ teaspoon ground cinnamon
- ⅓ cup butter or margarine, at room temperature
- 1 cup sugar
- 2 large eggs
- 1 cup mashed very ripe bananas
- 1 tablespoon minced fresh ginger
- 1 teaspoon finely grated lemon peel
- ½ cup buttermilk
  Vegetable oil cooking spray

1. In a medium-size bowl, stir together flour, baking powder, baking soda, and cinnamon. Set aside.

2. In a large bowl, beat butter and sugar with electric mixer on high speed until fluffy. Add eggs, one at a time, beating well after each addition. Beat in bananas, ginger, and lemon peel. Add flour mixture to egg mixture alternately with buttermilk, stirring just until thoroughly blended after each addition.

3. Coat a 9-inch-square baking pan or 5- by 9-inch loaf pan with cooking spray; pour batter into pan. Bake in a 350° oven until cake is golden brown and center springs back when lightly pressed (about 45 minutes for square pan, 50 minutes for loaf pan). Let cake cool completely in pan on a rack; then turn out of pan. Cut cake into squares or slices.

MAKES 9 SERVINGS

Per serving: 309 calories (25% calories from fat), 9 g total fat, 5 g saturated fat, 67 mg cholesterol, 262 mg sodium, 53 g carbohydrates, 1 g fiber, 5 g protein, 62 mg calcium, 2 mg iron

Apple-Berry Pie

Yes, you can have your pie and eat it too! Fill the bottom crust with a juicy blend of apples and fresh blackberries—then cover the fruit with an unusual streusel instead of a top crust. Replacing most of a traditional streusel's butter with marshmallow creme cuts the fat sharply and adds a subtle toasted-marshmallow flavor.

PREPARATION TIME: *About 20 minutes, plus 30 minutes to chill pastry and about 1 hour to cool baked pie*

BAKING TIME: *60 to 70 minutes*

- 1½ **cups all-purpose flour**
- ½ **cup plus 1½ tablespoons granulated sugar**
- ½ **teaspoon baking powder**
- ¼ **teaspoon salt**
- 2 **tablespoons cold butter or margarine**
- 2 **tablespoons solid vegetable shortening**
- 4½ **tablespoons ice-cold water**
- 3 **tablespoons quick-cooking tapioca**
- 1 **teaspoon grated lemon peel**
- 1 **teaspoon ground cinnamon**
- 4 **cups (about 1½ lbs.) peeled, thinly sliced Granny Smith apples**
- 3 **cups fresh blackberries**
- ⅓ **cup marshmallow creme**
- 2 **tablespoons butter or margarine, melted**
- ¼ **cup firmly packed brown sugar**
- ½ **cup regular rolled oats**

1. In a medium-size bowl, stir together 1 cup of the flour, 1½ tablespoons of the granulated sugar, baking powder, and salt. Using a pastry blender or 2 knives, cut in the 2 tablespoons cold butter until particles are pea-size; then cut in shortening until pea-size. Add cold water, 1 tablespoon at a time, tossing mixture gently with a fork. Gather pastry into a ball, pat into a 5-inch disk, wrap in plastic wrap, and refrigerate for 30 minutes.

2. Meanwhile, in a large bowl, combine remaining ½ cup granulated sugar, tapioca, lemon peel, and ½ teaspoon of the cinnamon. Mix in apples and blackberries. Let mixture stand for about 15 minutes to soften tapioca, stirring occasionally.

3. In a medium-size bowl, stir marshmallow creme and melted butter until smooth. Add remaining ½ cup flour, remaining ½ teaspoon cinnamon, brown sugar, and oats. Mix with your fingers to blend, then break streusel into small clumps.

4. On a lightly floured board, gently roll pastry out to a 12-inch round, lifting dough and reflouring board if necessary to prevent sticking. Ease pastry into a 9-inch pie pan. Fold under edge of pastry so it is flush with pan rim; then flute. Evenly fill crust with apple mixture. Pat streusel over filling to within 1 inch of rim.

5. Bake in a 375° oven until pie is bubbly (60 to 70 minutes); check after 45 minutes and cover lightly with foil if crust or streusel is getting too dark. Let cool on a rack for about 1 hour before serving.

MAKES 8 SERVINGS

Per serving: 372 calories (23% calories from fat), 10 g total fat, 5 g saturated fat, 16 mg cholesterol, 183 mg sodium, 70 g carbohydrates, 5 g fiber, 4 g protein, 56 mg calcium, 2 mg iron

Tarte Tatin

This luscious upside-down apple pie is low enough in fat for an occasional indulgence. To make it, you caramelize sugar with a little butter in an ovenproof frying pan, then spoon in sliced apples and top with pastry. At serving time, turn the warm tart over to let the caramel sauce flow over the apples. (You can also serve the tart cool; the apples will absorb most of the sauce.)

Avoid using a cast-iron pan for this dessert; it can darken the apples and give them a metallic flavor.

PREPARATION TIME: *About 15 minutes, plus 30 to 40 minutes to chill pastry and at least 2 hours to cool baked tart*

BAKING TIME: *55 to 60 minutes*

- ⅓ cup plus ¼ cup cold butter or margarine
- 1¼ cups all-purpose flour
- 1¼ cups sugar
- 1 large egg plus 1 large egg yolk (omit yolk if using margarine)
- 3½ pounds Golden Delicious apples
- 3 tablespoons lemon juice
- 5 to 6 cups vanilla fat-free ice cream

1. Cut ⅓ cup of the butter into chunks. Place in a food processor or a large bowl and add flour and ¼ cup of the sugar. Whirl or rub together with your fingers until mixture resembles fine meal. Add egg and egg yolk (if used); whirl or stir vigorously until pastry holds together. Pat pastry into a 5-inch disk, wrap in plastic wrap, and refrigerate for 30 to 40 minutes.

2. Peel and core apples, then cut lengthwise into ⅓-inch-thick slices; place in a large bowl and mix in lemon juice. Set aside.

3. Melt remaining ¼ cup butter in a 10-inch ovenproof frying pan over medium heat. Add remaining 1 cup sugar and cook, stirring often, until sugar melts, turns a deep caramel color, and just barely starts to smoke (6 to 8 minutes). Remove from heat. Quickly (to cool caramel) and carefully (to avoid spattering), spoon apples and juice over caramel, filling pan compactly.

4. On a board, overlap sheets of plastic wrap to make a 16-inch square. Unwrap pastry, dust with flour, and place on plastic wrap. Cover with more plastic wrap. With short, gentle strokes, roll pastry out to make an 11-inch round. Remove top sheets of plastic wrap; invert pastry round over apples and remove remaining plastic wrap. Tuck edge of pastry down between apples and pan. Cut three 2-inch-long vents near center of pastry.

5. Bake in a 375° oven until pastry is deep golden and juices start to bubble in center (55 to 60 minutes). Let cool on a rack until pan is no longer hot to the touch (at least 2 hours) or for up to 1 day.

6. To serve, loosen crust from sides of pan. If tart is very juicy, tip pan and spoon or siphon out some of the caramel sauce. Invert a rimmed serving plate over tart; holding plate and pan together, invert both to tip tart out onto plate. Lift off pan. Cut tart into wedges and serve with caramel sauce and ice cream.

MAKES 10 TO 12 SERVINGS

Per serving: 409 calories (24% calories from fat), 11 g total fat, 6 g saturated fat, 65 mg cholesterol, 156 mg sodium, 75 g carbohydrates, 3 g fiber, 5 g protein, 115 mg calcium, 1 mg iron

Chocolate–Crème de Menthe Pie

A splendid choice for special occasions, this dressy dessert stars chocolate all through, from the crunchy crust to the creamy layered fillings to the topping of deep, dark chocolate sauce. Make it the day before serving, since it needs nearly 10 hours in the freezer.

PREPARATION TIME: *About 30 minutes*
FREEZING TIME: *About 9 1/2 hours*

 3 **ounces semisweet chocolate**
 3 **tablespoons butter or margarine**
 1/4 **cup green crème de menthe**
 1 1/2 **teaspoons vanilla**
 1 1/4 **cups crisp rice cereal**
 1/2 **cup evaporated fat-free milk**
 2 **tablespoons unsweetened cocoa**
 2 **tablespoons light corn syrup**
 1 **teaspoon cornstarch**
 4 **cups vanilla nonfat frozen yogurt, softened**
    Dark Chocolate Sauce (recipe follows)
    Mint sprigs

1. Line a 9-inch pie pan with foil; fold foil over edge of pan and tuck beneath rim to secure. Set aside.

2. Combine chocolate and butter in top of double boiler set over (but not in) gently boiling water; cook, stirring occasionally, until chocolate and butter are smoothly melted. Add 1 tablespoon of the crème de menthe; cook for 1 minute, stirring constantly. Remove from boiling water; stir in 1 teaspoon of the vanilla, then cereal.

3. Spread chocolate-cereal mixture evenly over bottom and up sides of foil-lined pan. Cover and freeze for 45 minutes. Carefully lift crust from pan, using foil to help you; then carefully peel foil from crust. Return crust to pan. Cover and return to freezer.

4. While crust is freezing, combine milk, cocoa, corn syrup, and cornstarch in a small pan and stir until well blended. Bring to a boil over medium heat, stirring constantly; then cook, stirring, until mixture is slightly thickened (about 1 minute). Add 1 tablespoon of the crème de menthe and stir for 1 more minute. Remove pan from heat; stir in remaining 1/2 teaspoon vanilla. Let chocolate filling cool, then cover and refrigerate until cold.

5. In a large bowl, combine yogurt and remaining 2 tablespoons crème de menthe. Spread half the yogurt mixture in bottom of frozen chocolate crust; cover and freeze for 30 minutes. Also cover and freeze remaining yogurt mixture.

6. Remove pie from freezer, top with cold chocolate filling, and freeze for 10 minutes. Then spread remaining yogurt mixture over chocolate filling (soften yogurt mixture slightly, if necessary). Cover pie and freeze for at least 8 hours. Meanwhile, prepare Dark Chocolate Sauce.

7. To serve, let pie stand at room temperature for about 5 minutes; then cut into wedges. Top with Dark Chocolate Sauce and garnish with mint sprigs.

MAKES 10 SERVINGS

Dark Chocolate Sauce. In a small pan, combine 3 tablespoons **sugar**, 3 tablespoons **unsweetened cocoa**, 2 teaspoons **cornstarch**, 1 cup **water**, and 1 teaspoon **vanilla**. Bring to a boil, stirring constantly. Remove from heat and stir in 1 more teaspoon **vanilla**. Cover and refrigerate for at least 1 hour or up to 8 hours.

Per serving, including chocolate sauce: 228 calories (26% calories from fat), 6 g total fat, 4 g saturated fat, 10 mg cholesterol, 124 mg sodium, 38 g carbohydrates, 1 g fiber, 4 g protein, 124 mg calcium, 1 mg iron

Lemon Cheesecake Soufflé

Made with light ricotta and nonfat yogurt, this warm, puffy dessert has all the flavor of traditional cheesecake—but much less cholesterol and fat than you might expect. Spoon sliced fresh strawberries over each bowlful.

PREPARATION TIME: *About 30 minutes*
BAKING TIME: *About 45 minutes*

1 tablespoon butter or margarine, at room temperature
½ cup almond biscotti crumbs
1 carton (about 15 oz.) light ricotta cheese
1 cup plain nonfat yogurt
¾ cup sugar
¼ cup all-purpose flour
1 tablespoon grated lemon peel
¼ cup lemon juice
1 teaspoon vanilla
½ teaspoon salt
2 large egg yolks
1 tablespoon cherry-flavored liqueur
4 large egg whites (about ½ cup)
⅛ teaspoon cream of tartar
5 to 6 cups sliced fresh strawberries

1. Lightly butter bottom and sides of a 2½- to 3-quart soufflé dish. Then coat inside of dish with biscotti crumbs, leaving any loose crumbs in bottom of dish.

2. In a large bowl, combine ricotta cheese, yogurt, ½ cup of the sugar, flour, lemon peel, lemon juice, vanilla, salt, egg yolks, and liqueur. Beat with an electric mixer on medium speed until smooth.

3. In another bowl, using clean beaters, beat egg whites and cream of tartar on high speed until soft peaks form. Gradually add remaining ¼ cup sugar, continuing to beat until sugar is completely dissolved. Gently fold egg whites into ricotta mixture.

4. Pour into prepared dish and bake in a 350° oven until soufflé is golden brown and center feels firm when lightly pressed (about 45 minutes).

5. To serve, spoon warm soufflé into bowls; top with berries.

MAKES 10 TO 12 SERVINGS

Per serving: 190 calories (24% calories from fat), 5 g total fat, 2 g saturated fat, 53 mg cholesterol, 207 mg sodium, 28 g carbohydrates, 2 g fiber, 7 g protein, 123 mg calcium, 1 mg iron

Chocolate-Orange Cheesecake

Though it tastes unbelievably rich, creamy, and fudgy, this handsome cheesecake is a heart-healthy dessert: it's made with low-fat cottage cheese and fat-free cream cheese, and egg whites stand in for some of the whole eggs a traditional cheesecake would use.

PREPARATION TIME: *About 20 minutes, plus at least 2½ hours to chill*

BAKING TIME: *About 1 hour*

- ⅔ cup reduced-fat chocolate wafer crumbs
- 1½ tablespoons butter or margarine, melted
- 1 carton (1 lb.; about 1¾ cups) small-curd low-fat (2%) cottage cheese
- 1 large package (about 8 oz.) fat-free cream cheese, at room temperature
- 2 large eggs
- 2 large egg whites (about ¼ cup)
- 1 cup sugar
- ¾ cup unsweetened cocoa
- ¼ cup orange-flavored liqueur or orange juice
- 2 teaspoons grated orange peel
- ⅓ cup chopped semisweet chocolate

  Orange slices and shredded orange peel (optional)

1. In a small bowl, combine chocolate wafer crumbs and melted butter. Pat mixture evenly over bottom and about ½ inch up sides of a 9-inch cheesecake pan or a cake pan (at least 1¾ inches deep) with a removable rim. Bake in a 350° oven until crust is slightly toasted (10 to 12 minutes). Set aside.

2. Meanwhile, in a food processor or blender, combine cottage cheese, cream cheese, eggs, and egg whites. Whirl until very smooth.

3. In a large bowl, mix sugar and cocoa. Add cheese mixture, liqueur, and grated orange peel; stir until smoothly blended.

4. Place chocolate in a small microwave-safe bowl. Microwave on high (100%) in 5-second increments until soft. Stir until smooth, then scrape into cheese mixture. Beat with an electric mixer on medium speed until smoothly blended. Pour filling into crust.

5. Bake in a 350° oven until center of cheesecake barely jiggles when pan is gently shaken (40 to 45 minutes). Run a thin-bladed knife between cheesecake and pan rim. Then refrigerate cheesecake, uncovered, until cool (at least 2½ hours). If made ahead, cover airtight and refrigerate for up to 2 days.

6. To serve, remove pan rim. Garnish cheesecake with orange slices and shredded orange peel, if desired; then cut into wedges.

MAKES 12 SERVINGS

Per serving: 208 calories (23% calories from fat), 6 g total fat, 3 g saturated fat, 43 mg cholesterol, 355 mg sodium, 32 g carbohydrates, 0 g fiber, 10 g protein, 90 mg calcium, 1 mg iron

Iced Oatmeal-Raisin Cookies

Chewy oatmeal-fruit cookies are great for snacks or for tucking into lunchboxes. These are dressed up with a simple powdered sugar glaze.

PREPARATION TIME: *About 25 minutes*
BAKING TIME: *About 15 minutes*

  1 cup all-purpose flour
  ½ teaspoon baking soda
  ½ teaspoon salt
  ½ teaspoon ground cinnamon
  ¼ teaspoon cream of tartar
  ¼ cup butter or margarine, at room temperature
  ¾ cup granulated sugar
  2 teaspoons vanilla
  2 large egg whites (about ¼ cup)
  1 cup regular rolled oats
  ⅔ cup chopped raisins
    Vegetable oil cooking spray
1⅓ cups powdered sugar
  2 to 3 tablespoons fat-free milk or water

1. In a small bowl, stir together flour, baking soda, salt, cinnamon, and cream of tartar; set aside. In a food processor or a large bowl, whirl or beat butter, granulated sugar, vanilla, and egg whites until well blended. Add flour mixture to egg mixture; whirl or stir until combined. Stir in oats and raisins.

2. Coat 2 or 3 baking sheets with cooking spray. Drop dough by rounded teaspoonfuls onto baking sheets, spacing cookies 2 inches apart.

3. Bake in a 350° oven until cookies are light golden and firm to the touch (about 15 minutes), switching positions of baking sheets halfway through baking. Let cookies cool on baking sheets for about 3 minutes; then transfer to racks to cool completely.

4. In a small bowl, stir together powdered sugar and milk. Set each rack of cooled cookies over a baking sheet to catch any drips; drizzle icing evenly over cookies. Serve; or let stand until icing hardens (about 2 hours).

MAKES ABOUT 3 DOZEN COOKIES

Per cookie: 75 calories (18% calories from fat), 1 g total fat, 1 g saturated fat, 4 mg cholesterol, 66 mg sodium, 15 g carbohydrates, 0 g fiber, 1 g protein, 5 mg calcium, 0 mg iron

Spiced Biscotti

Fragrant with orange peel and spices and dotted with raisins and chopped dark chocolate, these delectable biscotti start with a homemade toasted almond paste. Serve them with hot coffee or tea or alongside a scoop of frozen yogurt.

PREPARATION TIME: *About 20 minutes*
BAKING TIME: *1 1/3 to 1 1/2 hours*

- 1/2 cup whole unblanched almonds
- 1 tablespoon vegetable oil
- 3 large eggs
- 3/4 cup sugar
- 2 tablespoons almond-flavored liqueur
- 1 tablespoon vanilla
- 1 tablespoon grated orange peel
- 1/2 teaspoon ground ginger
- 1/4 teaspoon ground cinnamon
- 1/8 teaspoon salt
- 1/8 teaspoon ground allspice
- 2 1/3 cups all-purpose flour
- 2 teaspoons baking powder
- 1/3 cup chopped raisins
- 1/3 cup chopped semisweet chocolate

1. Spread almonds on a baking sheet and toast in a 325° oven until golden beneath skins (10 to 15 minutes). Place oil and 1/4 cup of the hot almonds in a blender; whirl until a buttery paste forms. Chop remaining 1/4 cup almonds and set aside.

2. Scrape almond paste into a large bowl and add eggs and sugar; beat until blended. Stir in liqueur, vanilla, orange peel, ginger, cinnamon, salt, and allspice. In a small bowl, stir together flour and baking powder. Gradually add flour mixture to egg mixture, stirring until well blended. Then stir in chopped almonds, raisins, and chocolate.

3. Line a 14- by 17-inch baking sheet with cooking parchment (or grease baking sheet). Spoon batter down center of baking sheet; with floured hands, pat it into a flat log about 3/4 inch thick and 3 1/4 inches wide. Bake in a 325° oven until golden (about 25 minutes). Remove from oven and let cool for 5 minutes.

4. Reduce oven temperature to 225°. With a sharp knife, cut log crosswise into 1/2-inch-thick slices. Tip slices over so they lie flat on baking sheet; return to oven and continue to bake until cookies are golden all over (45 to 55 more minutes). Transfer cookies to racks and let cool. If made ahead, store airtight at room temperature for up to 1 week.

MAKES ABOUT 2 1/2 DOZEN COOKIES

Per cookie: 99 calories (27% calories from fat), 3 g total fat, 1 g saturated fat, 21 mg cholesterol, 49 mg sodium, 16 g carbohydrates, 1 g fiber, 2 g protein, 30 mg calcium, 1 mg iron

Anise Cookies

The crisp texture and distinctive anise flavor of these drop cookies may remind you of German springerle. Allowing the unbaked cookies to dry for several hours produces their unusual texture.

PREPARATION TIME: *About 50 minutes, plus at least 6 hours for unbaked cookies to dry*
BAKING TIME: *About 12 minutes per batch*

3	large eggs
1	cup sugar
1½	cups all-purpose flour
½	teaspoon baking powder
¼	teaspoon anise oil or 1 teaspoon anise extract

1. In a deep bowl, beat eggs with an electric mixer on high speed until foamy. Still beating, add sugar slowly, beating in 2 to 3 teaspoons per minute; allow 20 minutes to beat in all sugar. Continue to beat until sugar is thoroughly dissolved (about 4 more minutes); a little of the mixture rubbed between your fingers should feel smooth.

2. In a small bowl, stir together flour and baking powder. Stir anise oil into egg mixture; then add flour mixture and beat with mixer until dry ingredients are thoroughly incorporated.

3. Drop batter by teaspoonfuls onto heavily buttered and floured baking sheets, spacing cookies 1 inch apart. Stir batter frequently to keep ingredients mixed. Let unbaked cookies stand until tops feel dry and firm when touched (at least 6 hours) or for up to 1 day. Then bake in a 325° oven until cookies are pale golden brown on bottom and feel dry on top (about 12 minutes).

4. Transfer cookies to racks to cool. To store, package airtight and hold at room temperature for up to 1 week; freeze for longer storage.

MAKES ABOUT 9 DOZEN COOKIES

Per cookie: 17 calories (13% calories from fat), .20 g total fat, 0 g saturated fat, 6 mg cholesterol, 5 mg sodium, 3 g carbohydrates, 0 g fiber, 0 g protein, 2 mg calcium, 0 mg iron

Fudgy Brownies

The batter contains just one tablespoon of butter—but these brownies are lusciously moist. The secret? In place of fat, use prune baby food, a puréed prune-apple baking substitute, or applesauce (if made with applesauce, the brownies will have a more cakelike texture).

PREPARATION TIME: *About 15 minutes*
BAKING TIME: *22 to 24 minutes*

2	ounces unsweetened chocolate
1	tablespoon butter or margarine
1	cup sugar
1	large egg
1	large egg white (about 2 tablespoons)
6	tablespoons unsweetened apple-sauce or 3 tablespoons prune purée
2	teaspoons vanilla
½	cup all-purpose flour
2	tablespoons unsweetened cocoa
¼	teaspoon salt
¼	teaspoon baking soda

1. In a 2- to 3-quart pan, stir chocolate and butter over low heat until melted. Remove from heat and add sugar, egg, egg white, applesauce, and vanilla; stir until smooth. Sift flour, cocoa, salt, and baking soda into pan; stir to blend.

2. Spread batter in a lightly oiled 8-inch-square baking pan. Bake in a 350° oven until brownies pull from sides of pan (22 to 24 minutes; if they do not pull from sides, bake no longer than 25 minutes). Let cool completely in pan on a rack. To serve, cut into 2-inch squares.

MAKES 16 BROWNIES

Per brownie: 103 calories (28% calories from fat), 3 g total fat, 2 g saturated fat, 15 mg cholesterol, 71 mg sodium, 18 g carbohydrates, 1 g fiber, 2 g protein, 6 mg calcium, 1 mg iron

Apple-Cranberry Ice

A natural choice for autumn menus, this tangy ice is especially refreshing after a hearty stew or other filling main course. You'll need an electric ice cream maker to prepare it.

PREPARATION TIME: *About 30 minutes*
FREEZING TIME: *Varies with ice cream maker used*

- **3** cups water
- **1½** cups fresh cranberries
- **¾** cup sugar
- **⅔** cup unsweetened apple juice
- **2** tablespoons lemon juice

1. In a 2- to 3-quart nonaluminum pan, combine ½ cup of the water, cranberries, and ¼ cup of the sugar. Bring to a boil over medium heat; boil, stirring often, until berries pop (about 8 minutes). Remove from heat; let cool until no longer hot (about 15 minutes).

2. In a food processor or blender, whirl cranberry mixture until smoothly puréed. Strain purée through a sieve into a medium-size bowl; discard residue.

3. To bowl, add remaining 2½ cups water, remaining ½ cup sugar, apple juice, and lemon juice. Stir well. Cover and refrigerate until cold.

4. Pour cranberry mixture into an electric ice cream maker (at least 1½-quart size). Freeze according to manufacturer's directions until firm. If made ahead, cover airtight and freeze for up to 2 weeks.

MAKES 8 SERVINGS (ABOUT 4 CUPS TOTAL)

Per serving: 93 calories (1% calories from fat), .10 g total fat, 0 g saturated fat, 0 mg cholesterol, 1 mg sodium, 24 g carbohydrates, 1 g fiber, 0 g protein, 3 mg calcium, 0 mg iron

Peach Sherbet

A scoop or two of this creamy, honey-sweetened sherbet is the perfect close to a barbecue meal or a traditional fish dinner such as our Friday Night Fish Bake (page 55). In summer, make it with fresh peaches; at other times of year, use frozen fruit.

PREPARATION TIME: *About 10 minutes*
FREEZING TIME: *About 5 hours*

- **2** cups peeled, sliced ripe peaches; or 2 cups frozen unsweetened peaches, partially thawed
- **1** cup plain low-fat yogurt
- **½** cup orange juice
- **⅓** cup honey

1. In a food processor or blender, combine peaches, yogurt, orange juice, and honey. Whirl until peaches are finely chopped.

2. Pour mixture into an 8-inch-square metal pan; cover and freeze until almost firm (about 4 hours). Break mixture into large pieces with a heavy spoon and whirl in a food processor or blender until a smooth-textured slush forms.

3. Return mixture to pan, cover, and freeze until firm (about 1 hour). If made ahead, cover airtight and freeze for up to 2 weeks.

MAKES 6 SERVINGS (ABOUT 3 CUPS TOTAL)

Per serving: 114 calories (5% calories from fat), 1 g total fat, 0 g saturated fat, 2 mg cholesterol, 27 mg sodium, 27 g carbohydrates, 1 g fiber, 3 g protein, 75 mg calcium, 0 mg iron

PEACH SHERBET AND APPLE-CRANBERRY ICE

DESSERTS

Strawberry-Orange Smoothie

Serve this thick, chilly drink for dessert, breakfast, or an afternoon treat on a sultry day. If you like, use another flavor of yogurt, such as orange, banana-strawberry, or raspberry.

PREPARATION TIME: *About 5 minutes*

- 2 **cups unsweetened frozen strawberries**
- 1 **cup chilled orange juice**
- 1 **cup fat-free milk**
- 1 **cup strawberry low-fat yogurt**

1. In a blender, combine strawberries, orange juice, and milk; whirl just until strawberries are puréed. Add yogurt and whirl again just until blended.

2. Pour into chilled glasses and serve immediately.

MAKES 4 SERVINGS (4 TO 4½ CUPS TOTAL)

Per serving: 134 calories (5% calories from fat), 1 g total fat, 0 g saturated fat, 3 mg cholesterol, 67 mg sodium, 27 g carbohydrates, 0 g fiber, 5 g protein, 179 mg calcium, 1 mg iron

Mango-Peach Smoothie

Next time you crave something cool and exhilarating, satisfy your taste-buds with this combination of mango chunks, a fresh peach, and peach nectar. Lime juice intensifies all the fruit flavors.

PREPARATION TIME: *About 6 minutes*

- 1 **cup peeled mango chunks**
- 1 **large peach (about 8 oz.), peeled, pitted, and cut into chunks**
- 1 **cup chilled peach nectar**
- 2 **tablespoons lime juice**

1. In a blender, combine mango, peach, peach nectar, and lime juice. Whirl until smooth.

2. Pour into chilled glasses and serve immediately.

MAKES 1 OR 2 SERVINGS (ABOUT 3 CUPS TOTAL)

Per 1½-cup serving: 161 calories (2% calories from fat), .40 g total fat, 0 g saturated fat, 0 mg cholesterol, 13 mg sodium, 42 g carbohydrates, 2 g fiber, 1 g protein, 21 mg calcium, 0 mg iron

Hawaii 5-0

Tropical fruits combine with fat-free milk or vanilla yogurt in this smooth, creamy dessert drink. Coconut extract adds rich flavor—without the saturated fat found in coconut.

PREPARATION TIME: *About 7 minutes*

- 1 **cup cubed fresh pineapple**
- 1 **cup cubed papaya**
- ½ **cup chilled unsweetened pineapple juice or papaya nectar**
- 1 **medium-size ripe banana (about 6 oz.), peeled and cut into chunks**
- ½ **cup fat-free or low-fat (1%) milk (or vanilla nonfat or low-fat yogurt)**
- ⅛ **to ¼ teaspoon coconut extract**

1. In a blender, combine pineapple, papaya, pineapple juice, banana, milk, and coconut extract. Whirl until smooth.

2. Pour into chilled glasses and serve immediately.

MAKES 2 SERVINGS (ABOUT 3½ CUPS TOTAL)

Per serving: 171 calories (4% calories from fat), 1 g total fat, 0 g saturated fat, 1 mg cholesterol, 36 mg sodium, 40 g carbohydrates, 2 g fiber, 4 g protein, 108 mg calcium, 1 mg iron

Boysenberry & Blueberry Smoothie

It's deep purple and tastes it! You need just three ingredients—berry juice and two kinds of fresh or frozen berries—to concoct this treat in your blender.

PREPARATION TIME: *About 4 minutes*

1½ cups chilled boysenberry- or blackberry-flavored juice

1 cup fresh boysenberries or blackberries

1 cup fresh blueberries

1. In a blender, combine boysenberry-flavored juice, boysenberries, and blueberries. Whirl until smooth.

2. Pour into chilled glasses and serve immediately.

MAKES 1 OR 2 SERVINGS (ABOUT 3 CUPS TOTAL)

Per 1½-cup serving: 168 calories (3% calories from fat), 1 g total fat, 0 g saturated fat, 0 mg cholesterol, 23 mg sodium, 42 g carbohydrates, 5 g fiber, 1 g protein, 27 mg calcium, 1 mg iron

Raisin-Nut Brittle

Use your favorite nuts in this tempting candy; macadamias, walnuts, almonds, and cashews are all wonderful. To toast the nuts, spread them in a shallow baking pan and bake in a 325° oven just until golden (10 to 15 minutes); let cool slightly before using. Work quickly as you stir the nuts and raisins into the hot caramelized sugar—the candy hardens rapidly.

PREPARATION TIME: *About 5 minutes, plus at least 30 minutes to cool*
COOKING TIME: *12 to 15 minutes*

Butter or margarine

2 cups sugar

¼ teaspoon ground cinnamon

¾ cup toasted nuts

¾ cup golden raisins

1. Line a 10- by 15-inch baking pan with foil; lightly butter foil. Set pan aside.

2. In a wide nonstick frying pan, mix sugar and cinnamon. Place pan over medium-high heat and cook, shaking pan often, until almost all sugar is melted (about 10 minutes). Reduce heat to medium. Continue to cook, tilting pan to mix melted sugar with any remaining dry sugar, until all sugar is well mixed and turns amber colored (2 to 5 more minutes; do not scorch).

3. Remove pan from heat and quickly stir nuts and raisins into melted sugar; then immediately pour mixture into foil-lined pan. Working fast, use a spoon to spread candy into as thin a layer as possible. Let cool until firm (at least 30 minutes).

4. Remove cooled brittle from pan, using foil to lift it; then peel off foil. Break brittle into pieces. If made ahead, store airtight at room temperature for up to 3 days.

MAKES ABOUT 20 SERVINGS (ABOUT 1¼ LBS. TOTAL)

Per serving: 126 calories (22% calories from fat), 3 g total fat, 0 g saturated fat, 1 mg cholesterol, 5 mg sodium, 25 g carbohydrates, 0 g fiber, 1 g protein, 8 mg calcium, 0 mg iron

PHOTOGRAPHERS

Unless noted below, all photographs are by Chris Shorten.

Ralph Anderson: 43, 127, 131, 187, 200, 231.

Jim Bathie: 30, 44, 48, 58, 78, 170, 179, 220, 224.

PHOTO STYLIST

Unless noted below, all photos and food were styled by Susan Massey.

Kay E. Clarke: 30, 48, 58, 78, 127, 131, 187, 200, 231, 224.

Virginia R. Cravens: 43, 44, 179, 175, 220.